W9-AHF-168

*This book is dedicated to my wife and companion Lisa, who is always there for me, patient with me, and loves me in spite of my many faults. This book is dedicated to my kids, Felicia, Sarah, Jacob, Jared, and Elizabeth, who are the light of my life even if they don't know this all the time.*

## About the Author

**Robert G. Freeman** is a principal DBA and Team Manager at the Church of Jesus Christ of Latter-day Saints. He has been working with Oracle now for almost two decades and is the author of over a dozen different works on Oracle. He resides in Salt Lake City, Utah, with his lovely wife Lisa, three of his five kids, two grumpy cats, two airplanes, and a dog that whines all the time.

## About the Contributor

**Arup Nanda** has been an Oracle DBA for more than 12 years working on all challenges an Oracle DBA can possibly face—from modeling to performance tuning to disaster recovery and even people problems. He is a frequent speaker at many Oracle-related conferences and has coauthored four books and numerous articles including the Oracle Database 10*g* and 11*g* New Features series on Oracle Technology Network. In 2003, *Oracle Magazine* chose him as DBA of the Year. He lives in Connecticut with his wife Anindita and son Anish.

## About the Technical Editor

**Peter Sharman** has 18 years of IT experience designing, implementing, and managing the performance of Oracle solutions. As a solo consultant and team leader, Pete has provided administrative and technical leadership to leading Internet-based businesses, as well as several Fortune 100 and Fortune 500 companies. He has also completed world-class benchmarks and implementation reviews of the Oracle RDBMS, and performed high-impact performance tuning. A proven technical leader, Pete has acquired expert-level skills in Real Application Clusters (RAC) database design, administration, backup and recovery, operations planning and management, performance management, system management, and security and management of complex data centers. Pete has also presented at numerous conferences around the world, and written a book on Oracle architecture and administration. Pete has passed all the Oracle DBA Certifications, as well as being a qualified Oracle9*i*/10*g* Certified Master.

Currently, Pete is part of the RAC Quality Assurance group in Server Technologies Development at Oracle, testing the quality of all parts of the Oracle code base when run in a RAC environment.

# Contents

# Foreword

s of the publication of this book, I've been working for Oracle Corporation for a little over 14 years—and in those 14 years, I've seen 14 major releases of the Oracle Database go production—from version 6 through 7, 8, 8*i*, 9*i* and 10*g*—all the way to the current release, Oracle Database 11*g* Release 1.

Every new release brings with it hundreds of new features and changes, and Oracle Database 11*g* Release 1 is no exception.

Over time, the question everyone asks is "How do you keep up with all of this change?" Enter Robert Freeman and Arup Nanda, two very respected names in the Oracle community. Robert and Arup together continue their long tradition of educating and participating in the Oracle community with the release of this book *Oracle Database 11*g *New Features.* Both are active users of the Oracle Database software—engaged in the day-to-day production administration of large Oracle instances—and therefore write from the standpoint of someone who uses the software every day. It is this perspective, from the viewpoint of production DBAs, that makes this book both unique and useful.

This book introduces and provides examples of using many of the new 11*g* features and functions—educating the reader as to the overall intent and purpose of the functionality as well as demonstrating how it is implemented and how to use it.

Robert and Arup cover everything from new database management features to availability and recovery (the authors are well known in the Oracle universe for their solid knowledge of backup and recovery).

Oracle Database 11*g* Release 1 will forever change the way Database Administrators will approach upgrades and changes—with the introduction of Real Application Testing and the Database Replay feature. The authors dedicated an entire chapter of the book to this database option—a section I truly appreciate, given that real-world testing is the only way to introduce change in a production system. The authors give you the information you need to get started with this feature and understand what it does and does not do.

The chapter on performance tuning and large databases will be one many people will skip right to and start with. Over time, Oracle has added many features to the database to facilitate performance tuning as well as features to make things "go faster." The authors cover the most relevant new additions in Oracle Database 11*g* Release 1 including the new partitioning features and SQL plan management.

All in all, this book will make understanding what Oracle Database 11*g* Release 1 means to you. Filled with explanations written for DBAs and developers by a pair of DBAs/developers, this book will be a virtual roadmap to understanding this new release. Enjoy.

—Tom Kyte, Oracle Corporation

# Acknowledgments

R ight off the bat I should say that I don't like to name names. When you do that, inevitably people get forgotten, and feelings get hurt, so only a few names will be mentioned directly here.

The creation of any book takes the work of so many people. First and foremost, thanks to my wife and companion Lisa who puts up with me spending my time writing (at least that's what I'm calling it). Thanks to my kids, who constantly come into my office to remind me that I'm a father, not just a writer.

Thanks to my dad, who gave me my drive to succeed and never quit.

Thanks to all my co-workers and friends at the Church of Jesus-Christ of Latter-day Saints where I work. They are too numerous to mention here, but they are a great bunch of folks to work with.

An acknowledgement to all those whom I have worked with in the past is most in order. I dare not print a list of all those people for fear of leaving someone out. To all of you I owe more thanks than I can say. Thanks to previous employers who gave me wonderful opportunities.

Super-duper thanks to Tom Kyte for writing an incredible introduction. Thanks, Tom!!

Thanks to Arup Nanda for his great "Arup Says" contributions. Arup really adds so much value to this book and it is a much better work with his additions.

Thanks to Pete Sharman, my long-time friend and the technical editor of this book. He did a great job, and was brutally honest when something wasn't up to snuff.

A special thanks to Chapter 10 contributors Dan Norris and Kyle Brokaw. Without their assistance this book would not have been as complete. They each did an awesome job, and I appreciate their contributions.

Thanks to all the folks at Oracle who helped with this book as it was being written. Thanks to the beta staff and the metalink support staff and development for all the assistance I received from you!

Thanks to my friends, including those in and out of the Oracle community. One in particular was going through some rough times during the writing of this book. Divorce is an ugly business and I wish I could have been more help for you, my friend. I hope 2008 is a better year.

Last but not least, thanks to all the folks at Oracle Press who have made this book better than it would have otherwise been. Lisa McClain is tops. She's been there for the last several of my books and always keeps me in line. Vasundhara Sawhney was a great help getting this thing put together and Mandy Canales kept me on schedule, making sure this book got out on time. Thanks to everyone else at Oracle Press for the hard work and dedication!

# Introduction

racle Database 11*g* is the newest release of Oracle's flagship database product. It contains a number of new innovations, which we cover in the pages of this book. This is my third Oracle "New Features" book for Oracle Press, and I've actually been writing them since Oracle 8.0 was released. For each book, it's been an incredible experience to go through the product, find the new features, and learn how to use them.

It can be difficult to write books about new features. First, you don't start out running the production product. You write using a beta copy of the software, and just hope that the final release does not change too much. Also, the marketing reality is that publishers want to get books out to market. So there is always this battle between quality and delivery. In fact, the folks at Oracle Press/McGraw Hill are terrific about this, and understand the battle. In this book we have cut no corners. We wrote initially on the beta, and after the production code came out we went over the chapters with the production code looking for any changes.

The first new features book I wrote (in fact, my first book) was for upgrading from Oracle 7.3 to Oracle 8. This first book was written with the upgrade exam in mind. The book was written after Oracle 8 was released, so I had documentation at hand. The first book written from beta code was *Oracle9i New Features*. The 9*i* Beta was difficult. The documentation was not complete, and it was difficult to discover any information on the new feature sets that were being released. Oracle Database 10*g* was easier. The beta was a much easier process and documentation was more plentiful.

The Oracle Database 11*g* beta has been quite good in many respects. The documentation and ancillary information on what was in the Oracle Database 11*g* beta, and what was to come, was much more complete. As a result of this more mature beta, I think this book is so far the best of all the new features books that I've written. We started writing this book in early 2007, starting with the beta Oracle product, and then went over it chapter by chapter with the production product to make sure it was as accurate as it could be.

If you have read my new features books before, you will notice a bit of a difference in this volume. We have given OEM quite a bit more coverage this time. I can honestly say that I no longer hate OEM (which was not the case prior to, say, Oracle Database 10*g*). You will find much more coverage of OEM functionality. However, fear not; I've also tried to cover command-line methods as well, and in the few cases where it had to boil down to command-line or OEM coverage, I went with command line.

This is a book principally for the early adopter of Oracle Database 11*g*. It was written long before the Oracle certification exams were released, thus it is not a guide for those exams. Still, this book covers a great deal of the functionality that will no doubt be covered in the forthcoming certification process, so I suspect that it will help in one's attempt to pass the certification tests.

This book represents many hours of work on the part of numerous people. We all hope you enjoy this book and that it helps you in your efforts to master Oracle Database 11*g*.

# CHAPTER
## 1

# Oracle Database 11g
# Getting Started

nce again we set out on the adventure of discovery. As I did in my previous titles *Oracle9i New Features* and *Oracle Database 10g New Features*, I will introduce you to the wealth of new functionality of Oracle Database 11g! Joining us on this journey is none other than Arup Nanda. You probably know Arup for his *Oracle Database 10g New Feature* series that he wrote for Oracle Technology Network (OTN); it was very popular (and he's doing the same for Oracle Database 11g, a great companion web site to this book!). Arup will provide commentary thoughout this work, giving you his take and insights on specific features. Also, at the end of the book in the Appendix you will find Arup's top ten new features list.

This chapter is the place to begin, as we will discuss a number of "preflight" topics such as:

- Installing Oracle Database 11g

- Upgrading your database to Oracle Database 11g

- New parameters in Oracle Database 11g

- Changes to parameters in Oracle Database 11g

As always, this book is designed for early adopters, and for those who want to get a heads-up on what is available in Oracle Database 11g. Oracle Database 11g is a huge new release of the Oracle RDBMS product, and as such it has hundreds of new features, some obscure and perhaps even forgettable and some very important. In this volume I've done my best to give you concise information, including examples, on what I felt were the most important of the new features.

**NOTE**
*In this volume we are highlighting the changes to the Enterprise Edition of Oracle, so if you are running Oracle Standard Edition you might find that some of these features do not work.*

# Installing Oracle Database 11g

The Oracle Database 11g installer and the install process are not much different than that of Oracle Database 10g. The base install still comes on one CD, and a companion CD is available for ancillary products. There are a few changes to what is found on these install CDs, including:

- Oracle Application Express (APEX) is no longer installed on the companion CD. Instead it is installed when you install the base Oracle Database 11*g* product.

- The Data Warehouse Builder is installed when you install the base Oracle Database 11*g* product.

- All Enterprise edition installs will include Oracle Data Mining unless it is deselected.

One somewhat important change in the Oracle Database 11*g* install process is that it keys on the setting of the environment variable ORACLE_BASE to determine where it will install the Oracle software. ORACLE_BASE has actually been around for some time now, but it's never really been key to Oracle installs. Oracle Database 11*g* now uses the environment variable ORACLE_BASE when performing an install to ensure that the Oracle Database Installer will install the Oracle Database 11*g* software in a directory location that is compliant with Optimal Flexible Architecture (OFA). If you forget to set ORACLE_BASE, you will have the opportunity to set the value of ORACLE_BASE in the installer window (a default is supplied, which you should check carefully). Also ORACLE_BASE will now be stored in your Oracle inventory location. This is so that the Oracle Universal Installer (OUI) can reference ORACLE_BASE when installing other Oracle products.

**NOTE**
*It is recommended that you set the ORACLE_BASE environment variable in 11g, as Oracle indicates this environment setting will be required in the next major release of the Oracle RDBMS.*

If you are installing Oracle Clusterware 11*g*, you will need to enter the Oracle Cluster home location and ORACLE_BASE locations when running the Universal Installer. Both the Cluster home and ORACLE_BASE will default to the same directory level. You will need to change the Oracle Cluster Home location so that it is not under the ORACLE_BASE location, or the install will fail with an error.

**NOTE**
*Did you ever notice that when you install the companion disk components that have their own ORACLE_HOME, it is that ORACLE_HOME that gets put in the path first? This can cause problems if you don't set up your networking in the ORACLE_HOME of the companion disk.*

# The Database Configuration Assistant

The manual process of creating a database in Oracle Database 11*g* has not changed. The steps remain pretty much the same. However, when you are creating an Oracle database with the Oracle Database Configuration Assistant (DBCA), you might notice that a few things have changed.

In general the DBCA interface is not much different than what was available in Oracle Database 10*g*. One new feature is that when you are creating a database a new screen appears asking you if you want to use the enhanced 11*g* Database security settings, which include new default auditing settings and enabling the default password profile, or to use the pre-11*g* default security settings. See Chapter 4 for more information on these and other new security features. Other DBCA-related changes include:

- Oracle SQL Developer will be installed if you used a template-driven database install from the DBCA.

- Oracle XML DB will be installed in all Oracle databases when they are created.

- The Oracle Data Mining schema is created as a part of catproc.sql by default, and is no longer an option in the DBCA. Oracle Data Mining also no longer appears in the DBA_REGISTRY view.

Oracle Database 11*g* has also made it easier to switch managing your database between Database Control and Oracle Grid Control. The DBCA can now be used to easily switch between managing with DBCA and Oracle Grid Control.

# Upgrading to Oracle Database 11*g*

Oracle Database 10*g* provides a fairly easy upgrade path for users of older Oracle versions, and in fact, I think the upgrade process is slightly easier when moving from Oracle Database 10*g* to Oracle Database 11*g* than it was if you moved from Oracle9*i* to Oracle Database 10*g*! In this section we will provide an overview of each of the upgrade processes. We will discuss what versions you can upgrade from, and we will then discuss the different supported upgrade methods: the Database Upgrade Assistant (DBUA), manual upgrades, and export/import and data copy commands. However, before we dive into the specific coverage, I want to take a moment to discuss a few issues revolving around upgrades that I've seen come up before, and try to save you some time asking questions and making mistakes.

# Saving Time When Upgrading

I've been involved with the Oracle database product for a long time now—as of this writing not quite, but almost, two decades. I've done upgrades of every version since Oracle 7 (and have written books like this since the Oracle 7.3 to Oracle 8 days!). I'd like to share a few thoughts with you about the upgrade process that I think might help you save some time in the long run. So, let's get started.

## Please, Backup!

There is perhaps nothing more important to the entire upgrade process than backing up the database first thing. Please make sure you do this, and make sure it's a part of every database upgrade plan that you produce!

## Learn and Educate

This might seem obvious at first; you would think that everyone would take the time to learn about a new piece of software before they haul off and install it. It is so sad to say how many people I've talked to who proudly stated "We are on version x" and yet they know little or nothing about what is available on version x. Upgrading to a new version of Oracle is about more than just being able to still get support! Granted, caution must be exercised with the use of new features, but oh, some are so irresistible when you finally learn about them.

I remember when I first saw that you could rename a table, and you could rename a column in Oracle. Oh happy day!! No more dropping tables and re-creating them just to rename a column! What a great feature, and if I had not taken the time to learn about that feature, I might have wasted so much time doing things the "old" way. How much time do you have to burn?

So, then the question is, how do you figure out what you need to know about!? Well, you have purchased this book, which is a heck of a good start. Kudos to you on your wisdom to this point! What else should you do? Let me offer these suggestions:

1.  Read the manuals. Most Oracle manuals now have "new feature" sections in them that highlight the new features in the database that are part of the subject area of that manual. These often have links to the areas in the manual with more information. This is particularly helpful if you are using one of the ancillary Oracle features that we do not cover in any depth in this book.

2.  Read (or skim) the upgrade scripts that Oracle uses. Yeah, it may be tedious stuff, but there can be some really interesting information in there.

3.  Read (or skim) sql.bsq and its related scripts. This is the queen mother script that the **create database** command runs. Often you can find little tidbits of information in here that will teach you something new.

4. After installing a new version of the Oracle Database, use the Database Creation Assistant to create your first database. When you do so, make sure to have it create the scripts that it will use for that database creation. Then after the database creation is complete, review the scripts that it created. Often in these scripts you can see new feature-related parameters being used, or even simple changes in the way you might want to create your Oracle databases. Often you can learn a lot from these scripts.

## Don't Upgrade When Installing Oracle Database 11*g*

When you install Oracle Database 11*g* for the first time, it will display a list of the databases currently on your system and ask you if you want to upgrade them. I cannot tell you what a wholly bad idea this is, and how you should never ever allow Oracle to upgrade databases during an install. There are a number of reasons for this. First of all, you never know if the install will work correctly. There could be a lot of reasons why the installer might fail, but the bottom line is it can.

Of course, you hope that if it fails, the installer won't try to upgrade the databases— but never trust anything to work right if the installer fails. Another issue is that the installer might install Oracle successfully, but the migration might fail because your system is not really ready to migrate your database yet. Perhaps there are patches that need to be installed, or you missed some system configuration that needs to be updated (for example an obscure OS patch) before you haul off and start mucking with databases.

I strongly recommend that you install Oracle Database 11*g* first. After you have done that, run the DBCA (separately) and allow it to create a starter database for you under your new Oracle Database 11*g* Oracle Home. Make sure the database comes up, and run a few test queries against it. Also make sure your networking is working correctly. I'd create a database link in your test database and make sure that Oracle Net is working right. This kind of naturally leads us to our next topic.

## Test, Test, Test...

Testing might seem like the natural thing to do, but I've seen testing get the short end of the stick before, so I have to mention it here. For important applications it's not enough just to upgrade a database, start it up, and then run a few queries and anoint it as ready for prime time. While Oracle does a lot of testing on its products, I have yet to see one database product that didn't have a bug or two (or tens or hundreds!) in it. In fact, in my first week of testing the production version of 11*g* Release 1, I found and opened two different bugs.

As a result, regression testing of your important applications is critical before you migrate your production database to Oracle Database 11*g*. I've seen more than one upgrade project come to a screeching halt because of an Oracle bug, and I've seen production upgrades have to be rolled back for the same reason.

Another area where testing becomes really important is in the arena of performance. Changing Oracle versions can and does cause execution plans to change. Often these changes are for the better, but sometimes they can be for the worse. One shortcoming in test plans that I've seen is that they test functionality, but never volume. So you get the right answers, but once 250 concurrent users are asking the same question, it takes two hours to get a response. So, test in volume conditions, with real data volumes and realistic queries. Oracle Database 11*g* offers some new features that might help you in this regard, such as SQL Database Replay, which we discuss in Chapter 5 of this book.

## No, That's Not an Available Upgrade Path (or RTFM)

I'm getting older, my kids are getting more expensive, and I think I'm getting crankier as time goes on. So, if I sound a bit crotchety here, please understand. Over the years I have kept my eyes on the different Oracle newsgroups (Oracle-L, LazyDBA, and the Quest Pipelines are among my favorites). I love these newsgroups because they offer such a sharing of knowledge and really have the opportunity to help people solve problems more quickly than ever. But...

Some people have become lazy. They make assumptions; they don't read the manual or briefly scan it and don't really catch the details. Some people seem unable to research and make semi-educated guesses, and then seem even more unable to actually test these guesses. There are people out there who literally seem to think that Oracle leaves it up to them to craft an upgrade strategy to move their database.

For example, I've seen more than one person ask if you could migrate to version *x* of the database by using transportable tablespaces. The answer is: even if you could, check the Oracle upgrade manual; it's not a supported upgrade method. If you do, you are a test pilot and Oracle isn't likely to provide you with much support. It's kind of like me pulling the engine out of my airplane and reinstalling it without an A&P (Airframe and Powerplant) mechanic certifying the work was done correctly, and without reading the maintenance manual to figure out how much torque to apply to the engine mount bolts. Yeah, I can probably do it, but why take the risk and why guess at it when the information is right there for me?

So, please read the upgrade manual. If you are not well acquainted with the Oracle upgrade process (it has not changed much for you old hands but read through it once for the Gipper, OK?), then read it again. Having done that, you won't ask a question in a public forum that clearly indicates you have not read the manual, and I won't have to flame you. OK, I'm not that crotchety yet, but there are those who will flame you if you have not read the manual.

## Upgrade Prerequisites

Depending on the other Oracle software you may be using, database upgrade prerequisites will vary. Typical prerequisites would include upgrading Oracle Clusterware and upgrading ASM before you upgrade databases using these components.

Again, carefully read the upgrade documentation before you attempt any upgrade to ensure that you are following the correct upgrade path for your configuration.

Another area to pay special attention to is the OS and the Oracle related requirements for OS versions and patches. In many cases, the Oracle Universal Installer (OUI) will point out if you are not meeting the minimum required configuration. There may well be cases in which OS patches need to be applied and the OUI is not aware of these requirements. Check with Oracle Metalink and your vendors for more information on this issue.

### Give Back to the Community

I suppose I could bring in a celebrity at this point to give this message, but I'll do it anyway. Please give. Give generously. The Oracle community needs your experience with this and every new version that comes out of the chute. If you have problems, don't just find a workaround and move on. Let us hear about them. Use the newsgroups I mentioned before and share your problems with the Oracle community because it makes us stronger. Please, don't just give up if something doesn't work right; open a service request with Oracle and get them to fix it and share your discovery with the world. Blogs are great things, and I'd hope that after only a few hours of Oracle Database 11*g* production availability we will see blogs on your experience show up and fill Google search results unto eternity. Please, give until you can give no more—we will all be thankful.

## Supported Upgrade Paths

Generally Oracle Database 11*g* supports upgrades from Oracle9*i* Releases 1 and 2, and Oracle Database 10*g* Releases 1 and 2. Table 1-1 provides more detail on the upgrade support for Oracle Database 11*g*.

| Your Database Version | Requirements for Upgrading to Oracle Database 11*g* |
| --- | --- |
| Any Oracle version < = 9.0.1.4 | Upgrade to Oracle Database 10.2 using a supported upgrade path(s). Direct migration to Oracle Database 11*g* is not supported unless you use import/export or the SQL*Plus copy method. |
| Oracle 9.2.0.4 (or higher), Oracle Database 10.1.0.2 (or higher) Oracle Database 10.2.0.1 (or higher) | Direct upgrade via supported upgrade methods is supported. |

**TABLE 1-1.** *Oracle Database 11g Supported Upgrade Paths*

## Supported Upgrade Methods

Oracle Database 11*g* supports four different methods of upgrading your database:

- The Database Upgrade Assistant (DBUA)

- Manual database upgrade

- Export/import

- Data copy

In the next sections we will look at each of these methods in detail.

## Upgrade with DBUA

I must confess up front that I don't use the DBUA much. I'm a command-line kind of guy, and so I prefer the more granular control that I get with the manual upgrade process. However, the manual upgrade process can be tedious, so in my opinion the DBUA is a nice tool to have when you have a number of databases you need to upgrade, and you want to do the upgrade with as little muss and fuss as possible. In this section we will introduce you to the DBUA and then we will talk about the logs created by the DBUA that you can review after you have upgraded the database.

### Using the DBUA

**NOTE**
*If you have multiple versions of Oracle installed, make sure you are running the correct version of DBUA (use the DBCA executable in the ORACLE_ HOME directory of the Oracle Database version you are upgrading to). Although you will get an error message if you are running the wrong version, it can take some time for that message to appear.*

The DBUA will step you through the process of doing a database upgrade of both a clustered Oracle database and a nonclustered Oracle database. The DBUA also provides the option to upgrade an ASM instance.

The DBUA will make various recommendations as to configuration changes that you might want to make as a part of the database upgrade. For example, if your optimizer statistics are stale, DBUA will recommend that you exit the DBUA and update those statistics before you do the upgrade.

**NOTE**
*If you did not make the required time zone patch
updates to your Oracle9i or Oracle 10g database,
the DBUA will fail to upgrade your database until
you have applied these patches!*

After you have started the DBUA, it will present you with a list of databases you
can upgrade as seen in Figure 1-1. This list shows you the ORACLE_HOME and
database name of each Oracle instance on the system. Because this list is generated
from the /etc/oratab file in UNIX OS's or the list of available Oracle Database
Services in Windows, you will find all Oracle databases on your system included on
the list (even those that may not be functioning). From this list, select the database
you wish to upgrade

After you have started the DBUA, it will present you with a list of databases you
can upgrade as seen in Figure 1-1. This list shows you the ORACLE_HOME and
database name of each Oracle instance on the system. Because this list is generated
from the /etc/oratab file, you will find all Oracle databases on your system included
on the list (even those that may not be functioning). From this list, select the database
you wish to upgrade.

The DBUA will prompt you to enter a value for the new **diagnostic_dest** parameter.
This parameter replaces the old background, user, and core dump destination
directories. The DBUA will provide you with a default destination that you can choose,

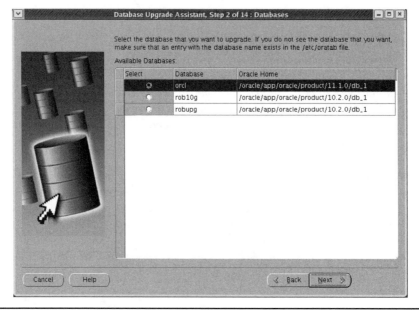

**FIGURE 1-1.**  *The Database Upgrade Assistant: select database screen*

or you can enter an alternative directory location for these files to be stored in. We will discuss the **disgnostic_dest** parameter and other new parameter-related information later in this chapter.

As with previous versions of the DBUA, you can choose to have Oracle back up the database before the upgrade, or you can indicate that you have already backed up the database. If you allow the DBUA to back up the database, then the backup will be a cold backup, so be aware that you will be adding to the total time the database will be down for the upgrade if you are going to have DBUA perform the backup.

If you want to perform your own backup, I'd suggest you use Recovery Manager (RMAN) to perform the backup. Oracle Press has a great book on RMAN called *Oracle Database 10g RMAN Backup and Recovery* that can guide you on your RMAN backup. Here is an example of an RMAN command that you can use to back up your database:

```
RMAN> shutdown immediate
RMAN> startup restrict
RMAN> backup database plus archivelog
format 'backup_destination_here' tag before_upgrade;
RMAN> shutdown immediate
RMAN> startup
```

**NOTE**
*Of course, backups are very important, particularly when an upgrade fails for whatever reason. I'd prefer to back up the database before the upgrade. If you are using RMAN you can validate the backup and make sure it's complete. If you have the time and resources, I'd do a test restore on the backup just to cover yourself completely.*

The DBUA also gives you the option of moving your database datafiles during the upgrade process if you so desire. You can move them from file system to file system, from a file system to ASM, or from ASM to a file system. Personally, I think I'd do this independent of an upgrade, but that's just me.

The DBUA also gives you the option of configuring the Flash Recovery Area (FRA). This is particularly handy if you are moving from Oracle9*i*, which did not offer the FRA, or if you did not use the FRA in previous Oracle Database 10*g* databases.

Another choice you will make from the DBUA is the option to recompile invalid objects after the upgrade. This is similar to running the utlrp.sql package from the SQL command line. The default option is to recompile packages, and I recommend you take this option.  Finally the DBUA provides the option to backup the database (again, I prefer to do this before hand, manually). Having decided to backup or not backup, DBUA will provide a summary of your choices, and warnings related to the database upgrade. You simply click on the finish button, and your upgrade will begin! Note that once you start the upgrade, you will not be able to use the database until the upgrade is complete. Figure 1-2 is an example of the DBUA window as it is upgrading a database.

### DBUA-Related Logging

Notice at the bottom of the DBUA output shown in Figure 1-2 that the logging directory for the DBUA is listed (in our case $ORACLE_HOME/cfgtoollogs/dbua/db_name). In this directory you will find the logs related to a DBUA upgrade. After each upgrade you should review the logs in this directory for errors after the migration is complete.

Note the location of the log files in the DBUA window. The logs can be very handy in solving upgrade problems should that arise. The DBUA will create a number of logs in the directory listed. Note that each separate upgrade of a database will have its own log directory (thus, old logs are not removed). For example, in Figure 1-2 the DBUA has put logs into the $ORACLE_HOME/db_1/cfgtools/dbua/rob10dbua/upgrade2 directory. In this case we see that the rob10dbua database has had one upgrade attempt previous to this upgrade attempt (the first upgrade attempt would be in the upgrade1 directory).

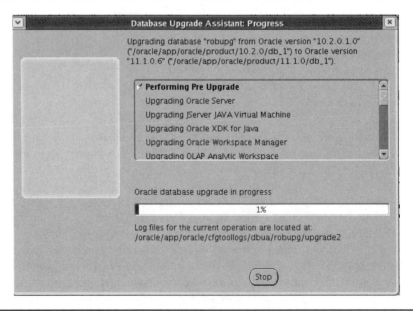

**FIGURE 1-2.** *The Database Upgrade Assistant: progress screen*

**Arup Says…**

I find it extremely useful to let the log files scroll by as the entries are written to them. In Unix-based systems, it is rather trivial. A simple command in another terminal, **tail -f <logfile>**, shows a continuous display of the tail end of the file. As new material is added to it, I see it. This gives a little bit more educated insight into the process than just looking at the upgrade screen with a slider bar and a percentage indicator.

Within the DBUA log file directory there are a number of logs you might be interested in. Table 1-2 provides a list of the log files of most interest to you.

### How Do I Know If the Upgrade Is Successful?

Of course, if you watch the DBUA to completion, then you will know the upgrade is successful (and that you can patiently outwait a very boring bit of screen output). The DBUA will provide you with the screen seen in Figure 1-3 which indicates success.

After you click on OK, the DBUA will display the Upgrade Results page. This page provides summary information about the completed upgrade that includes

| Log Name | Purpose |
| --- | --- |
| UpgradeResults.html | This is a summary of what the DBUA intends to upgrade. This HTML file is displayed by the DBUA before the upgrade begins. |
| Trace.log | Provides detailed tracing information on the entire upgrade process. Any errors reported by the DBUA will be recorded in this log. |
| Oracle_Server.log | This file (which can be quite large) provides details of the execution of the entire migration project. If an error occurs you can find more details in the text of this file. If something in the upgrade fails, this is where you are likely to find information pertinent to the failure. |
| Post_Upgrade.log | Log file for details on post upgrade operations. You can look in this file to determine if the upgrade was successful or not. |

**TABLE 1-2.**   *Oracle Database 11g DBUA Logs of Interest*

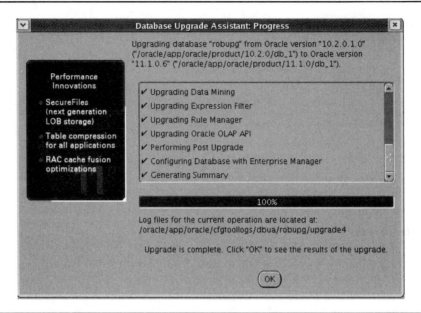

**FIGURE 1-3.** *The Database Upgrade Assistant: Successful Upgrade*

information including the new ORACLE_HOME location, parameters that have been added or updated, and parameters that have been removed. Also you can configure database passwords from the DBUA Upgrade Results page.

If you feel that the upgrade was not successful in some way, the DBUA Upgrade Results page also provides the ability to rollback the upgrade. If you had the DBUA backup the database before it started the upgrade then DBUA will restore the database and reset configuration parameters. If you did your own backup, then this option will only reset various configuration settings and you will need to manually restore the database. Figure 1-4 provides an example of the DBUA Upgrade Results page.

Once your upgrade is complete, you should backup your new database again. Also, backing up other related database files that have changed (like the listener.ora, or the tnsnames.ora) would be a good idea after a successful upgrade.

It may be that you will walk away from the process and then during your absence some horrific thing like the system rebooting will occur (or as happened in my case, your dog gets under your desk and kills the power). So, how do you know if the upgrade was successful in this case? You will want to do the following:

1. Review the Oracle_Server.log (see the previous section for more on this log file). Look for ORA- errors in the log. If there are any in the log that are not expected, you will want to check with Oracle and determine what needs to be done. One problem is that our friends at Oracle have filled this log with

comments that include ORA- in them, so a simple search and find will not work very well. Many times I will just go to the bottom of the log and look to see if there is an error there or near the bottom. Often if an error occurs it will be toward the end of the log.

Another place to look is the Post_Upgrade.log file. This logs all operations that occur after DBUA has actually upgraded the database. Look at the bottom of the file for a successful call to dbms_registry_sys.validate_components call. If it was completed successfully, then odds are that your upgrade was successful.

2. Check the alert log of the database for errors during the migration. There have been some changes to the way the alert log is managed. See Chapter 2 for more details on the new **diagnostic_dest** parameter and how it impacts database logging.

3. You can check the DBA_REGISTRY view to make sure all of the components have the correct version number assigned to them. If they do not, you will need to determine why this is the case (it may be as simple as a bug where one of the components is not getting updated correctly in the registry; that has happened before).

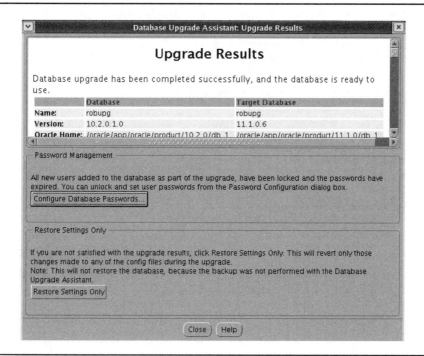

**FIGURE 1-4.**   *The Database Upgrade Assistant: Upgrade Results*

## Going Back

So, what if you see some errors during the upgrade process and the DBUA failed? What if you find errors in the logs and you want to go back? If you had DBUA backup your database, you can have it restore your database. In other cases, you are going to have to restore the database that failed to migrate yourself.

In the DBUA interface, the last screen will give you an option to recover your database if there was an error on the DBUA. However, as in our earlier example, if the power went out and the DBUA session ended as a result, you no longer have that option. This is one reason I just prefer to do a manual backup/restore. DBUA does place all the files used to backup/restore your database into the logging directory. Therefore another option is to go to the logging directory and use the files contained there.

In the case of a power outage (or perhaps the Blue Screen of Death from Windows), you need to review the logs carefully. If you can determine from the logs that the upgrade process failed, you can manually restart the upgrade process from that point. However, if you prefer to stick to using the DBUA to do your upgrades, then the best course of action will be to recover the pre-upgrade database image from the backup you took before the upgrade, and restart the upgrade.

DBUA does a simple copy of your data files when it does a backup rather than use RMAN. You will find your backup files in the directory ORACLE_BASE/admin/ <database_name>/backup. Here you will find a script file or batch file (the name varies by platform) that you can run to restore your database to the pre-Oracle Database 11*g* version. If you are running the script on Windows, it will also drop and re-create the Oracle Windows service for you.

If you backed up your database via RMAN before the upgrade, then restoring the database is as simple as issuing the following RMAN command (note we assume you tagged your backup with the tag "before_upgrade").

```
STARTUP NOMOUNT
RUN
{
    RESTORE CONTROLFILE FROM 'save_controlfile_location';
    ALTER DATABASE MOUNT;
    RESTORE DATABASE FROM TAG before_upgrade
    RECOVER DATABASE NOREDO;
    ALTER DATABASE OPEN RESETLOGS;
}
```

After the restore is complete, you will need to reset your environment variables to point to the old Oracle software locations. If you are using Windows you will need to drop and re-create your Oracle service.

# Manual Upgrades

The downside to manual upgrades is that they can be tedious and you have to manage a number of steps. The upside is that you have a great deal more control over the upgrade process. If something fails and you are doing a manual upgrade, it is often much easier to recover from that failure than if you are using the DBUA.

If you are going to opt for a manual upgrade, the first thing I'd do is read the upgrade manual carefully. I'd then create a checklist for you to follow. Each of the upgrade steps can vary a little bit by platform (for example, Windows installs require that you drop and re-create services). So it's important to read the manual.

In the next sections we will divide the manual process up into pre-upgrade, upgrade, and post-upgrade sections. In each section we will provide some direction and insight into that part of the upgrade process. Finally, we will discuss rolling back the upgrade if that becomes necessary.

## Before You Upgrade to Oracle Database 11*g*

Before you just haul off and run the database upgrade scripts, a bit of pre-planning is in order. While we present an ordered list in Table 1-3 of pre-upgrade steps to follow, you must reference the Oracle Database 11*g* Upgrade Manual as well as the Readme and other related files for the most current information on the steps to follow when upgrading. We have found in the past that things tend to change between different versions (and operating systems), and of course the specific version you are upgrading to may be different than the version we used when we wrote this book (we used the first production version of Oracle Database 11*g* for this book).

Another thing we must mention (again) is that you need to test, test, test (we actually had 10 pages of the word "test" here, but our editor/publisher decided that might be a bit much) before you do anything else. Table 1-3 provides a summary of the pre-upgrade steps that you will want to make sure you take when performing an Oracle Database 11*g* upgrade:

You will notice we mentioned the Oracle Pre-Upgrade Information Tool in step 8 in Table 1-3. It is critical to the smooth upgrade of your database that you run this tool every time you do an upgrade. I have seen cases where the tool was run on development and test databases without any problem findings being noted, only to have an upgrade fail in production. This was because the DBA assumed that there would be no problems with the production upgrade since there were not any problems in the other upgrades. Don't make this mistake.

**NOTE**
*If you are upgrading a clustered database, you will shut down all but one of the instances of the cluster, which will be the node you upgrade. Check out the Oracle upgrade documentation for specific actions that might need to be completed on each node (such as installing the new software on each node and so on).*

| Step | Action |
|------|--------|
| 1 | Read this book! Read the Oracle Database Upgrade guide! |
| 2 | Upgrade your OS and any other vendor software as required to support Oracle Database 11*g*. |
| 3 | Install the Oracle Database 11*g* software. I always like to create a little test database after installing the Oracle software just to make sure everything works right. |
| 4 | Test the upgrade on a non-production database first! |
| 5 | Back up the database. (Earlier in this chapter we provided you with an example RMAN script that you can use.) |
| 6 | Prepare the new **oracle_home** location. Copy the old configuration files (SPFILE, IFILE, password file, and so on) to the new Oracle Database 11*g* locations. Review these files and update them to include any new or changed parameters. |
| 7 | Check the redo log file size and ensure that it is greater than 4MB in size. The Oracle Database 11*g* upgrade process will fail if the online redo logs are smaller than 4MB in size. You can run this query to determine the size of the online redo logs:<br>```Select name, bytes```<br>```FROM V$LOGFILE;``` |
| 8 | Run the Oracle Pre-Upgrade Information Tool (utlu111i.sql in our version) to determine what you will need to change in your database to make the upgrade successful. You will find this tool in ORACLE_HOME/rdbms/admin directory of your Oracle Database 11*g* software install. Changes you may need to make include:<br>a. Remove obsolete database parameters.<br>b. Adjust parameter settings to reflect minimum values indicated by the output of the pre-upgrade tool. For example the **sga_target** parameter might need to be increased.<br>c. Increase tablespace sizes.<br>d. You may wish to adjust the **compatible** parameter to 11.0 so you can use the new features of Oracle Database 11*g* after the upgrade. Note that once you modify the **compatible** parameter, you cannot change the **compatible** parameter to a lower setting without recovering your database to a point in time that was before the change of the **compatible** parameter.<br>*Note that during the upgrade, the **compatible** parameter must be set to at least 10.0.0. You can reset it to 9.2.0 after the upgrade if you wish to ensure that you can only use the 9.2.0 feature set.*<br>e. Adjust all paths in the parameter file to reflect the new **oracle_home** structure as needed.<br>f. If you are going to upgrade a cluster, make sure **cluster_database** is set to false for the upgrade. |
| 9 | Determine if there are any new Oracle parameters that you want to use. Determine if there are any parameters that you want to change. You will make these changes after the database upgrade. |
| 10 | Determine if any users are currently using the **CONNECT** role. This role is depreciated in Oracle Database 11*g* and has all privileges stripped from it except the create session privilege. |
| 11 | If you are using OEM, you will want to save your OEM Control Data should you need to downgrade. Refer to the Oracle Database 11*g* Upgrade Manual for more information on this process. |
| 12 | Create a listener for the Oracle Database 11*g* Database. This will need to be done before you can upgrade to Oracle Database 11*g*. |

**TABLE 1-3.** *Oracle Database 11g Pre-Upgrade Steps*

## Upgrade to Oracle Database 11*g*

Once all the pre-upgrade work is done, it's time for the fun part, upgrading the database! Cowboys on the American plains might have said "yeeeehhhhaaawwww" at this point. Again we provide a table with a general list of steps to follow when upgrading your database. I can't say it enough—please check out the Oracle upgrade manual and make sure nothing has changed or that there are no OS-specific things you need to do. Table 1-4 presents my list.

One of two things, lack of memory or lack of tablespace space, causes many upgrade failures. If your failure is due to one of these, you can simply correct the problem (for example, increase memory, extend the tablespace, or enable **autoextend**) and then **shutdown abort** the database. Then restart the database with the **startup upgrade** command and rerun the catupgrd.sql script again.

If you have started the upgrade with the catupgrd.sql script and you determine that for whatever reason you cannot complete it, you will need to restore your database with the backup you took of it. There is no "flashing back" an incomplete upgrade.

### Re-Run the Upgrade

In the case of an error during a manual upgrade, you can often re-run the upgrade. Simply follow these steps:

1.  Correct the problem.

2.  Shutdown the database (**shutdown immediate**).

3.  Restart the database with the **startup upgrade** command.

4.  Re-start the upgrade process from step 9 in Table 1-4.

### After You Upgrade to Oracle Database 11*g*

Once the upgrade script has completed the upgrade, you are almost done! Now we need to perform some post-upgrade steps to check the upgrade status and complete the process. One last time we will provide a table with a general list of steps to follow when upgrading your database. Also one last time we remind you to first check out the Oracle upgrade manual and make sure nothing has changed. Table 1-5 gives you our list.

**NOTE**
*We can't say it enough: These are the general steps you will need to take. You must reference the upgrade guide, and your OS-specific documentation for the complete enchilada! Don't cry for me, Argentina—you must prepare before you do!*

| Step | Action |
| --- | --- |
| 1 | Shut down the database. You should shut down the database in a consistent manner using **shutdown immediate**. If you must use **shutdown abort**, restart the database in restricted mode and then do a **shutdown immediate**. |
| 2 | *If you are using Windows*, you will need to stop the Oracle service for the database you are upgrading. You will then use the oradim utility to remove the service for the database you are migrating. Then use the oradim utility to re-create the new Oracle Database 11*g* service. |
| 3 | *If you are using UNIX*, you will need to make sure your environment variables are pointing to the new Oracle Database 11*g* directories. This would include **oracle_home**, **path**, **classpath**, and **ld_library_path** as well as any OS-specific environment variables you may need to set. |
| 4 | Open a command-line window/prompt and change to the ORACLE_HOME\rdbms\admin directory. |
| 5 | Start SQL*Plus (make sure you are using the 11*g* version of SQL*Plus!) and connect to the database as a user with SYSDBA privileges. |
| 6 | From the SQL*Plus prompt, start up the database in upgrade mode using the following command:<br><br>**startup upgrade**<br><br>Confirm that the banner says the database was started with Oracle Database version 11. There is no need to stop the upgrade process if errors appear indicating that obsolete initialization parameters are in use. You can correct those errors after the upgrade has completed. |
| 7 | If you are upgrading from Oracle 8.1.7 or Oracle9*i*, you will need to create a **sysaux** tablespace. Follow the direction in the upgrade guide to complete this step. |
| 8 | Use the **spool** command to start spooling the results of the upgrade to a log file.<br>`SQL> spool upgrade.log` |
| 9 | Using the catupgrd.sql script, start the upgrade process!<br>`SQL> @catupgrd.sql`<br>Once this script has completed, it will shutdown the database. |
| 10 | Restart the newly upgraded database with the **startup** command. |

**TABLE 1-4.** *Oracle Database 11g Upgrade Steps*

| Step | Action |
|------|--------|
| 1 | Run any post-install actions required by any ancillary Oracle features that you might have installed in your database (for example, Oracle Text). These steps will be listed in the Oracle Database 11*g* upgrade guide, or in the component-specific user guide. |
| 2 | Run the post-upgrade tool (in our version, utlu111s.sql) to display the status of the database components. Ensure that all components show a valid status. |
| 3 | Run the catuppst.sql script from $ORACLE_HOME/rdbms/admin. This script contains upgrade related steps that do not require the database to be started in upgrade mode. |
| 4 | After the catuppst.sql script has completed, run the utlrp.sql script contained in $ORACLE_HOME/rdbms/admin. Note that catuppst.sql and utlrp.sql can be run at the same time. After running utlrp.sql, you should make sure that no unexpected objects are still invalid. SQL that can help you make this determination might include:<br>`SELECT count(*) FROM dba_invalid_objects;`<br>`SELECT distinct object_name FROM dba_invalid_objects;` |
| 5 | Shut down the database. As before, you should shut down the database in a consistent manner using **shutdown immediate**. |
| 6 | Remove any obsolete parameters from the parameter file. Add or change any Oracle Database 11*g*-specific parameters you identified during the pre-upgrade steps. |
| 7 | Start up the database with the **startup** command. |
| 8 | If you are using Oracle Label Security, you will need to run olstrig.sql to re-create the data manipulation language (DML) triggers on the tables with Oracle Label Security policies. |
| 9 | Recompile all stored PL/SQL and Java code with utlrp.sql. Check that all packages and classes are valid. |
| 10 | Check the component Registry (DBA_REGISTRY) and make sure that each component has been properly upgraded. |
| 11 | Back up your database. |
| 12 | Perform any final post-upgrade tasks as required. Such tasks might include:<br>a. Upgrading the RMAN Recovery catalog<br>b. Upgrading any statistics tables that you might have created.<br>c. Changing passwords for newly created Oracle-supplied accounts.<br>d. Enabling passwords to enforce case sensitivity.<br>e. Enabling any other new Oracle 11*g* features you might wish to use.<br><br>Check the upgrade guide for a complete list of possible post-upgrade tasks that you might need to complete. |

**TABLE 1-5.**   *Oracle Database 11*g* Post-Upgrade Steps*

Be extra aware of additional things you might need to do depending on what options you are running. For example, if you are using packages such as **utl_tcp, utl_smtp, utl_mail, utl_http, or utl_inaddr** then you are going to want to review new features revolving around Access Control Lists (ACL) in Oracle Database 11*g*. Until you have configured ACL's in 11*g*, you will not be able to use these functions anymore. We discuss ACL's in chapter 6 of this book.

## Rolling Back Your Upgrade to Oracle Database 10*g*

In America we say, "When all else fails, punt".… When your newly upgraded database just isn't working and you need to go back, what do you do? The most obvious answer is to restore the backup you took before the upgrade. This is the simplest and most straightforward way of rolling back an upgrade.

Oracle Database 11*g* supports downgrading to the 10*g* major version of the release that you upgraded from (note that downgrade to 9*i* is not supported). So, if you went from 10.1 to 11.1, you can downgrade to 10.1 but not to 10.2. Of course, you will need to make sure that you have not used any new Oracle Database 11*g* features before you downgrade, and the **compatible** parameter can not have been changed to 11. There are some version specific downgrade requirements, depending on which version you upgraded from. Please reference the Oracle Database Upgrade Guide for more details with regards to downgrading to the version of Oracle you are upgrading from.

**NOTE**
*You can use export/import to downgrade to any previous version, but that takes a lot of time. We discuss this topic more later in this chapter.*

As a part of the pre-upgrade process, I'd strongly recommend performing a rollback test where you roll back a test database. This way you will be familiar with the process. You might also want to talk to Oracle support and check Metalink to make sure there are no gotchas waiting for you if you have to rollback. The Oracle Upgrade Manual provides a concise set of instructions on downgrading your Oracle Database to its previous version.

**NOTE**
*Any time you have to downgrade, you should consider that you are at risk. If things are bad enough with the version of the software that you are on that you have to downgrade, you need to consider that the software can equally go wrong when you are trying to use it to downgrade (for example, perhaps a bug has introduced block corruption). When crafting an upgrade plan, you must consider the possibility that downgrading will not be an option.*

**Arup Says...**

Before you upgrade, you should create a script to create the control file. You can do it very easily by issuing **alter database backup controlfile to trace**. This command will generate a trace file in the user_dump_dest directory. Locate that file, open it, trim off all the fat from the top (the stuff like the Oracle version, date, and so on) and save it in some location as a file named cr_cntfile.sql. This file is a script to re-create the control file. If all else fails, you can at least create a control file from this script to restore the database to the previous version. If that is not reason enough, consider the contents of this script file: It contains the database parameters like **maxdatafiles**; the names of all the redo log and data files; temporary tablespace files; database characterset, and many other things. Think of this as a quick documentation of the database. You should keep this file and the pre-11*g* initialization file in some safe location.

# Using Export/Import for Upgrades and Rollback

You can use the Export/Import utilities (or Data Pump if you are using Oracle Database 10*g* Release 1 or later) to perform both upgrades and rollbacks if you prefer. In this section we will discuss both of these options, starting with using export to upgrade the database. We will then discuss rolling back using export/ import. While most of these sections will also apply to using Oracle Data Pump, our final section will address the few issues that differ when Data Pump is in use.

## Upgrade with Export/Import

I've talked to a number of DBAs who prefer to use the export/import method of upgrading to a new database. Using export/import is a supported migration method, as is using the Oracle Data Pump utilities introduced in Oracle Database 10*g*. For a smaller database, or for cases where you would like to move your database to another environment, export/import can be a good solution. Smaller is key here though, as the export/import process can take a very long time on larger databases, certainly much longer than using the DBUA or manually upgrading a database.

The export/import method requires that you have first created an Oracle database. You can easily create a database with the Oracle Database Configuration Assistant, or manually if you prefer. Once that is done then you can export the database from the database to be upgraded, and import it into your new Oracle Database 11*g* database.

Export/import comes in very handy if your database is at a version of Oracle that does not support a direct upgrade path to Oracle Database 11*g*. This can reduce the time to upgrade the database, since you don't need to perform multiple upgrades. I've also run into cases in the past where we could not find the CDs to the intermediate version of Oracle that we needed to upgrade to, so we just opted to export and import. This was just a much easier solution.

Exports from lower versions are always upward compatible. So if you are migrating from a 7.3 database to an 11*g* database via export, there should be no problems.

## Downgrade with Export/Import

Downgrading via an export, such as when you are trying to roll back from an upgrade, is a different issue. In these cases you need to make sure you are using the correct version of the Oracle export/import utility. The general rule is that when you are exporting from a higher version of the Oracle database with intent to import the file into a lower-level Oracle database, then you should use the lower version of the export and import utilities. For example, to export from Oracle Database Version 11*g* to Oracle Database Version 10*g*, you would use the Oracle Database 10*g* versions of export and import.

Along with making sure you use the correct version of the export/import utilities, you will also need to make sure that you have the correct version of the export views loaded in the database. This only applies in cases where you are exporting from a newer database with the intent of importing the data into an older database. For example, suppose you intend to export from Oracle Database Version 11*g* to Oracle Database Version 10*g*. In this case, you would first load catexp.sql from the Oracle Database 10*g* ORACLE_HOME into the Oracle Database 11*g* database. Once the export is complete, run catexp.sql from the Oracle Database Version 11*g* ORACLE_HOME in the database to update the views to the correct version of Oracle.

One more issue with regard to rolling back with export/import is the issue of object compatibility. If you have started to utilize some of the features of Oracle Database 11*g* in your schemas and you decide you need to roll back the database to an earlier version, you might be in for a nasty surprise. For example, if you exported from Oracle 8.0.5 into an Oracle Database 11*g* database and then created a table using list partitioning, you would have a problem if you tried to rollback to Oracle 8.0.5. The bottom line is: be careful after you upgrade if you make any schema changes using new Oracle Database 11*g* features.

## What about Oracle Data Pump?

The biggest difference when using Oracle Data Pump has to do with the issue of version differences. Data Pump makes it so much easier to move data between different versions of the database. Oracle Data Pump comes with a **version** parameter that allows you to define the version of the database that you are creating the export for. So, for example, if you are exporting from an Oracle 11*g* database and you wish to import that file into an Oracle 10.2.0 database, you would include

**version=10.2.0** in the **expdp** command line. As with export/import, Oracle Data Pump can read a dump file created by an older version of the database when importing into a newer version.

## Upgrade Using Data Copying

Oracle Database 11*g* also supports upgrades via the SQL*Plus copy command through database links. This is a handy way to upgrade smaller databases, or if you wish to only upgrade a small subset of a given schema (or perhaps subsets of rows in a given schema).

If you choose this approach you will have to create the new Oracle Database 11*g* database along with the tablespaces, the needed schemas/users, and the database links before you could begin the migration process.

# Oracle Parameter Changes

Each new Oracle version includes changes to the parameters within the database. This section covers these changes so you can consider them in your upgrade plans. In this section we will cover new parameters, deprecated parameters (ones that still work but you need to consider replacing), and obsolete parameters (ones that no longer work and you need to remove). We will only be covering the more commonly used parameters in this section. We will not cover changes to hidden, obscure, rarely used or OS-specific parameters.

## New Parameters

A number of new parameters are available in Oracle Database 11*g*. A number of these new parameters will be covered in various parts of this book. Parameters discussed in this book are marked with the symbol (*). You can reference the index for specific pages where these parameters are discussed. The new parameters in Oracle Database 11*g* include the following:

- **asm_preferred_read_failure_groups** (*)

- **client_result_cache_lag** (*)

- **client_result_cache_size** (*)

- **commit_logging** (*)

- **commit_wait** (*)

- **control_management_pack_access**(*)

- **db_lost_write_protect**

- **db_securefile**
- **db_ultra_safe**
- **ddl_lock_timeout** (*)
- **diagnostic_dest** (*)
- **global_txn_processes**
- **java_jit_enabled** (*)
- **ldap_directory_sysauth**
- **memory_max_target** (*)
- **memory_target** (*)
- **optimizer_capture_sql_plan_baselines** (*)
- **optimizer_use_invisible_indexes** (*)
- **optimizer_use_pending_statistics** (*)
- **optimizer_use_sql_plan_baselines** (*)
- **parallel_io_cap_enabled**
- **plscope_settings**
- **redo_transport_user**
- **resource_manager_cpu_allocation**
- **result_cache_max_result** (*)
- **result_cache_max_size** (*)
- **result_cache_mode**(*)
- **result_cache_remote_expiration**(*)
- **sec_case_sensitive_logon**(*)
- **sec_max_failed_login_attempts** (*)
- **sec_protocol_error_further_action**
- **sec_protocol_error_trace_action**

- **sec_return_server_release_banner**

- **xml_db_events**

# Deprecated Parameters

Deprecated parameters are parameters that Oracle eventually plans on making obsolete. They work normally, but warnings will appear as the database is starting up on the console and in the database alert log. You can also determine if a parameter is deprecated by using the column **isdeprecated** in the **v$parameter** view. If the parameter is deprecated, this column will be set to TRUE.

Three parameters in Oracle Database 11*g* are deprecated (since Oracle Database 10*g* Release 2) in favor of the **diagnostic_dest** parameter. These are

- **background_dump_dest**

- **core_dump_dest**

- **user_dump_dest**

Remaining deprecated parameters (since Oracle Database 10*g* Release 2) include:

- **commit_write**   This parameter is replaced by the new **commit_logging** and **commit_wait** parameters.

- **instance_groups**   See Chapter 10 for more information on Real Application Cluster changes in Oracle Database 11*g*.

- **log_archive_local_first**

- **plsql_debug** Replaced by **plsql_optimize_level**

- **plsql_v2_compatibility**

- **remote_os_authent**

- **standby_archive_dest**

- **transaction_lag attribute**

NOTE
*You can find a complete list of deprecated parameters from various versions of Oracle in the Oracle Database Upgrade Guide for 11g Release 1.*

> **Arup Says...**
> I strongly recommend setting the parameter **diagnostic_dest** when you upgrade
> the database or create a new database under Oracle 11*g*. Oracle ignores the
> parameter **background_dump_dest**, even if it is defined in the initialization
> parameter file. Instead it assumes the parameter **diagnostic_dest** to be
> **$oracle_base**. In that directory, it creates a subdirectory, diag; then another one
> under that, rdbms; yet another subdirectory under that, <database name>; and
> so on, and stores the text alert log there. So don't be surprised if you suddenly
> find the alert log of the older database not being updated any more. It will be
> under the **diagnostic_dest** directory.

## Obsolete Parameters

A database with obsolete parameters will start, but warnings on the console and in
the alert log will appear. Parameter in Oracle Database 11*g* that have been made
obsolete include:

- **Ddl_wait_for_locks**

- **Logmnr_max_persistent_sessions**

- **Plsql_compiler_flags**

## Undo_Management Parameter Madness

One final parting thought on changes to parameters in Oracle Database 11*g*. That is
that the **undo_management** parameter default is now AUTO. Manual undo is still
available but you will have to enable it in order to use it.

# Oracle Dictionary View Changes

Amazingly, no static data dictionary views were deprecated in Oracle Database 11*g*.
The **v$datafile** view had the column **plugged_in** removed. A large number of new
views have been added. Review the Oracle Database Reference manual for more
information on the different views that have been added.

Additionally, Oracle Database 11*g* does not deprecate any dynamic views
either. A large number of new views have been added. Review the Oracle Database
Reference manual for more information on the different views that have been
added.

# End of Line

The word Summary or Chapter Summary seems so old fashioned. "End of Line" therefore will be my summary at the end of these chapters. For those of you who don't know, "End of Line" was used in the movie *Tron*. The MCP would say "End of Line" after finishing his communications.

Thus we are at End of Line for this chapter. We have discussed the rather involved process of upgrading to Oracle Database 11*g*. We have discussed both automated upgrades and manual upgrades, and hopefully I've given you a proper feel for each, so you can decide which way you want to go. Successfully finishing an upgrade is ultimately satisfying. Successfully finishing the upgrade of 200+ databases is wholly satisfying.

Now, get out there and upgrade those databases and read the rest of this book to figure out what great things lie in wait for you with Oracle Database 11*g*!

End of line…

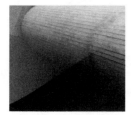

# CHAPTER
## 2

# Oracle Database New
# Management Features

hey say the winters in Russia are long and cold. I must say that this chapter kind of feels like a Russian winter. It's long, and may seem a bit dry instead of cold, but it's full of important Oracle Database 11*g* stuff. Oracle Database 11*g* has a number of new features and enhanced functionality in it that simplify database management. These features include:

- Automatic Storage Management (ASM)

- Automatic Memory Management

- Automatic Database Diagnostic Monitor (ADDM)

- Automatic Workload Repository (AWR)

- Scheduler AutoTask automated maintenance tasks

- Parameter file management changes and new features

- Resource Manager

- Finer-grained dependencies

- DDL WAIT

- Add column with defaults

Let's start by looking at new features and changes related to ASM.

# ASM-Related Changes and New Features

Automatic Storage Management (ASM) has a number of new features that are designed to make using ASM easier and more efficient. New ASM features include:

- New documentation

- ASM disk group attributes

- ASM fast disk resync

- ASM compatibility attributes

- ASM preferred mirror read

- ASM rolling upgrade

- Other ASM enhancements

- New SYSASM role

## New ASM-Related Documentation

Oracle Database 11*g* has added additional documentation dedicated to storage management. The *Oracle Database Storage Administration Guide* is now a part of the overall database documentation set and covers installing, configuring, and using ASM in great detail.

## ASM Disk Group Attributes

A new ASM **attribute** clause is available that allows you to assign attributes directly to ASM disk groups (as opposed to using templates). Some of these attributes already existed in Oracle Database 10g, but there are also new attributes you can assign to a diskgroup (which we will discuss in later sections in this chapter), and the **attribute** clause is new. Both the **create diskgroup** and the **alter diskgroup** commands allow you to define or modify these settings as required. The following table shows a list of the attributes you can set with the new **attribute** clause.

| Attribute | Description |
|---|---|
| **au size** | This is the allocation unit size that defaults to 1MB. This attribute can only be set when the disk group is created. The AU size can be defined using any power of 2 (1,2,4, 8, etc.) from 1M to 64M. For example, 4M would be 4194304. |
| **compatible.rdbms** | See the section "ASM Compatibility Settings" later in this chapter. Example '11.0'. The default value is 10.1. This value cannot be rolled back to a previous, lower version setting. |
| **compatible.asm** | Defines the format of the data on the ASM disks. See the section "ASM Compatibility Settings" later in this chapter. Example '11.0'. The default value is 10.1. |
| **disk_repair_time** | Causes the resync process to begin to keep track of changes to disk extents that belong to an offline disk. See the section "ASM Fast Disk Resync" later in this chapter. Valid values are from 0 to 136 years. Support for this attribute is only available if both **compatible** attributes (**compatible.rdbms** and **compatible.asm**) are set to 11.1 or higher. |

You can query the V$ASM_ATTRIBUTE view to see the individual attributes assigned to a given disk group. Here is an example:

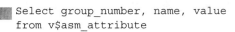

```
Select group_number, name, value
from v$asm_attribute
```

```
order by group_number, name;
GROUP_NUMBER NAME                         VALUE
------------ -------------------- --------------------
           1 au_size              1048576
           1 compatible.asm       11.1.0.0.0
           1 compatible.rdbms     11.1.0
           1 disk_repair_time     600M
```

## ASM Fast Disk Resync

Oracle Database 11*g* introduces ASM fast disk resync. This new feature allows you to resynchronize ASM disks within an ASM disk group with a surviving disk group after a failure group becomes unavailable for a period of time (for example, due to a disk controller failure). As long as the failure does not cause the attached disk media to become corrupted, ASM fast disk resync can resynchronize the missing disks as soon as the interruption is corrected. The time to perform the resync is dependent on a number of factors, but it often can be much quicker than rebuilding the entire disk group. During the resync operation your ASM disks can be fully operational. You should consider that there will be performance degradation during the time of the disk repair. Also you will need to consider the loss of redundancy during the overall outage and resynchronize time.

Typically, ASM will drop a disk not long after it has been taken offline. To enable the use of fast disk resynchronization (and prevent the disk from being taken offline), you will need to set the **disk_repair_time** attribute for a given disk group. When the **disk_repair_time** attribute is set, the resync process will begin to keep track of changes to disk extents that belong to an offline disk. When the disk is brought back online, the resync process will synchronize the disk and bring it back into the disk group.

You define the disk repair time in units of minutes or hours (using m/M or h/H to indicate the unit). You can also define partial hours by use of a decimal indicator (for example, 3.5H). The default (if you set the **disk_repair_time** attribute without a time setting) is 3.6 hours if you do not indicate a time in the **disk_repair_time** attribute (so if you are using the default, you better hustle when fixing those bad disk cables!). If you stock disk cards, cables, and the like in your computer room and you sleep on a cot not far away, then 3.6 hours may be long enough. However, if you are like me and you live a fair distance away and your outages always happen at hours that are not conducive to getting replacement hardware within 3.6 hours, you might consider increasing the size of this attribute. The repair time will reset after a disk is brought back online; therefore, if it goes offline again, the clock starts counting from 0.

If a disk goes offline and the disk repair time elapses, then the disk will be dropped. If you have a disk that goes offline and you want to drop it before the repair time expires, you can issue the **alter diskgroup ... disk offline** statement using the **drop after** clause.

**NOTE**
*You cannot set a **disk_repair_time** attribute for a disk
that is already offline.*

Here are some examples of setting a disk group's disk repair time attribute:

```
ALTER DISKGROUP DG1 SET ATTRIBUTE 'DISK_REPAIR_TIME'='18H';
ALTER DISKGROUP DG2 SET ATTRIBUTE 'DISK_REPAIR_TIME'='12.5H';
ALTER DISKGROUP DG3 SET ATTRIBUTE 'DISK_REPAIR_TIME'='600M';
```

## ASM Compatibility Settings

Oracle Database 11*g* provides for granular control of compatibility with regard to
ASM disk groups. This is done through the setting of two different compatibility
attributes via the **alter diskgroup** command. The first is the *Oracle disk group
compatibility* attribute. The Oracle disk group **compatibility** attribute setting
defines the format of the data on the ASM disks, and should always be equal or
greater than the **compatibility** parameter of the Oracle database accessing the ASM
disk. The **compatible.asm** attribute must always be set to a value that is equal to or
greater than the **compatible.rdbms** attribute. Once this attribute is set, it cannot be
rolled back.

You set the Oracle disk group compatibility setting via the **alter diskgroup**
command setting the **compatible.asm** attribute as seen in this example:

```
ALTER DISKGROUP DG1 SET ATTRIBUTE 'compatible.asm'='11.1.0';
```

You can also set this parameter when using the **create diskgroup** command as
seen here:

```
CREATE DISKGROUP dgroup4 EXTERNAL REDUNDANCY
DISK '/oracle/asmdata/asm_dgroup1_04.asm'
ATTRIBUTE 'compatible.asm' = '11.1';
```

The second attribute is the *Oracle database compatibility* attribute, which is
defined by setting the ASM disk group **compatible.rdbms** attribute. This attribute
defines the minimum version of an Oracle database that can mount a given disk group.
This attribute should be set to a value that is equivalent to the lowest compatibility
setting of any Oracle database that will be mounting that disk group. Once this
attribute is set, it cannot be rolled back since it has implications on the format of the
messages that the ASM instance and the associated database instances are passing back
and forth. Oracle does allow you to roll forward the setting, obviously.

Note that each disk group can have its own compatibility settings, and thus multiple versions of the Oracle database can connect to any given ASM instance. Here is an example of setting the database compatibility attribute:

```
ALTER DISKGROUP DG1 SET ATTRIBUTE 'compatible.rdbms'='11.1.0';
```

An example of how these attributes influence each other can be seen by looking at the relationship between the **disk_repair_time** attribute and the **compatible.asm** attribute. If you accept the default **compatible.asm** setting and try to set the **disk_repair_time** attribute, you will get this error:

```
ORA-15032: not all alterations performed
ORA-15242: could not set attribute DISK_REPAIR_TIME
ORA-15283: ASM operation requires compatible.rdbms of 11.1.0.0.0 or higher
```

This message indicates that you need to set the **compatible.asm** attribute for the disk group being configured. Set the **compatible.asm** attribute from the default of 11.0.0 to 11.1.0 as seen in the following example, and all will be well:

```
ALTER DISKGROUP DG1 SET ATTRIBUTE 'compatible.asm'='11.1.0';
```

So, the compatibility parameter not only controls which databases can connect to your ASM disk groups; it also controls the features available in ASM (just like the database compatibility parameter). You can see the compatibility settings for disk groups using the V$ASM_ATTRIBUTE view.

One example of the interaction of the **compatible.asm** and **compatible.rdbms** attributes might be a case where **compatible.rdbms** is set to a value of 10.2, and **compatible.asm** to a value of 11.1. This will restrict the ASM disk group management to versions of Oracle greater than 11.1, but the individual disk groups can manage Oracle database instances with the compatible parameter set to 10.2 or greater.

## ASM Preferred Mirror Read

Some ASM configurations involve remote mirroring to disks that are a fair distance away (and may also involve remote instances). In these cases, the primary disk group may not be the best set of disks for a given instance to read from. For example, you might have two Real Application Clusters (RAC) instances on hardware 30 miles apart. One set of disks might be stored with each RAC system. In this case, you want the local RAC instance to be able to read from the closest ASM disk that is available to ensure the best performance.

ASM preferred mirror read is only available on RAC configurations, and generally used only with clustered ASM instances. ASM preferred mirror read allows you to read from a mirrored extent rather than the primary extent. To take advantage of this feature, you should configure a mirrored extent copy that is local to each distant node in the cluster. Use the new parameter, **asm_preferred_read_failure_groups**, to configure the instance with a list of preferred disk failure group names to use when accessing ASM disks. The format of the parameter is *diskgroupname.failuregroupname* where *diskgroupname* is the name of the disk group that the failure group belongs to and *failuregroupname* the name of the preferred failure group. You can include multiple diskgroup/failgroup names by separating each preferred read group defined with a comma as seen in this example:

```
Asm_preferred_read_failure_groups=dgroup1.fdisk2, dgroup2.fdisk2
```

If ASM cannot read from the preferred disk failure group, it will proceed to read from the preferred group and then from any additional failure group that might be defined. You can use the PREFERRED_READ column of the V$ASM_DISK view to determine if a given disk in a disk group is a preferred read disk or not.

## ASM Rolling Upgrades

Oracle Database 11*g* now supports rolling upgrades once you have upgraded to Oracle Database 11*g*. Rolling upgrades from Oracle Database 10*g* to Oracle Database 11*g* are not supported. As a part of this rolling upgrade feature, you can upgrade ASM instances as a rolling upgrade. When attempting to perform rolling upgrades, you must take care to ensure that dependent components are upgraded first (for example, you must upgrade Cluster Ready Services [CRS] before you can upgrade ASM).

Oracle has added new syntax to support rolling upgrades. You use the **alter system** command along with the new **start rolling migration** parameter. Each migration will require that a different set of parameters be provided along with the **alter system start rolling migration** command including the version number, release number, update number, port number, and the port update number. Consult the upgrade documentation for the correct time and format of the command for your upgrade.

When you issue the **alter system start rolling migration** command, ASM will first try to determine whether any ASM rebalancing operations are occurring. If rebalancing operations are occurring, then the command will fail. If no rebalancing operations are occurring, then the operational characteristics of the ASM cluster will change as follows:

■  You can only mount and dismount disk groups (no alter, create, or drop).

■  Database can open and close files in disk groups.

- Files can be resized or removed.

- Access to views and fixed packages will be limited. Global views on a clustered ASM instance will be disabled.

After altering the instance to start the migration, you will shut down and upgrade each instance one at a time. Once the upgrade is complete you can restart the ASM instance, and it will join the cluster. Once the upgrade is complete you end the upgrade process using the **alter system** command:

```
Alter system stop rolling migration;
```

If during the upgrade you encounter problems, you can simply reverse the process to roll back. One at a time shut down an ASM node, roll it back to the previous software, and then restart it. Once the rollback is complete you can end the migration. Note that once you end the migration you cannot roll back.

**NOTE**
*As you might imagine, we strongly suggest that you read the upgrade instructions before you do any upgrade and make sure that you can use this procedure for that upgrade.*

# ASM Support for Variable Allocation Unit Sizes

As mentioned in the earlier section "ASM Disk Group Attributes", ASM now supports variable extent sizes, which can reduce the memory requirement associated with large ASM disk files, and thus improve performance. Now as file sizes increase Oracle can allocate multiple extents of varying size. Since the maximum size of an ASM file is dependent on the size of its extent, this means that your files can be larger than the previous limit of 35TB for external redundancy disk groups.

You can also define disk groups such that the files created in them will be created with a different AU size. AU sizes can vary from 1MB to up to 64MB in size. See the earlier section "ASM Disk Group Attributes" for more on how to set the **au** attribute. The ability to define different allocation units allows ASM disk groups with external redundancy to have a maximum file size of 128TB, as opposed to 35TB in Oracle Database 10*g*.

# New SYSASM Role

Oracle has created a new role, SYSASM, that you should use when connecting as an administrator to an ASM instance. You should start using SYSASM instead of SYSDBA because, in the future, SYSDBA connections to an ASM instance will likely not be supported. The authentication requirements for connecting as SYSASM are the same as when you connect as SYSDBA.

**Arup Says...**

The support for variable extent sizes is perhaps the most important addition to ASM in Oracle Database 11g. Prior to 11g, the number of extents, especially in a large database, were simply too high, which made the extent maps too big to be manageable in the shared pool and caused performance issues as well as the dreaded **ORA-4031 Unable to allocate x bytes in shared pool** errors. To alleviate the issue, Oracle Database 10g allowed an allocation unit to be defined in much larger sizes through the use of an underscore parameter, as shown in the following example:

```
_asm_ausize=16777216
```

This parameter, although an underscore one, is supported by Oracle and is documented in MetaLink. The preceding line creates 16MB AUs. In large databases over 10TB, that is a recommended size. The default value is 1048576, or 1MB, even in Oracle Database 11g. But this one-size-fits-all fix was not a solution in all cases. You could set the parameter if you knew well in advance how big your database will grow, but in many cases you may not know that in advance. In Oracle Database 11g, this problem is solved by decoupling the extent size from the AU size. In 11g, one extent may span more than one AU and the extent size grows as the database size grows, keeping the extent map under a manageable limit that improves performance.

However, this also means that extents will become somewhat fragmented on the disk over a period of time. This is usually negligible in many cases, even if you drop and create database objects a lot. This will be a serious problem only if you do a lot of data file creations and deletions. If you see performance issues, you could defragment the disk by using the **alter diskgroup ... rebalance** operation.

An example of connecting to an ASM instance using the new SYSASM role is seen here:

```
[oracle@localhost ~]$ sqlplus / as sysasm
SQL*Plus: Release 11.1.0.3.0 - Beta on Sat Feb 24 19:48:10 2007
Copyright (c) 1982, 2006, Oracle.  All rights reserved.
Connected to:
Oracle Database 11g Enterprise Edition Release 11.1.0.3.0 - Beta
With the Partitioning, OLAP and Data Mining options
SQL>
```

You can also use the normal connect commands such as **connect sys/robert as SYSASM** and the like.

## New asmcmd Commands

It's funny how many people I've talked to who use ASM but have neither used nor heard of **asmcmd**. **Asmcmd** was first released in Oracle Database 10*g* Release 2 to make it easier to navigate ASM disks and their contents. Oracle Database 11*g* has added additional features to **asmcmd** that we will cover in this section. These features include the ability to back up and recover ASM metadata, the new **lddsk** command, the **repair** command, and some new flag options for existing **asmcmd** commands.

### ASM Diskgroup Metadata Backup and Recover

**Asmcmd** comes with a new set of commands that allow you to back up and restore the metadata associated with all your ASM disk groups. The **md_backup** command will create a backup of all the ASM metadata, or a subset of ASM metadata, depending on the parameters that you use. Here is an example of using the **md_backup** command to back up the entire ASM metadata repository:

```
[oracle@localhost ~]$ asmcmd
ASMCMD> md_backup
```

Once this command has completed running, a file will be created in the current working directory. On my Linux system this file was called ambr_backup_intermediate_file, but this filename may well vary on different operating systems. The backup file is pretty much text-based, so you can read through it. More advanced use of the **md_backup** command allows you to control where the backup file will be created, specify the disk groups that you want to back up, and to override various options.

The **md_restore** command is used to restore disk group backups taken with the **md_backup** command. You can restore from the backup without any changes, or the **md_backup** command gives you numerous options to override settings too. Here is an example of doing a metadata restore:

```
[oracle@localhost ~]$ asmcmd
ASMCMD> md_restore -b ambr_backup_intermediate_file
```

Both commands can be run as a parameter when you start **asmcmd** as in this example:

```
[oracle@localhost ~]$ asmcmd md_backup
```

Also be aware that the **md_backup** command will not overwrite a previous backup file. So you will need to move the file somewhere after the backup so the next backup will be successful.

So, why would you use **md_restore** and **md_backup**? As with Oracle databases there is a possibility that the ASM metadata stored in the ASM diskgroups could

> **Arup Says...**
> I can't say enough about the usefulness (and timeliness) of the metadata
> backup/restore functionality. In addition to the possibility of metadata
> corruption as Robert mentions, there is also a possibility of someone running a
> **dd** command to overwrite the contents of the disk header. This has actually
> happened to me! The key thing to understand is that the header tells what is
> located where on the disk. Overwriting the header removes that information,
> but not the actual data itself. So, if you can reinstate the header, you may be
> able to recover the data through the database. So, always run the **md_backup**
> command and keep the output file in a safe location.
>     This **md_restore** command can also reinstate dropped disks, in some cases.
> Another use of that is developing an automatic change control process
> whenever you add, change, or drop disks.

become corrupt (perhaps because of some in-memory OS corruption). While it is
(hopefully) a rare situation, it is in cases like these that your ASM metadata backups
could come in handy. I recommend that, if you are using ASM, a metadata backup
become one of your new daily backup operations.

### Lsdsk Command
The **lsdsk** command lists the disks that are visible to ASM. Here is an example:

```
[oracle@localhost ~]$ asmcmd lsdsk
Path
/oracle/asmdata/asm_dgroup1_01.asm
/oracle/asmdata/asm_dgroup1_02.asm
```

### Remap Command
The **remap** command can be used to repair a range of physical blocks on your ASM
disks. The command takes as parameters the disk group name, the disk name, and
the block range to remap. Note that while this command might make the disk
usable again (due to physically or logically corrupted blocks), it will not recover lost
or corrupted data for you. Here is an example:

```
[oracle@localhost ~]$ asmcmd remap dgroup1 disk_001 2000-4000
```

### New Options for ls, lsct, and lsdg
The **ls** command has two new parameters, **-c** and **-g**. The **-c** parameter uses the
V$ASM_DISKGROUP view for the source of its output. If the **-g** parameter is used, then
GV$ASM_DISKGROUP will be used as the source of the output of the command.

The **lsct** command also has a new **-g** parameter, which will cause it to select from the GV$ASM_CLIENT view rather than the V$ASM_CLIENT view.

Finally the **lsdg** command also has added the **-c** and **-g** parameters. The **-c** parameter uses the V$ASM_DISKGROUP view for the source of its output. If the **-g** parameter is used, then GV$ASM_DISKGROUP will be used as the source of the output of the command.

# Automatic Memory Management

Oracle has made more changes to automated memory management features in Oracle Database 11*g*. Oracle Automatic Memory Management can now automatically manage both the system global area (SGA) and the program global area (PGA). This additional functionality is controlled through the use of some new parameters, **memory_target** and **memory_max_target**. Also related to this new functionality are some changes to the advisors and some new views. We will discuss each of these topics in the next sections.

## Overview of Automatic Memory Management

Automatic memory management is added onto the existing Oracle Automated Memory Management structure and also allows for the use of the various parameter settings that can be used to configure minimum settings for the pools that the parameters are associated with. Automatic Memory Management adds two new memory parameters, **memory_max_target** and **memory_target**. You can see the relationship of the various memory parameters in Figure 2-1.

There are two parameters that have been added to support Automatic Memory Management, **memory_ target** and **memory_max_target**. Let's look at these parameters next.

### The memory_target Parameter

The **memory_target** parameter is somewhat a combination of the **sga_target** parameter value and the **pga_aggregate_target** parameter, representing the total amount of memory that Oracle has to allocate between the various SGA and PGA structures. The **memory_target** parameter is dynamic and can be changed up to and including the value of **memory_max_target**, which we discuss next.

### The memory_max_target Parameter

The **memory_max_target** parameter allows you to dynamically change the value of the parameter **memory_target** within the confines of **memory_max_target**. Thus you can adjust the total amount of memory available to the database as a whole at any time.

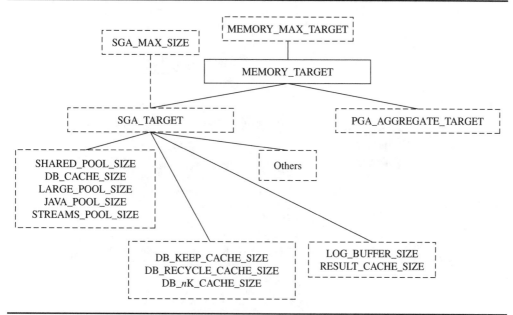

**FIGURE 2-1.**   *Relationship of memory parameters*

The **memory_max_target** parameter is set either manually or derived and defaults to a value equal or greater than the value of the **memory_target** parameter. Oracle will default **memory_max_target** to a value equal to **memory_target** if **memory_max_target** is not set and **memory_target** is set. Oracle will set **memory_max_target** to a value of 0 if **memory_target** is not set. If **memory_target** is not set but **memory_max_target** is set to a non-zero value, then you can modify memory settings dynamically by changing **memory_target**, or by changing the other specific memory parameter settings. Figure 2-2 illustrates the auto memory parameter dependency.

**NOTE**
*The **memory_target** and **memory_max_target** parameters cannot be used when LOCK_SGA has been set. Also **memory_target** and **memory_max_target** cannot be used in conjunction with huge pages on Linux.*

When upgrading you may want to configure the **memory_target** parameter, or you can choose to do it later. When you configure **memory_target** you should take into consideration the current settings for the **sga_target** and **pga_aggregate_target**

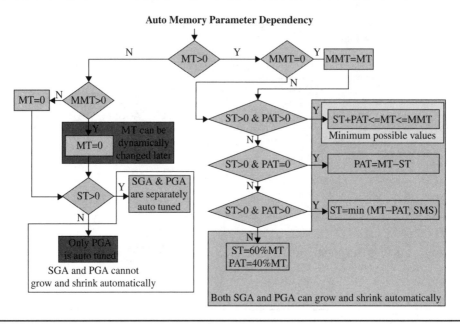

**FIGURE 2-2.**  *Auto memory parameter dependency*

parameters. In most cases, you will want to sum up the sizes of **sga_target** and **pga_aggregate_target** and set **memory_target** to this value. Then set **sga_target** and **pga_aggregate_target** to zero values.

**NOTE**
*Some platforms can give you grief about setting* ***memory_target****. For example, on Linux you need to make sure that /dev/shm (or its equivalent) is allocated with an amount of space slightly larger than what you wish to set the* ***memory_target*** *value to. Failure to do this will result in the following error:*

```
ORA-00845: MEMORY_TARGET not supported on this system
```

In determining how to size memory, you can still choose to leave the **sga_target** and **pga_aggregate_target** parameters set to their current values. In doing so, you indicate minimum amounts of memory that should be allocated to these structures. In this case, Oracle can allocate more memory to either structure but will not be able to reduce memory available to these structures below the setting of the associated parameter. This implies that if you convert to these new parameters during the upgrade process, leaving **sga_target** and **pga_aggregate_target** set as configured, that **memory_target** >= (**sga_target** + **pga_aggregate_target**). Failure to configure this properly will keep the instance from starting due to an ORA-00838 error.

Something else to be aware of is that if you set **memory_max_target** and start the instance, Oracle will grab an amount of free memory equivalent to the setting of **memory_max_target**. This may vary by OS, but this is what we found in the Linux and Windows OS environments. So be aware of the potential implications of setting this parameter.

**NOTE**
*Be careful when changing settings if you are converting to automated memory management. You will want to make sure that the sga_max_size and sga_size are not set when converting to memory_ max_target and memory_target. Although setting these parameters at the same time is supported, you need to do so carefully so as to avoid unexpected consequences.*

## New Memory Advisor Functionality and Views

Oracle has added a new view, V$MEMORY_TARGET_ADVICE, which provides recommendations on how to set the **memory_target** parameter. Here is an example query against this view:

```
SQL> select * from v$memory_target_advice order by memory_size_factor;
MEMORY_SIZE MEMORY_SIZE_FACTOR ESTD_DB_TIME ESTD_DB_TIME_FACTOR    VERSION
----------- ------------------ ------------ ------------------- ----------
        176                .5          126              1.1443          0
        264                .75         110                   1          0
        352                 1          110                   1          0
        440               1.25         110                   1          0
        528                1.5         109                 .99          0
        616               1.75         109                 .99          0
        704                 2          109                 .99          0
```

In this example, we see that increasing memory on our database will have no positive impact. The current **memory_size** setting is 352MB (if the SIZE_FACTOR is 1, then this is the current size) which seems more than sufficient. Increasing it by 25 percent to 440MB (SIZE_FACTOR of 1.25) will only result in a minimal performance increase as shown by the difference in the ESTD_DB_TIME column from 110 to 109. Note that this view will display no data until automated memory management is enabled (setting the **memory_target** parameter at a minimum).

**NOTE**
*The data in these views is dependent on AWR snapshots. If you have disabled AWR, or if you have just created a database, you may see nothing when you query these views. Also the result sets from these views are going to be very dependent on load and use of the system. The output will look very different on an idle system compared to a very busy and dynamic one.*

Another view, V$MEMORY_DYNAMIC_COMPONENTS, provides a peek into the various memory components of the database and how they are sized by Oracle's automated memory management facility. Here is an example of a query against this view showing us the memory components currently configured. Note that in addition to the normal memory pools, there are entries for SGA Target and PGA Target:

```
select component, current_size curr_size, min_size, max_size,
user_specified_size uss, granule_size gs from v$memory_dynamic_
components where current_size > 0;


COMPONENT           CURR_SIZE    MIN_SIZE    MAX_SIZE          USS          GS
---------------  ----------  ----------  ----------  ----------  ----------
shared pool        67108864    62914560    67108864           0     4194304
large pool          4194304           0     4194304           0     4194304
java pool           4194304     4194304     4194304           0     4194304
SGA Target        218103808   218103808   218103808           0     4194304
DEFAULT buffer    134217728   134217728   138412032    83886080     4194304
cache
Shared IO Pool      8388608     8388608     8388608     8388608     4194304
PGA Target        150994944   150994944   150994944           0     4194304
```

## How Is Oracle Managing My Memory?

You can monitor how Oracle is managing your memory by reviewing the V$MEMORY_RESIZE_OPS view. This view contains a list of the last 800 SGA resize requests handled by Oracle. Here is an example:

```
select parameter, initial_size, target_size, start_time
from v$memory_resize_ops
where initial_size > 0 and final_size > 0
order by parameter, start_time;


PARAMETER               INITIAL_SIZE TARGET_SIZE START_TIME
-------------------     ------------ ----------- -------------------
db_cache_size              121634816   117440512 04/28/2007 19:33:45
db_cache_size              121634816   117440512 04/28/2007 19:33:45
db_cache_size              117440512   113246208 04/28/2007 19:33:45
```

```
db_cache_size            113246208   109051904 04/28/2007 19:33:45
db_cache_size            109051904   104857600 04/28/2007 19:34:10
db_cache_size            104857600   100663296 04/28/2007 19:34:33
db_cache_size            100663296    96468992 04/28/2007 19:34:35
pga_aggregate_target     125829120   335544320 04/28/2007 19:39:20
shared_pool_size          58720256    62914560 04/28/2007 19:33:45
shared_pool_size          54525952    58720256 04/28/2007 19:33:45
shared_pool_size          62914560    67108864 04/28/2007 19:34:10
shared_pool_size          67108864    71303168 04/28/2007 19:34:33
shared_pool_size          71303168    75497472 04/28/2007 19:34:35
```

As you can see from this output, Oracle was busy making changes to the database cache and the shared pool!

## Automatic Memory Management and OEM

Oracle Enterprise Manager (OEM) fully supports automatic memory management. From the OEM home page, you click on the Server tab at the top, and then proceed to click on memory advisors. From this page you can enable or disable automatic memory management, set the total and maximum memory size parameters, and review the memory allocation history. Figure 2-3 is an example of the OEM Memory Advisor page.

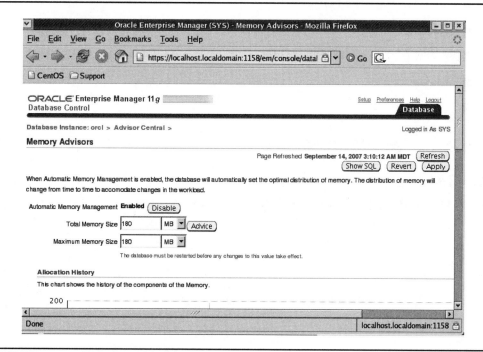

**FIGURE 2-3.**  *OEM Memory Advisor page*

Automatic Memory Management also has an interface into the memory advisor function that you can use (it's a graphic built off the V$MEMORY_TARGET_ADVICE view) to determine how you should allocate memory to the instance.

## Converting to Automatic Memory Management

You can manually convert to Automatic Memory Management or do so though OEM. You can also configure a new database to use Automatic Memory Management through the Database Configuration Assistant (DBCA). Those upgrading to Oracle Database 11*g* might ask if it's worth changing to Automatic Memory Management. As with anything else new, I'd do so with caution, testing it out carefully in your development environments. If you have an immediate need to convert, then do so, but if you can wait, I would not put existing production systems at risk. With regard to new databases built on the 11*g* stack, I will probably configure them to use Automatic Memory Management and test them carefully.

# ADDM New Features

Oracle Database 11*g* offers a number of new ADDM features. These new features include:

- New ADDM-related views
- ADDM now RAC-aware
- A new package called **dbms_addm** that you can use to manage ADDM
- Classifications
- Directives

Let's look at each of these new features next!

## ADDM New Views

Oracle Database 11*g* has added new ADDM-related views as seen in the following table:

| View Name | Description |
| --- | --- |
| DBA_ADDM_TASKS | Provides a historical representation of previous ADDM tasks |
| DBA_ADDM_INSTANCES | Displays instance-level information for ADDM tasks |
| DBA_ADDM_FINDINGS | Provides additional information for the various advisor views |
| DBA_ADDM_FDG_BREAKDOWN | Provides information on the contribution of the given finding for each instance |
| DBA_ADDM_SYSTEM_DIRECTIVES | |
| DBA_ADDM_TASK_DIRECTIVES | |

Note that each DBA_ view has a corresponding USER_ view except DBA_ADDM_SYSTEM_DIRECTIVES.

## ADDM Now RAC-Aware

There are several performance issues that are very RAC-specific. Prior to Oracle Database 11*g*, the only way to analyze the cluster component of a RAC configuration was through the use of a number of GV$ views. Oracle Database 11*g* has added a new layer of analysis to ADDM called Database ADDM. With Database ADDM, Oracle ADDM is now RAC-aware and will include a RAC cluster analysis as a part of the overall ADDM database analysis process.

As with Instance ADDM, the new Database ADDM processes are run after each AWR snapshot by default. Database ADDM can provide reporting on the following conditions:

■ Excessive use of global resources such as IO and global locks

■ High-load SQL and resulting hot blocks

■ Global cache interconnect traffic

■ Network latency issues

■ Skewing in instance response times

You enable Database ADDM by calling the **set_default_task_parameter** attribute of the Oracle-supplied **dbms_advisor** PL/SQL package. Through this call you can set the value of the **instances** parameters, which will indicate which instances should receive Database ADDM analysis. The following table provides a look at the different settings you can use for the instances parameter.

| Instances Setting | ADDM Analysis Mode Enabled |
| --- | --- |
| UNUSED | Disables Database ADDM for all instances |
| Comma-separated list of instances | Database ADDM will be done only for the instances listed |
| ALL | Enables ADDM for all instances |

Here are some examples of setting this parameter:

```
-- Disable Database ADDM for all instances
Exec dbms_advisor.set_default_task_parameter('ADDM','INSTANCES','UNUSED');
-- Configure Database ADDM for instances 1 and 3 only
Exec dbms_advisor.set_default_task_parameter('ADDM','INSTANCES','1,3');
-- Configure Database ADDM for all instances
Exec dbms_advisor.set_default_task_parameter('ADDM','INSTANCES','ALL');
```

The results of this additional level of analysis will appear in several places in OEM, such as the Cluster database home page in the performance analysis page. From there you can drill down into other detail pages. Manual reporting is also available with the new **dbms_addm** package, which we will discuss in the next section.

## Managing ADDM Through DBMS_ADDM

Oracle Database 11*g* introduces the **dbms_addm** package to assist the DBA in administration of Oracle ADDM. This package provides the ability for the DBA to direct that an ADDM analysis begin, to print a report, or to remove a previous analysis.

Some of the more commonly used programs in **dbms_addm** and their purpose are listed in the following table (we will discuss directives shortly, so they are not in this list).

| | |
|---|---|
| **analyze_db** | Schedules a database-specific ADDM analysis, based on two provided snapshot ranges |
| **analyze_inst** | Schedules an instance-specific ADDM analysis based on two provided snapshots |
| **analyze_partial** | Schedules a partial database ADDM analysis based on two provided snapshots and a listed set of instances |
| **delete** | Deletes a specified ADDM task |
| **get_report** | Provides the default ADDM report for the listed ADDM task |

Here is an example of using the **dbms_addm** package to execute a database-wide ADDM analysis and report on the results:

```
-- Get the list of valid snapshots within the last 4 hours
select instance_number, snap_id
from wrm$_snapshot
where end_interval_time < systimestamp - interval '4' HOUR
order by 1,2;
INSTANCE_NUMBER     SNAP_ID
--------------- ----------
              1         24
              2         23
              2         25
              2         26

Var tname varchar2(60);
BEGIN
    :tname:='ADDM Database Task';
    dbms_addm.analyze_db(:tname, 25, 26);
END;
/
set long 1000000
Spool /tmp/dbreport.rpt
SELECT dbms_addm.get_report(:tname) FROM dual;
spool off
```

The resulting report generally follows the same format of the standard ADDM report (addmrpt.sql) that you can run on Oracle Database 10g. You could remove the ADDM analysis later buy using **dbms_addm.delete** as seen in this example:

```
exec dbms_addm.delete('ADDM Database Task');
```

## Finding Classifications

The Oracle Advisor framework was introduced in Oracle Database 10*g*. ADDM is one example of these advisors. In that framework we have symptoms, problems, warnings, and informational types of findings. A finding name has been added to the Advisor framework in Oracle Database 11*g*. The finding name provides additional information that helps to classify the finding being given. For example, one finding might be that CPU usage is too high, as seen in this example:

```
select task_name, finding_name,
type, impact_type from dba_advisor_findings
where rownum < 2;

TASK_NAME               FINDING_NAME TYPE          IMPACT_TYPE
--------------------    ------------ -----------   ------------------------------
ADDM:2209966315_1_3     CPU Usage    PROBLEM       Database time in microseconds.
```

The FINDING_NAME column is a new column in Oracle Database 11*g* that classifies the finding into a specific classification, in this case CPU Usage. This column is also added to the USER_ADVISOR_FINDINGS view.

This new classification of findings can be used to perform additional analysis as in this case, where we try to see if the CPU usage problems seem to group around a specific time (late morning seems popular here):

```
select to_char(execution_end, 'hh24') hour , count(*)
from dba_advisor_findings a, dba_advisor_tasks b
where finding_name='CPU Usage'
and a.task_id=b.task_id
group by to_char(execution_end, 'hh24')
order by 1;

HO    COUNT(*)
--    ----------
04            1
05            1
07            1
11            3
12            3
13            2
15            1
16            2
17            1
```

There are about 80 different classifications of findings, which can be found in the DBA_ADVISOR_FINDING_NAMES table.

# Directives

When running ADDM it might be desirable to direct the analysis to ignore certain conditions. For example, if there is a ROBERT schema with well-known shortcomings it would make sense to exclude ROBERT from an ADDM analysis. To exclude various ADDM analysis and findings from appearing, you can set directives. These directives can be assigned to a specific ADDM task, or can be set as a system directive. Directives can be set via command line, or from within OEM. The following sections discuss creation and removal, and provide example use of directives.

## Creation of Directives

The procedures used to set directives are found in the following table:

| Directive Type | Procedure Name | Description |
| --- | --- | --- |
| Insert finding | **dbms_addm. insert_finding_directive** | Limits the ADDM report to specific finding types (see "Finding Classifications" earlier in this section). |
| Insert parameter | **dbms_addm. insert_parameter_directive** | Creates a directive that prevents ADDM from suggesting actions to alter the value of a specific system parameter (**v$parameter**). |
| Insert segment directive | **dbms_addm. insert_segment_directive** | Creates a directive that will keep ADDM from suggesting actions related to specific owner, segment, subsegment, or a specific object number. |
| Insert SQL directive | **dbms_addm. insert_sql_directive** | Creates a directive that will keep ADDM from suggesting actions based on specific SQL IDs. Further filtering includes the ability to limit the SQL to a minimum number of active sessions, or minimum response time in microseconds. |

## Removal of Directives

**Dbms_addm** provides procedures to remove directives as seen in the following table:

| Directive Type | Removal Procedure Name |
| --- | --- |
| Delete finding | **dbms_addm.delete_finding_directive** |
| Delete parameter | **dbms_addm.delete_parameter_directive** |
| Delete segment directive | **dbms_addm.delete_segment_directive** |
| Delete SQL directive | **dbms_addm.delete_sql_directive** |

## Determining If Directives Are Defined

A new column, FILTERED, which can be found in a number of views, indicates if a particular row in the view was filtered out by a directive. Views with the FILTERED columns include:

- DBA and USER_ADVISOR_FINDINGS

- DBA and USER _ADVISOR_RECOMMENDATIONS

- DBA and USER _ADVISOR_ACTIONS

## Using Directives: Example

An example of the use of these directives might be a case where we do not want ADDM to report on the ROBERT schema at any time. In this example we exclude the ROBERT schema, and execute the report:

```
var tname VARCHAR2(60);
var inst_num number;
BEGIN
-- This will run on just the current instance.
select instance_number into :inst_num from v$instance;
-- Give the analysis a name.
:tname := 'mydb_instance_analysis';
-- Create the task.
DBMS_ADVISOR.CREATE_TASK('ADDM', :tname);
-- Snapshot to start the analysis
DBMS_ADVISOR.SET_TASK_PARAMETER(:tname, 'START_SNAPSHOT', 242);
-- Snapshot to end the analysis
DBMS_ADVISOR.SET_TASK_PARAMETER(:tname, 'END_SNAPSHOT', 243);
-- Set the instance for the task.
DBMS_ADVISOR.SET_TASK_PARAMETER(:tname, 'INSTANCE', :inst_num);
-- Set the directive.
DBMS_ADDM.INSERT_SEGMENT_DIRECTIVE(:tname, 'Segment directive ID', 'ROBERT');
```

```
-- Fire the task.
DBMS_ADVISOR.EXECUTE_TASK(:tname);
END;
/
-- report on the task.
set long 1000000
SELECT dbms_addm.get_report('mydb_instance_analysis') FROM dual;
exec dbms_addm.delete_segment_directive(NULL,'Segment directive ID');
exec dbms_addm.delete('mydb_instance_analysis');
```

And, we can also produce the ADDM report and have it ignore the restriction set by using the **dbms_advisor.get_task_report** procedure, as seen in this example:

```
SELECT DBMS_ADVISOR.GET_TASK_REPORT('mydb_instance_analysis', 'TEXT', 'ALL')
FROM DUAL;
```

# AWR New Features

Oracle Database 11*g* has enhanced the Oracle Database Automated Workload Repository (AWR), which was introduced in Oracle Database 10*g*. New features make management of your database even easier. New and enhanced features include:

- Default retention of AWR snapshots changed

- New AWR baseline features

- Adaptive metric thresholds

## Default Retention of AWR Snapshots Changed

By default, Oracle Database 11*g* will now retain eight days of AWR snapshot information (as opposed to seven). As always you can override the default. This value will only be set on new databases. Databases that are upgraded will keep the AWR retention value already set for them.

## AWR Baseline New Features

Oracle Database 11*g* consolidates the previous baseline features introduced in Oracle Database 10*g*. The term applied to these consolidated features is the *AWR baseline*. In addition to the various features available in Oracle Database 10*g*, Oracle Database 11*g* has added new features that make AWR baselines even more useful to the DBA. This includes:

- New types of AWR baselines

- Adaptive thresholds

### New Types of AWR Baselines

Oracle Database 11*g* offers some new twists on the AWR baseline. These include the following:

- **Moving window baselines**   A moving baseline typically based on the entirety of the statistical data contained in AWR

- **Single baseline**   Allows you to define a baseline to be captured for a single specified period of time in the future

- **Repeating baseline**   Allows you to define a baseline to be captured for a repeating period of time in the future

The next sections will discuss these new types of baselines. We will also discuss AWR baseline templates, data dictionary views related to baseline templates, and removal of baseline templates.

### Moving Window Baselines

A new feature in Oracle Database 11*g* is the moving window baseline. The moving window baseline is always called SYSTEM_MOVING_WINDOW, and you can see details of this baseline in the WRM$_BASELINE view. The SYSTEM_MOVING_WINDOW baseline start-and-stop window period will correspond to the time between the earliest and latest snapshot available in Oracle Database 11*g*. As a result the period of time that this baseline represents is controlled by the retention setting for AWR, and it is constantly moving (hence the clever name, moving window baselines).

The default moving window baseline window size can be adjusted from the defaults via a call to **dbms_workload_repository.modify_baseline_window_size** as seen in this example:

```
exec dbms_workload_repository.modify_baseline_window_size ( -
                    window_size => 30);
```

The value of **window_size** must be set to a value in days equal to or less than the overall AWR retention setting or you will get an ORA-13541 error.

You can use the moving baseline with OEM to compare current statistics to baseline statistics to assist you in determining how well your database is performing. For example, the OEM performance page allows you to define the baseline to which you wish to compare the statistics being reported. You can use the system moving baseline, a manually defined baseline, or no baseline at all.

The moving window baseline implies that your baselines will continue to reflect a current performance baseline of your system. The baseline data is kept fresh, whereas manual baselines will become staler over time and will cease to reflect the accurate baseline state of your database. Having said that, it's probably a good idea to maintain some manual baselines for comparison purposes to ensure that your database does not just slowly crawl into performance oblivion.

### Single Baseline

Single baselines in some ways are much like baselines in Oracle Database 10g, in that you can define a single baseline over an existing set of AWR snapshots. However, single baselines also allow you to define a baseline for a future period of time. For example, if you have special processing that happens on an irregular basis and you know it will happen this weekend, you may want to create a single baseline to schedule the generation of that baseline.

You can configure a single baseline from OEM. To do so, select the Server tab from the OEM database home page. There under Statistics Management you will see an option titled AWR Baselines. From this page you can create a single baseline. OEM will have you define the start time and end time of the baseline, or the start-and-stop AWR snapshot range.

If you create a single baseline based on previous AWR snapshots, no baseline template is created. If you create a single baseline based on a future time period, a baseline template will be created in order to schedule that baseline execution. Until the baseline template is executed, it will now show up on the list of available AWR baselines in OEM. You can also define an expiration date for a given baseline with the **expiration** parameter. This expiration time is based on the **end_time** parameter of the baseline that is created.

The **dbms_workload_repository.create_baseline_template** PL/SQL procedure can be used to manually create single baselines, as seen in this example in which we create a baseline for a future time (September 30th) and set it to expire 30 days from the **end_time** of the baseline:

```
Alter session set nls_date_format='yyyy-mm-dd hh24:mi:ss';
BEGIN
    DBMS_WORKLOAD_REPOSITORY.CREATE_BASELINE_TEMPLATE (
                    start_time => '2007-09-30 13:00:00',
                    end_time => '2007-09-30 14:00:00',
                    baseline_name => 'baseline_093007',
                    template_name => 'template_093007', expiration => 30);
END;
/
```

You can review the results of all baseline executions from the OEM AWR Baselines page by clicking on the baseline you are interested in. You can also use various data dictionary views to review these baseline results, including DBA_HIST_BASELINE and DBA_HIST_BASELINE_DETAILS, and you can also use the manual reporting scripts awrddrpt.sql and awrddrpt.sql.

**Arup Says...**
Repeating baselines are extremely useful in solving performance issues that are tied to a specific time, or an interval. For instance, imagine a data warehouse database where Extract, Transform, and Load (ETL) jobs run during the night and reports run during the day. A repeating baseline that repeats every night at certain intervals helps establish a pattern over a period of days. By examining the AWR reports for each of these baselines, you can identify whether there is a pattern to these performance problems, which comes in handy for resolving the issue.

## Repeating Baselines

Repeating baselines can be defined to occur on a regular basis at a fixed time interval. For example, if you have report processing that occurs every Saturday from 6 P.M. until 11 P.M., you may want to create a repeating baseline that runs during that time period. This can be useful to track the overall efficiency of processing over a longer period of time, or in troubleshooting important processing that is suddenly suffering from performance problems.

You can configure a repeating baseline from OEM. To do so, select the Server tab from the OEM Database home page. There under Statistics Management you will see an option titled AWR Baselines. From this page you can create a repeating baseline. OEM will have you define the start time and duration of the baseline, as well as the frequency (daily, monthly, and so on). You will also need to enter a date/time to expire the baseline (these repeating baselines do expire eventually). Finally OEM gives you the ability to define how long the baseline should be retained. OEM will then create the repeating baseline for you. After you create a repeating baseline, Oracle will create a template that represents that baseline. See the next section for more on baseline templates. As each moving baseline is generated, that execution will appear on the AWR Baselines page in OEM.

The **dbms_workload_repository.create_baseline_template** PL/SQL procedure can be used to manually create repeating baselines, as seen in this example where we have a repeating baseline that executes every Sunday at 1 p.m for three hours. The baselines expire after 30 days, and will start on 5/31/2007, and the last baseline will execute on the Sunday before or on 12/31/2007:

```
BEGIN
    DBMS_WORKLOAD_REPOSITORY.CREATE_BASELINE_TEMPLATE (
                    day_of_week => 'sunday', hour_in_day => 13,
                    duration => 3, expiration => 30,
                    start_time => '2007-05-31 17:00:00',
                    end_time => '2007-12-31 20:00:00',
```

```
                                 baseline_name_prefix => 'baseline_Sunday_reports _',
                                 template_name => 'template_Sunday_reports');
END;
/
```

### AWR Baseline Templates

AWR baseline templates are created when you create a repeating baseline. It is this
template that will be used each time the scheduled baseline is executed. You can
view the template from OEM, which will show you various information on the
repeating baseline that has been created.

### AWR Baseline Templates and the Data Dictionary

You can use the DBA_HIST_BASELINE_TEMPLATE data dictionary view to access
information on baseline templates. Here is an example of the use of this view:

```
SQL> select template_name, template_type from dba_hist_baseline_template;
TEMPLATE_NAME                    TEMPLATE_
-------------------------------- ---------
robert_test_002                  SINGLE
template_070526                  SINGLE
template_Sunday_reports          REPEATING
test_repeating                   REPEATING
```

### Removing Baseline Templates

OEM provides an easy way to remove baseline templates. From the Server tab on
the OEM Database home page, simply select AWR Baselines. On the AWR
Baselines page there is a link to the AWR Baseline Templates page. From the AWR
Baseline Templates page you can view the status and configuration of existing
baseline templates, and you can choose to remove them.

   Use the **dbms_workload_repository.drop_baseline_template** PL/SQL procedure
to remove existing baseline templates from the system as seen in this example:

```
BEGIN
   DBMS_WORKLOAD_REPOSITORY.DROP_BASELINE_TEMPLATE (
                     template_name => 'template_Sunday_reports');
END;
/
```

# Adaptive Metric Thresholds

Setting alerting thresholds in OEM can be hit and miss. Because metrics with regards
to performance can be hard to define, and can vary based on workload, baselines
can be used to define a set of metrics that reflect the system more accurately. This is
doubly hard if you have a new database, and no historical information on which to
base your thresholds. Adaptive metric thresholds in Oracle Database 11g allow you

to move beyond that in that they will use AWR baselines to automatically set metric thresholds for you. OEM also makes it easy to apply these adaptive metric thresholds, with just a couple of clicks. The other benefit of adaptive metric thresholds is that as your system workload changes, the alerting thresholds will evolve to reflect the current state of the database.

Through OEM's Baseline Metric Thresholds page (a link is available on the AWR Baselines page already discussed in the previous section), you can allow Oracle to perform a quick configuration of your thresholds. Based on the type of workload your system will most often be doing (online transaction processing [OLTP], Warehouse, or Alternating workloads), OEM will define your metric thresholds for you. Once Oracle Database configures the initial thresholds, you can then choose to edit them as required from the Basic Metric Thresholds page.

The thresholds that are generated automatically will adapt to the given workload on the system as reflected in the baseline used to generate the metric. Thus, if you have a heavier reporting workload in the evenings, with few online users, the metric for average active sessions will likely be less in the evenings and higher in the daytime. As the AWR moving baseline statistics change over time, any metric defined as an adaptive metric may find its alerting threshold changed. You can determine if a given metric is set as adaptive from the OEM Baseline Metric Thresholds page.

# Scheduler AutoTask Automated Maintenance Tasks

Oracle Database 10g introduced new automated maintenance tasks such as automated statistics gathering. Oracle Database 11g adds a new component to the Oracle infrastructure called AutoTask. The job of AutoTask is to provide a central component that is responsible for management of scheduled maintenance tasks. In the following sections we will look at the AutoTask architecture, dictionary views, and managing AutoTask tasks with OEM and manually. Finally we will look at AutoTask maintenance windows.

## AutoTask Architecture

AutoTask builds on much of the existing architecture of Oracle Database 11g. The AutoTask architecture consists of the following:

■ **AutoTask Background Process** This background process (ABP) is spawned by MMON and is responsible for managing the AutoTask features. It coordinates the AutoTask clients and the scheduler. It also maintains AutoTask-related history, which can be seen in the DBA_AUTOTASK_TASK view.

- **AutoTask clients**   Automated maintenance tasks that are scheduled by AutoTask. Oracle Database 11*g* includes clients for statistics gathering, the Segment Advisor, and the Automatic SQL Tuning Advisor.

- **The AutoTask maintenance windows**   Different maintenance windows exist for different days of the week. These windows can be modified as required.

- **Resource Manager**   A resource plan is enabled that is designed to limit the amount of resources that the AutoTask tasks can consume. This resource plan can be modified as required (see the section titled "AutoTask Resource Management") for more on the new resource plan associated with AutoTask).

- **OEM**   OEM allows you to manage the start time and duration of the various AutoTask maintenance windows and add or remove maintenance tasks. You can also use OEM to enable or disable maintenance tasks.

- **The Scheduler**   AutoTask operations rely heavily on the scheduler. The AutoTask architecture uses scheduler windows and the scheduler infrastructure to execute AutoTask tasks.

## AutoTask Dictionary Views

New views have been created to support the AutoTask infrastructure. Oracle Database 11*g* has removed the old jobs from the DBA_SCHEDULER_* views, and moved them to DBA_AUTOTASK_* views (such as the SQL Tuning Advisor). The following views have been added for AutoTask:

- **DBA_AUTOTASK_CLIENT**   This view lists the different clients that AutoTask will run. You can use the DBA_AUTOTASK_CLIENT view to look at a great deal of information including the names of the different AutoTask tasks that will be run, the status of the tasks, the consumer group they are assigned to, and how long the mean durations of the job are run. Other information that the view provides is CPU consumption by the task over time, maximum duration of the client, the name of the window group the client is assigned to, and many other client-related attributes. Here is an example of the use of the DBA_AUTOTASK_CLIENT view:

```
select client_name, status, consumer_group, mean_job_duration
from dba_autotask_client;

CLIENT_NAME                              STATUS    CONSUMER_GROUP
MEAN_JOB_DURATION
-------------------------------- -------- -----------------------------
```

```
auto optimizer stats collection    ENABLED   ORA$AUTOTASK_STATS_GROUP
+000000000 00:04:26.000000000
auto space advisor                  ENABLED   ORA$AUTOTASK_SPACE_GROUP
+000000000 00:00:45.272727272
sql tuning advisor                  ENABLED   ORA$AUTOTASK_SQL_GROUP
+000000000 00:05:53.000000000
```

**NOTE**
*The documentation says the MEAN_JOB_DURATION column is an average and not a true mean of the duration of the job. The bottom line is that these views are using average times, not mean times as the column name suggests.*

- **DBA_AUTOTASK_CLIENT_HISTORY**  This view provides a historical representation of the AutoTask client execution events per window. This allows you to look at historical run information for each AutoTask client based on the given window that the AutoTask executed in. Here is an example of a query against the view to determine when the automated statistics collection clients ran:

```
select client_name, window_name, jobs_created, jobs_started,
jobs_completed
from dba_autotask_client_history
where client_name like '%stats%';
```

| CLIENT_NAME | WINDOW_NAME | JOBS CREATED | JOBS STARTED | JOBS COMPLETED |
|---|---|---|---|---|
| auto optimizer stats collection | THURSDAY_WINDOW | 1 | 1 | 1 |
| auto optimizer stats collection | SUNDAY_WINDOW | 3 | 3 | 3 |
| auto optimizer stats collection | MONDAY_WINDOW | 1 | 1 | 1 |
| auto optimizer stats collection | SATURDAY_WINDOW | 2 | 2 | 2 |
| auto optimizer stats collection | SUNDAY_WINDOW | 4 | 4 | 4 |
| auto optimizer stats collection | TUESDAY_WINDOW | 1 | 1 | 1 |

- **DBA_AUTOTASK_CLIENT_JOB**  Provides information on AutoTask jobs currently defined and executing. This view will typically be empty unless an AutoTask job is running.

- **DBA_AUTOTASK_JOB_HISTORY**  This view provides information on the history of each AutoTask client execution.

```
select client_name, job_status, job_start_time, job_duration
from dba_autotask_job_history
where client_name like '%stats%'
```

```
order by job_start_time;

CLIENT_NAME                          JOB_STATUS JOB_START_TIME
JOB_DURATION
------------------------------------ ---------- ------------------------------------
--------------
auto optimizer stats collection SUCCEEDED  18-FEB-07 02.43.45.598298 PM -07:00
+000 00:00:24
auto optimizer stats collection SUCCEEDED  18-FEB-07 06.49.51.326230 PM -07:00
+000 00:02:21
auto optimizer stats collection SUCCEEDED  18-FEB-07 10.59.53.677261 PM -07:00
+000 00:00:55
auto optimizer stats collection SUCCEEDED  23-FEB-07 12.57.25.844519 AM -07:00
+000 00:12:49
auto optimizer stats collection SUCCEEDED  24-FEB-07 06.17.02.045879 PM -07:00
+000 00:13:09
auto optimizer stats collection SUCCEEDED  05-MAR-07 10.00.06.955011 PM -07:00
+000 00:04:32
```

■ **DBA_AUTOTASK_OPERATION**   This view provides information on the attributes assigned to each AutoTask operation. For example, an AutoTask client job may be marked as SAFE TO KILL if it can be interrupted in the middle of its operation without negative effect. An example of this can be seen in this output where the ATTRIBUTES column for the "auto optimizer stats collection" job lists is marked as SAFE TO KILL:

```
select * from dba_autotask_operation
where client_name like '%stats%';

CLIENT_NAME                          OPERATION_NAME           OPE PRIORIT
------------------------------------ ------------------------ --- -------
ATTRIBUTES                           USE_R STATUS
------------------------------------ ----- --------
auto optimizer stats collection      auto optimizer stats job OPT INVALID
ON BY DEFAULT, VOLATILE, SAFE TO KILL FALSE ENABLED
```

■ **DBA_AUTOTASK_SCHEDULE**   Provides the start time and duration for each AutoTask window.

■ **DBA_AUTOTASK_TASK**   This view provides information on each individual AutoTask task. It provides a great deal of information from statistics on the last run of the given task to estimated statistics for the next run of the task.

```
select client_name, task_name, task_target_type
from dba_autotask_task;

CLIENT_NAME                    TASK_NAME                TASK_TARGET_TYPE
------------------------------ ------------------------ ----------------
```

```
auto optimizer stats collection gather_stats_prog     System
auto space advisor               auto_space_advisor_prog  System
sql tuning advisor               AUTO_SQL_TUNING_PROG     SQL Workload
```

**NOTE**
*Here is one place where we see AutoTask meet the scheduler. Note the TASK_NAME column in the DBA_AUTOTASK_TASK view. This relates the AutoTask tasks to the programs stored in the scheduler, which can be seen in the DBA_SCHEDULER_PROGRAMS view as seen here:*

```
select program_name
from dba_scheduler_programs
where program_name='GATHER_STATS_PROG';
PROGRAM_NAME
------------------------------

GATHER_STATS_PROG
```

- **DBA_AUTOTASK_WINDOW_CLIENTS**  This view provides information on the different windows associated with AutoTask Clients.

- **DBA_AUTOTASK_WINDOW_HISTORY**  This view provides information on the AutoTask windows.

## Managing AutoTask Tasks via OEM

OEM provides an interface into AutoTask task management via the Scheduler Central page. A link to Scheduler Central can be found at the bottom of the OEM home page. From the scheduler home page you can see both automated maintenance tasks running via AutoTask, regular scheduler jobs, or Enterprise Manager jobs. Figure 2-4 provides an example of the OEM Scheduler Central page, displaying Automated Maintenance Tasks scheduled to be run.

You can see from the OEM page that the different kinds of available jobs are listed at the top. Each of these is a hyperlink that takes you to a page that allows you to further manage those types of jobs. For example, I can click on the Automated Maintenance Tasks link and OEM will display the page seen in Figure 2-5, which will allow me to manage automated maintenance tasks.

From the page in Figure 2-5 you can see if the tasks are executing within their scheduled windows, or if they are exceeding the window times. Notice the three options at the top under schedulers. These allow you to manage different kinds of scheduled tasks. For example, if you wanted to manage an Automated Maintenance Task, you would click on that link, finding yourself on the page shown in Figure 2-6.

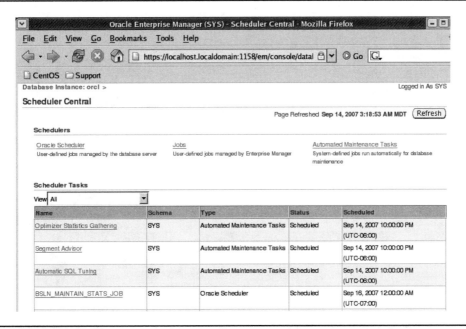

**FIGURE 2-4.**   *OEM Scheduler Central and Automated Maintenance Tasks*

From the page in Figure 2-6, you can manage automated maintenance tasks by clicking on the Configure button at the top of the page. Lower on the page you'll find specific automated maintenance tasks listed, and you can see the past and future task execution schedule in a graphic format. You can click on some tasks for detailed recommendations provided by the tasks as a part of the advisor framework. For example, if we click on Segment Advisor on the page, we will find ourselves on the Segment Advisor Recommendations OEM page.

We mentioned configuring automated maintenance tasks by clicking on the Configure button as seen in Figure 2-6. OEM provides the ability to enable or disable automated maintenance tasks either on a global level, or on a very granular level. You can enable or disable specific tasks, and enable or disable specific scheduled task executions. Some of the tasks have a Configure button that you can click on that will allow you to further configure that specific task. Figure 2-7 provides an example of the Automated Maintenance Tasks Configuration page of OEM.

## Managing AutoTask Tasks Manually

In Oracle Database 10*g* you used the **dbms_scheduler** package to administer new automated scheduler jobs such as the out-of-the-box collection of database statistics. With the advent of AutoTask you will start using a new package to manage these jobs

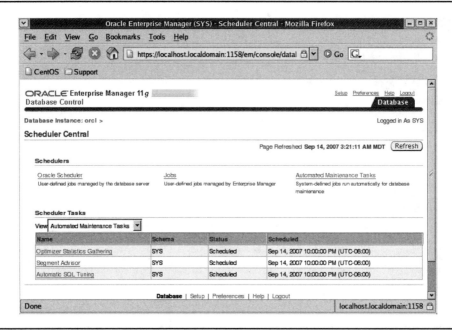

**FIGURE 2-5.** *OEM Scheduler Central showing Automated Maintenance Tasks*

with the **dbms_auto_task_admin** package. OEM now uses this package to manage these automated jobs too.

You will use the **dbms_auto_task_admin.disable** subprogram to disable any of the AutoTask tasks. Note that there are no default values for any of the parameters, so you will need to include them all in the call. In this example we will disable the automatic collection of statistics:

```
BEGIN
dbms_auto_task_admin.disable(client_name => 'auto optimizer stats collection',
operation => NULL, window_name => NULL);
END;
/
```

The **window_name** parameter allows you to define a specific window that you wish to disable (as opposed to the entire task). Out of the box there are seven windows, one for each day of the week. These windows are called MONDAY_WINDOW, TUESDAY_WINDOW, and so on. If I did not want the statistics collection to run on Sunday (because, perhaps, I load new records into my data warehouse on Sundays), I could disable the AutoTask execution for that day with this command:

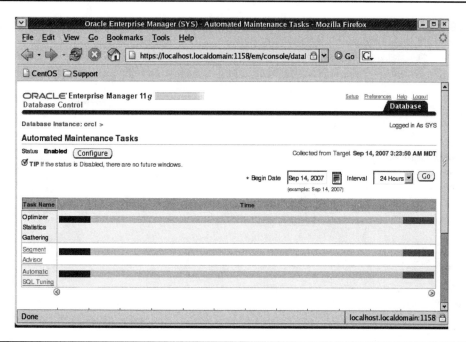

**FIGURE 2-6.** *OEM Automated Maintenance Tasks page*

```
BEGIN
dbms_auto_task_admin.disable(client_name => 'auto optimizer stats collection',
operation => NULL, window_name => 'SUNDAY_WINDOW');
END;
/
```

Conversely, to re-enable a given task you will use the **dbms_auto_task_
admin.enable** subprogram. Again, you must include all the default values as seen
in this example:

```
BEGIN
dbms_auto_task_admin.enable(client_name => 'auto optimizer stats collection',
operation => NULL, window_name => NULL);
END;
/
```

# AutoTask Maintenance Windows

As mentioned earlier, AutoTask tasks are built to execute during AutoTask maintenance
windows. There are seven default windows, one for each day of the week. The
weekday windows (MONDAY_WINDOW, TUESDAY_WINDOW, and so on) have

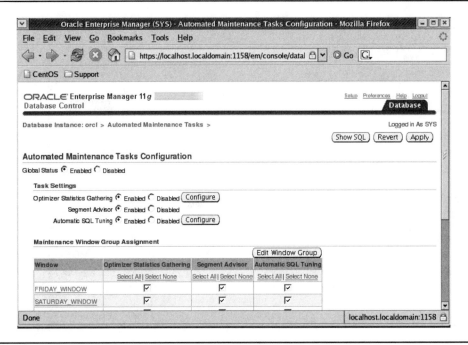

**FIGURE 2-7.** *OEM Automated Maintenance Tasks Configuration page*

a duration of four hours and start at 10 P.M. local time. The weekend windows have a duration of 20 hours and are scheduled to start at 6 A.M. local time.

**NOTE**
*The \*_WINDOW windows replace the WEEKEND_WINDOW and WEEKNIGHT_WINDOW windows available in Oracle Database 10g. These windows are still defined in Oracle Database 11g, however.*

These windows are assigned to a resource plan, DEFAULT_MAINTENANCE_PLAN, which is enabled automatically when the maintenance windows are opened. The DEFAULT_MAINTENANCE_PLAN resource plan has a number of consumer groups assigned to it and various associated tasks including:

- **ORA$AUTOTASK_SQL_GROUP** Automatic SQL Tuning tasks are assigned to this consumer group.

- **ORA$AUTOTASK_SPACE_GROUP**   Segment Advisor tasks are assigned to this group.

- **ORA$AUTOTASK_STATS_GROUP**   Automatic statistics gathering is assigned to this group.

Each of these groups control resource utilization of specific AutoTask maintenance tasks (for example, allowable CPU load).

# Parameter File Management Changes and New Features

Oracle has made several changes with regard to how server parameter files (or SPFILES) are managed. These include:

- Read/write error handling of SPFILES

- Easier conversion to the use of SPFILES

- Users are prevented from setting invalid values in SPFILES

Let's look at each of these changes in more detail.

## Read/Write Error Handling of SPFILES

Oracle Database 11*g* is more protective of SPFILES. If a read/write error occurs while reading from or writing to the SPFILE, Oracle will generate an error in the alert log, and future writes to the parameter file will be ignored. In this situation you can opt to shut down the database and restore the parameter file. You can also opt to create a new parameter file using the new **create spfile from memory** option (discussed in the next section). Finally, in the case of an error with the SPFILE, you can continue to run the database.

## Easier Conversion to the Use of SPFILES

Alas, there are those of you who have still not been converted to starting with an SPFILE. Oracle has made it even easier for you to create and start using an SPFILE. You can now use the new **create spfile from memory** command. This command will take the in-memory settings and dump them out to an SPFILE for use. You can also use this method to create a backup of your SPFILE using your current memory settings should you desire to do so. This is a handy way to back up the SPFILE before you start making changes to it with the **alter system** command.

By default Oracle will create the SPFILE in a default location as defined by the operating system (often ORACLE_HOME/dbs). You can also specify where to create the SPFILE by defining the name and location of the SPFILE as seen in this example:

```
Create spfile='/oracle/util/spfilename.sp' from memory;
```

## Users Are Prevented from Setting Invalid Values in SPFILES

Oracle Database 11*g* has added additional error checking when you make changes to database parameters. Now in many cases, when you change a parameter and are using incorrect syntax, Oracle will advise you that you are using the wrong value. Unfortunately, this does not seem to be a consistent thing in Oracle Database 11*g*, but it's a start. Here is an example:

```
SQL> alter system set control_management_pack_access = 'Wrong_Value'
scope=spfile;
alter system set control_management_pack_access = 'Wrong_Value' scope=spfile
*
ERROR at line 1:
ORA-00096: invalid value Wrong_Value for parameter
control_management_pack_access, must be from among DIAGNOSTIC+TUNING,
DIAGNOSTIC, NONE
```

# Resource Manager Changes and New Features

Oracle Database 11*g* has included a number of new features associated with the resource manager. These new features include

- The ability to measure the maximum IO throughput of the system (IO calibration)

- The default maintenance plan

- Built-in resource plans

- Resource Manager statistic histories stored in AWR

- Resource Manager plan new directives

## IO Calibration

The Oracle Database Resource Manager has a new procedure that allows you to run IO calibration tests on your database and review the results of that test. When run, the **dbms_resource_manager.calibrate_IO** procedure will generate a workload

across all nodes of the cluster. The procedure takes two input parameters, and
returns three values as seen in the following tables:

| Input Parameter | Type | Meaning |
|---|---|---|
| **num_physical_disks** | **pls_integer** | This is the approximate number of physical disks being used by the database. Default 1. |
| **max_latency** | **pls_integer** | Maximum latency in milliseconds allowed for IO requests of size **db_block_size**. Default 20. |

| Output Parameter | Type | Meaning |
|---|---|---|
| **max_iops** | **pls_integer** | Maximum number of randomly distributed IO requests of **db_block_size** that can be sustained by the system. |
| **max_mbps** | **pls_integer** | Maximum number of megabytes per second that can be sustained by the system. Based on randomly distributed, 1MB reads. |
| **actual_latency** | **pls_integer** | Average latency of **db_block_size** IO requests at a rate of MAX_IOPS in ms. |

**NOTE**
*You must be using asynchronous IO in order to use*
*this feature.*

Here is an example of the use of the **dbms_resource_manager.calibrate_io**
procedure:

```
Declare
      v_max_iops        PLS_INTEGER:=1;
      v_max_mbps        PLS_INTEGER:=1;
      v_actual_latency  PLS_INTEGER:=1;
```

```
begin
    dbms_resource_manager.calibrate_io(
        max_iops=>v_max_iops,
        max_mbps=>v_max_mbps,
        actual_latency=>v_actual_latency);
    dbms_output.put_line('Results follow: ');
    dbms_output.put_line('Max IOPS: '||v_max_iops);
    dbms_output.put_line('Max MBPS: '||v_max_mbps);
    dbms_output.put_line('Actual Latency: '||v_actual_latency);
end;
/
```

We can view the status of a calibration exercise (current or historical) by querying the V$IO_CALIBRATION_STATUS view, as seen in this example:

```
Select status from v$io_calibration_status;
STATUS
-------------
IN PROGRESS
```

We can review the results by using the DBA_RSRC_IO_CALIBRATE table as seen in this example:

```
select * from dba_rsrc_io_calibrate;

STATUS          LATENCY    MAX_IOPS   MAX_MBPS   NUM_DISKS
------------- ---------- ---------- ---------- ----------
CALIBRATION_TIME
-----------------------------------------------------------
READY                 19         77          6          1
27-MAY-07 09.50.15.421 PM
```

# Default Maintenance Plan

As with previous versions of Oracle there is typically no resource manager plan active by default. There is one exception to be aware of, and that is related to the DEFAULT_MAINTENANCE_PLAN resource plan that we discussed earlier in this chapter. When the scheduler maintenance window is opened, and if a plan is associated with that window (as is the case during the maintenance window), then the plan associated with that scheduler window will become active in the system.

If you do not wish the scheduler to define a resource plan, you can use the **dbms_scheduler.set_attribute** procedure to set the **resource_plan** attribute to a blank string, which will disable this feature. You would need to alter all the maintenance windows defined in Oracle Database 11*g* to completely prevent the DEFAULT_MAINTENANCE_PLAN plan from being set. Similarly, if you wish to assign a different resource plan, you can use the same process to assign the changed resource plan name to the given schedule.

**Arup Says...**

IO calibration is nothing new in the information technology sector. There are several other technologies that can provide IO calibration—from hardware vendors as well as OS vendors. Even Oracle has a tool called Orion that accomplishes part of it. So what extra functionality can this IO calibration tool in 11*g* provide?

Plenty. First of all, all the other tools merely do a lot of IO to the disk and develop a profile based on the actual transfer. Some tools may go an extra mile or two by adding more granularity, more intelligence, and so on; but they are all the same more or less. The IO calibration procedure in the package **dbms_resource_manager** is unique in the sense that it executes the *same* routines the Oracle Database makes, not some generic IO request. This makes the calibration truly representative of the actual Oracle database calls, which affects the performance significantly. So, conceivably, if there is a bug in the Oracle kernel code in the IO area, the bug will affect the calibration as well, and, that will be, well, highly desirable. The similarity in the output of the bug will be desirable, not the bug itself, of course.

If you generally like the idea of the DEFAULT_MAINTENANCE_PLAN being used by the scheduler, but there are times when you do not want the current resource plan to be overridden, you can configure the **resource_manager_plan** database parameter with a **force** attribute, which will prevent the plan from being overwritten as seen in this example:

```
Alter system set resource_manager_plan='force:rf_plan' scope=both;
```

You can also use the **dbms_resource_manager.switch_plan** PL/SQL procedure to pin a plan. To remove the **force** attribute, you issue the **alter system** command as seen in the preceding example and simply remove the **force** attribute as seen here:

```
Alter system set resource_manager_plan='rf_plan' scope=both;
```

## Built-In Resource Plans

Oracle Database 10*g* came with a built-in resource plan called SYSTEM_PLAN. The SYSTEM_PLAN in and of itself was not a particularly useful resource plan. Oracle Database 11*g* comes with a new plan, the MIXED-WORKLOAD PLAN which provides resource management for a mixed environment consisting of OLTP and DSS/batch jobs.

## Resource Manager Statistics in AWR

One of the nice features of AWR is that it provides a persistent repository for historical statistical data. Since the V$ views are cleared when the database is shut down, AWR becomes the best place for an accurate historical representation of the performance of your database. To make it easer to track the effectiveness of the Oracle Database Resource Manager, AWR now contains views that provide historical information on Resource Manager performance. These new views are

- **DBA_HIST_RSRC_PLAN**   Contains the historical data from V$RESOURCE_PLAN

- **DBA_HIST_RSRC_CONSUMER_GROUP**   Contains historical data from V$RESOURCE_CONSUMER_GROUP

Each of these views is associated with a given AWR snapshot and can be materialized through OEM. Additionally Oracle Database 11*g* adds the V$RSRCMGRMETRIC view, which contains historical metrics for Resource Manager consumption of resources by the various consumer groups.

## Resource Manager Plan Directive New Features

New attributes can be associated with Resource Manager plan directives in Oracle Database 11*g*. The new parameters are

- **switch_io_megabytes**   This defines the amount of IO in megabytes that a given session can consume before the directive action is taken. Defaults to NULL (unlimited).

- **switch_io_reqs**   This defines the number of IO requests that a given session can execute before the directive action is taken. Defaults to NULL (unlimited).

- **switch_for_call**   This replaces the SWITCH_TIME_IN_CALL parameter, which is deprecated in Oracle Database 11*g*. If this parameter is set to TRUE, the consumer group will be restored to its original consumer group at the end of the top call if the action is taken as a result of the **switch_time**, **switch_io_megabytes**, or **switch_io_reqs** parameters.

- **mgmt_p1 to mgmt_p8**   These parameters replace the CPU_P1 to CPU_P8 parameters, which are deprecated in Oracle Database 11*g*. If the plan has the CPU_MTH parameter set to EMPHASIS, this defines the CPU percentage to allocate to the various levels (1 through 8). Only MGMT_P1 is applicable if CPU_MTH is set to RATIO (which is typically used for simpler plans with only a single level of CPU allocation), in which case it defines the weight of CPU usage.

Examples of the use of the new parameters can be seen here:

```
-- Create the resource plan
BEGIN
     DBMS_RESOURCE_MANAGER.CREATE_PENDING_AREA();
END;
/

BEGIN
     DBMS_RESOURCE_MANAGER.CREATE_CONSUMER_GROUP (
     CONSUMER_GROUP => 'OLTP',
     COMMENT => 'OLTP');
END;
/

BEGIN
     DBMS_RESOURCE_MANAGER.CREATE_CONSUMER_GROUP (
     CONSUMER_GROUP => 'HIGH_IO_GROUP',
     COMMENT => 'OLTP');
END;
/
BEGIN
     DBMS_RESOURCE_MANAGER.CREATE_CONSUMER_GROUP (
     CONSUMER_GROUP => 'EXCESSIVE_IO_GROUP',
     COMMENT => 'OLTP');
END;
/
BEGIN
     DBMS_RESOURCE_MANAGER.CREATE_CONSUMER_GROUP (
     CONSUMER_GROUP => 'REPORTING',
     COMMENT => 'REPORTING');
END;
/

BEGIN
   DBMS_RESOURCE_MANAGER.CREATE_PLAN(
     PLAN => 'DAYTIME',
     COMMENT => 'More resources for OLTP applications');
END;
/
BEGIN
     DBMS_RESOURCE_MANAGER.CREATE_PLAN_DIRECTIVE (
     PLAN => 'DAYTIME',
     GROUP_OR_SUBPLAN => 'OLTP',
```

```
        COMMENT => 'OLTP group',
        MGMT_P1 => 75,
        SWITCH_GROUP => 'HIGH_IO_GROUP',
         SWITCH_IO_REQS => 100,
         SWITCH_IO_MEGABYTES => 250,
         SWITCH_FOR_CALL => TRUE);
END;
/

BEGIN
        DBMS_RESOURCE_MANAGER.CREATE_PLAN_DIRECTIVE (
        PLAN => 'DAYTIME',
        GROUP_OR_SUBPLAN => 'REPORTING',
        COMMENT => 'Reporting group',
        MGMT_P1 => 15,
        PARALLEL_DEGREE_LIMIT_P1 => 8,
        ACTIVE_SESS_POOL_P1 => 4);

        DBMS_RESOURCE_MANAGER.CREATE_PLAN_DIRECTIVE (
        PLAN => 'DAYTIME',
        GROUP_OR_SUBPLAN => 'OTHER_GROUPS',
        COMMENT => 'This one is required',
        MGMT_P1 => 10);
END;
/
BEGIN
        DBMS_RESOURCE_MANAGER.CREATE_PLAN_DIRECTIVE (
        PLAN => 'DAYTIME',
        GROUP_OR_SUBPLAN => 'EXCESSIVE_IO_GROUP',
        COMMENT => 'High IO group',
        MGMT_P1 => 15,
        PARALLEL_DEGREE_LIMIT_P1 => 2);
END;
/
```

# Finer-Grained Dependencies

Prior to Oracle Database 11*g*, changes to database objects could inadvertently render a dependent object invalid when in fact the dependent object would not need to be invalidated. For example, prior to Oracle Database 11*g*, if you add a column to a table, this can result in the invalidation of a dependent view.

Oracle Database 11*g* now records dependency metadata at a greater level of granularity, so that things like adding columns or removing columns to a table, which do not impact a dependent object, will not cause that dependent object to go invalid.

# DDL WAIT Option Now Default

In Oracle Database 10*g*, by default DDL commands would not wait if the object was locked. Instead an error would be generated and the attempted change would fail with an ORA-00054, indicating the resource was locked. Now, in Oracle Database 11*g*, Oracle in many cases will not only not return an error, but will execute the change without a wait being required. For example, you can now do the following in Oracle Database 11*g*:

```
Session 1:
SQL>insert into test values (1);
1 row created.
Session 2:
SQL>alter table test add (id2 number);
Table altered.
```

Note in the preceding example that session 2 did not need to wait for session 1 to be committed. In fact, if you do a **describe** of the TEST table from session 1, even before a **commit**, you will see the new column added, and you could insert a row into that column.

### Arup Says...

The DDL WAIT option is a really useful feature. How many times have you tried to alter a table being used in production and were frustrated to find that someone is using the table at that very instance? Your **alter** statement would fail with something like **ORA-00054: resource busy and acquire with nowait...** All you need is a miniscule time window to get an exclusive lock on the table and make your changes. The DMLs on the table can continue afterwards. But, alas, you couldn't do it in 10*g* and earlier.

I had to resort to techniques like placing the DDL in a loop and executing it several times hoping that it would get the lock sometime—a very crude approach but the only feasible one. In Oracle 11*g*, you do not need to do much. In the session you want to issue a DDL statement, issue this SQL first:

```
alter session set ddl_lock_timeout = 10;
```

This will make the subsequent DDL statements wait for 10 seconds before timing out. Next, when you issue the DDL statement, and it can't get the exclusive lock due to DML activities in other sessions, this statement will not fail with ORA-00054; rather it will hang (actually wait to get a lock). The moment it acquires a lock, the statement succeeds. If the lock is not acquired within the 10-second period, then the DDL statement fails with ORA-00054 error.

This feature is extremely useful in busy systems for making DDL changes.

You can also use the new **ddl_lock_timeout** parameter at the session level to indicate that a DDL statement should wait for the DDL lock to be released. Here is an example:

```
SQL> alter session set ddl_lock_timeout=30;
Session altered.
```

# New Add Column Functionality

Oracle Database 11*g* now allows you to add a NOT NULL column with a default value to a table in one, quick, easy operation. The default value is stored as metadata in the database, and the default value is not actually physically stored in the table. This makes the process of adding a column with a default value much faster.

### Arup Says...

This is a great feature for availability. Prior to Oracle 11*g*, when you add a column with not null constraint and with a default value, Oracle actually populates the value in *all* the rows of the table. *All* the rows, ouch! Imagine a multimillion-row table where the data will be updated several million times and how much redo and undo it will generate. In addition, it will also lock the table for the entire duration preventing DDLs. This caused a lot of consternation among users.

In Oracle 11*g*, the statement **alter table emp add (grade varchar2(1) default 'X' not null)** does not actually update the table at the same time this DDL is run. You can check this by setting the event 10046 before running the DDL and checking the trace file afterwards:

```
SQL> alter session set events '10046 trace name context forever,
level 16';
Session altered.
SQL> alter table emp add (grade varchar2(1) default 'X' not null);
Table altered.
SQL> alter session set events '10046 trace name context off';
Session altered.
```

Now check the trace file; you will not see a reference to the **update emp ...** statement. This behavior results in significantly less redo and undo, and also completes faster.

Another great use of this feature is while adding a NOT NULL column to a table without a default value.

# End of Line

We have covered a lot in this chapter. Clearly, Oracle Database 11*g* is full of neat stuff, and I think some of the handiest features are the simplest ones like the DDL WAIT option (certainly it lacks the complexity of some of the other features!) or the new add column functionality. Hard-core users of ASM will find that new functionality helpful too. I think Arup has done a bang-up job in this chapter too, so all hail Arup! All in all, a load of information and we are not done yet. Chapter 3 is hot on the heels of this chapter and it's even more fun, if you can believe that! Hang on tight, it's going to be an exciting ride!

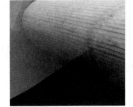

# CHAPTER
## 3

# Oracle Database
# New Availability and
# Recovery Features

racle Database 11*g* has a number of new features in it that simplify database backup and recovery. These features include:

- Fault diagnosability infrastructure

- RMAN

- Flashback database

- High availability

Let's look at these new features now in more detail.

# Fault Diagnosability Infrastructure

Oracle Database 11*g* introduced a new feature called the fault diagnosability infrastructure. This infrastructure is designed to assist in preventing, detecting, diagnosing, and resolving problems such as database bugs and various forms of corruption. This new infrastructure changes some things such as where the alert log is generated, and adds a great deal of new functionality to Oracle Database. In the next several sections we will cover the new fault diagnosability infrastructure components:

- The Automatic Diagnostic Repository (ADR)

- The alert log

- Trace, dump, and core files

- The Support Workbench

- ADR Command Interpreter (ADRCI) command-line utility

- Other ADR contents

## The Automatic Diagnostic Repository (ADR)

The ADR is the repository for the files associated with the fault diagnosability infrastructure. The files are stored on the host operating system, which has a standard directory structure. Each instance stores data in its own ADR home. The ADR provides for standardization of the location for files that Oracle is required to support. This standardized file structure also makes it easy for Oracle to package these files, a feature we will discuss shortly.

The new **diagnostic_dest** parameter defines the root of the ADR and deprecates the **user_dump_dest**, **core_dump_dest**, and **background_dump_dest** parameters that you are probably familiar with. As a result, if you create a new Oracle Database 11*g* database with the DBCA, you will not find the alert log or user trace files where you would have previously expected them. By default the **diagnostic_dest** parameter is set to $ORACLE_BASE. If $ORACLE_BASE is not set, then it is set to the value of $ORACLE_HOME. The root directory of the ADR directory structure starts with a directory called diag, under which is a subdirectory that references the product type. For example, for the database the product is called rdbms. Under rdbms is a directory for each database, and then a directory for each individual instance.

For example, if $ORACLE_BASE is /u01/oracle and the database name is mydb, database instance is mydb1, then the structure of the ADR directory for that database will be /u01/oracle/diag/rdbms/mydb/mydb1. This directory structure is called the ADR home, and each instance has its own ADR home. If you are using RAC, you can used shared storage for ADR, or individual storage on each node. We would recommend shared storage in an RAC environment since you can see the aggregate diagnostic data from any node. Also a shared ADR allows for more robust recovery options for the data recovery advisor.

Under this directory structure will be a number of other directories. Some of the most common directories include the following:

- **Alert** This is the location of the XML-formatted alert log. See the next section titled "The Alert Log" for more information (it's not your father's alert log!).

- **Cdump** This is the location of the core dumps for the database.

- **Trace** This contains trace files generated by the system, as well as a text copy of the alert log.

- **Incident** This directory contains multiple subdirectories, one for each incident.

In Figure 3-1 we see a diagram of the ADR base structure.

A new view, V$DIAG_INFO, provides information on the various ADR locations, as well as information related to ADR, such as active incidents. Here is an example of a query against the V$DIAG_INFO view:

```
SQL> select * from v$diag_info;
    INST_ID NAME                          VALUE
---------- ---------------------------- ---------------------------------------
         1 Diag Enabled                  TRUE
         1 ADR Base                      C:\ORACLE\PRODUCT
         1 ADR Home                      C:\ORACLE\PRODUCT\diag\rdbms\rob11gr4\ro
                                         b11gr4
```

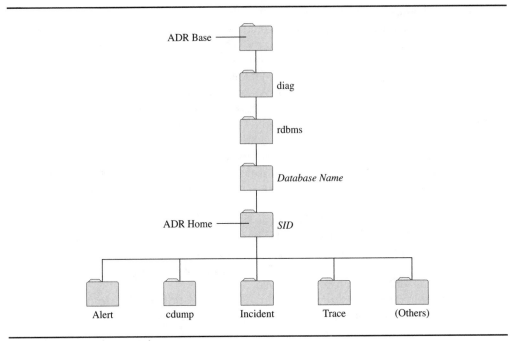

**FIGURE 3-1.** *The ADR base structure*

```
1 Diag Trace               C:\ORACLE\PRODUCT\diag\rdbms\rob11gr4\ro
                           b11gr4\trace
1 Diag Alert               C:\ORACLE\PRODUCT\diag\rdbms\rob11gr4\ro
                           b11gr4\alert
1 Diag Incident            C:\ORACLE\PRODUCT\diag\rdbms\rob11gr4\ro
                           b11gr4\incident
1 Diag Cdump               C:\ORACLE\PRODUCT\diag\rdbms\rob11gr4\ro
                           b11gr4\cdump
1 Health Monitor           C:\ORACLE\PRODUCT\diag\rdbms\rob11gr4\ro
                           b11gr4\hm
1 Default Trace File       C:\ORACLE\PRODUCT\diag\rdbms\rob11gr4\ro
                           b11gr4\trace\rob11gr4_ora_7832.trc
1 Active Problem Count     1
1 Active Incident Count    1
11 rows selected.
```

We will discuss problems and incidents in more detail later in this section.

## The Alert Log

In Oracle Database 11*g* the alert log is now stored in two formats in the ADR. The
first is the old text format, and the second is a copy that is formatted with XML tags.
This allows tools to process the alert log more efficiently and gather more detailed
information. The alert log is stored in the ADR directory called alert. If you wish to

look at the old text copy of the alert log you will find it in the ADR directory called cdump.

OEM provides a way to look at the alert log with the XML tags stripped out of it. You can also use the new ADR Command Interpreter (**adrci**) command-line utility to strip out the XML tags from the alert log. **Adrci** has some interesting features. For example, you can view the alert log using the **tail** option, as shown in the following example. This will allow you to watch the alert log as records are generated, much like using the UNIX **tail** command:

```
C:\oracle\product\11gBetaR4\db_01\NETWORK\ADMIN>adrci
ADRCI: Release 11.1.0.4.0 - Beta on Sat Jun 2 01:09:30 2007
Copyright (c) 1982, 2006, Oracle.  All rights reserved.

ADR base = "C:\oracle\product"
adrci>>show alert -tail
ADR Home = C:\oracle\product\diag\rdbms\rob11gr4\rob11gr4:
*************************************************************************
2007-06-02 00:42:47.398000 -06:00
Logminer Bld: Lockdown Complete.  DB_TXN_SCN is
UnwindToSCN (LockdownSCN) is 1832443
2007-06-02 00:42:48.929000 -06:00
db_recovery_file_dest_size of 2048 MB is 83.44% used. This is a
user-specified limit on the amount of space that will be used by this
database for recovery-related files, and does not reflect the amount of
space available in the underlying filesystem or ASM diskgroup.
2007-06-02 00:43:45.586000 -06:00
SYS_AUTO_SQL_TUNING_TASK created SQL Profile named
"SYS_SQLPROF_0144bacb369c0000" for sql_id g0jvz8csyrtcf
during execution "EXEC_1_7".
2007-06-02 00:45:20.916000 -06:00
SYS_AUTO_SQL_TUNING_TASK created SQL Profile named "SYS_SQLPROF_0144bacb94b60001" for
sql_id d89c1mh5pvbkz during execution "EXEC_1_7".
2007-06-02 00:55:09.970000 -06:00
Thread 1 advanced to log sequence 91
Current log# 1 seq# 91 mem# 0: C:\ORACLE\ORADATA\ROB11GR4\ROB11GR4\REDO01.LOG
```

We will discuss other functionality of the **adrci** command-line utility throughout this chapter.

## Trace, Dump, and Core Files

Trace files, dump files, and core files are now all stored in the ADR. Because these files are often associated with a database incident (such as an Oracle code bug), having them all stored in a consistent directory structure makes it easier for Oracle to package these files for support purposes.

## The Support Workbench

One of the main purposes of the ADR is to support the new Oracle Database 11g feature, the Support Workbench. The Support Workbench provides the ability to investigate errors and report them to Oracle. In some cases the Support Workbench

## Arup Says...

The absence of the alert log file, at least the way it is accessed, may pose some interesting problems. For instance, consider the case where there are two Oracle SIDs on the host running from the same Oracle Home. Here two alert logs are produced. Since the SIDs are on the same Oracle Home, you have to call the **adrci** command from the same source, that is, $OH/bin. When you issue **show alert**, which alert log will be shown? And, more important, how can you ask for a specific alert log to be shown? In case of multiple Oracle SIDs, you will get the following error:

```
adrci> show alert -tail
DIA-48449: Tail alert can only apply to single ADR home
```

The answer to the issue lies in another command in **adrci**—**set homepath**. While you're at the **adrci** command prompt, issue the following command to see all the homes (ADR homes, not Oracle Homes) that **adrci** can access:

```
adrci> show homes
ADR Homes:
diag/rdbms/probe2/PROBE2
diag/rdbms/probe1/PROBE1
diag/asm/+asm/+ASM11
diag/tnslsnr/prolin2/listener
```

Here you can see the homes **adrci** can access. To see the alert log of the SID PROBE2, you will point **adrci** to that home:

```
adrci> set homepath diag/rdbms/probe2/PROBE2
```

Now, when you issue **show alert**, the alert log of the PROBE2 instance is shown.

To confirm this, or to find out later which home is set, use the following command:

```
adrci> show homes
ADR Homes:
diag/rdbms/probe2/PROBE2
```

You can change the home at any time by issuing the **set homepath** command.

But as you can see, it can become tedious after a while. You almost always tail the alert log of a specific SID, and you would want that to be the default.

To save typing the **set homepath** command every time, you can use an ADRCI script, a small text file with contents as shown in the following example:

```
set homepath diag/rdbms/probe2/PROBE2
show alert -tail -f
```

Name this file adrci.cmd. Now you can call this script directly as

```
$ adrci -script=adrci.cmd
```

It will execute the commands inside the file, much like a Unix shell script. In addition to the alert log, the listener log is also in XML now, so you will not find a file called listener.log under $OH/network/log any more. The file will be called $ORACLE_BASE/diag/tnslsnr/prolin2/listener/alert/log.xml. You can examine the file using the ADRCI utility as well.

```
adrci> set homepath diag/tnslsnr/prolin2/listener
adrci > show alert -tail -s
```

can even correct errors, suggesting the use of advisors designed to correct specific problems. The Support Workbench is a shortcut to opening a service request (SR) with Oracle, providing a streamlined method of opening the SR and collecting the information that Oracle Support will request to service the SR.

The Support Workbench is supported by many different interfaces. Typically one would use Oracle Enterprise Manager, but the **adrci** command-line utility is available, as are PL/SQL packages **dbms_hm** and **dbms_sqldiag**. In the next few sections we will discuss using the Support Workbench to correct Oracle Database errors.

The principal way to access the Support Workbench is through OEM. The Support Workbench has its own OEM page. To access it, select Software and Support from the OEM Database home page as seen in Figure 3-2.

## Using the Support Workbench—Workflow

Usually the use of the Support Workbench is a result of an Oracle error, though sometimes it might be in response to an alert in OEM. There are several steps that need to be followed when using Support Workbench to deal with an incident, as seen in Figure 3-3. We cover these steps in more detail in the next few sections.

**Step 1: View Critical Alerts and Errors**   Step 1, viewing critical alerts and errors, should already be something that you do as a DBA. You probably have had experience with Oracle errors such as the ORA-600 and reviewing alerts from OEM.

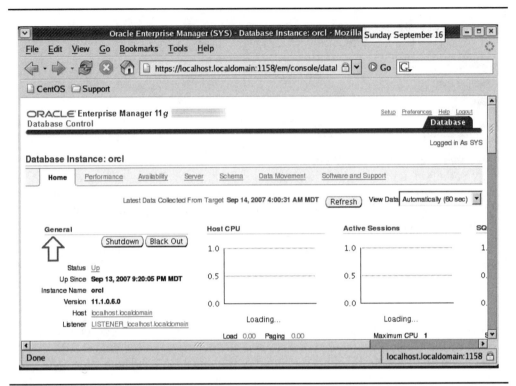

**FIGURE 3-2.** *OEM Database Home page*

The Support Workbench augments your monitoring by automatically detecting many errors that might occur in your database and creating problem records for those errors. Within the context of the Support Workbench, each error type is typically a *problem*. A given problem can have many occurrences (for example. the same ORA-0600 can occur many times). Each occurrence is called an *incident*. A given problem, then, may have one or more incidents associated with it. The Support Workbench Page provides a summary of each problem, and allows you to drill down into the different incidents. Figure 3-4 provides a screen print of the OEM Support Workbench Page.

**Step 2: Review the Details**   Step 2 is equally something that a DBA should be used to dealing with, the details of given errors. Step 3 involves gathering additional information on the error from OEM or perhaps doing some research on the error. Upon reviewing the details, you may well discover a solution to the error.

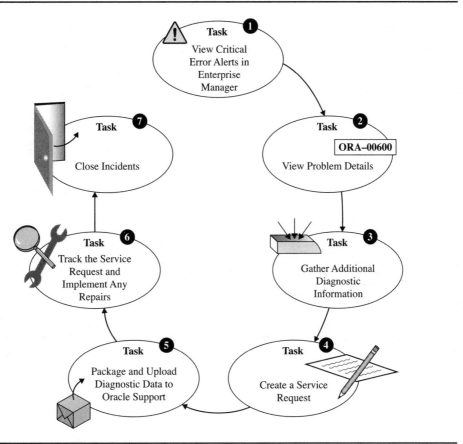

**FIGURE 3-3.** *Steps to use Oracle Database Support Workbench*

**Step 3: Collect Additional Information: Health Checks**   If you have not found a solution to the error in Step 2, then Step 3 involves collecting additional diagnostic information. This may include running database health checks with the new Oracle health checks. The health checks analyze the database looking for various types of corruption, and then generate a report of any findings. Along with the generated report there may be recommendations on how to solve the problem. There are a number of different health checks available to run. These are listed in the following table.

| | | |
|---|---|---|
| All Control Files Check | Data Block Integrity Check | Logical Block Check |
| All Datafiles Check | Dictionary Integrity Check | Redo Integrity Check |
| Archived Log Check | Failure Simulation Check | Redo Revalidation Check |
| Block IO Revalidation Check | HM Test Check | Single Datafile Check |
| | IO Revalidation Check | Transaction Integrity Check |
| CF Member Check | Log Group Check | Txn Revalidation Check |
| DB Structure Integrity Check | Log Group Member Check | Undo Segment Integrity Check |

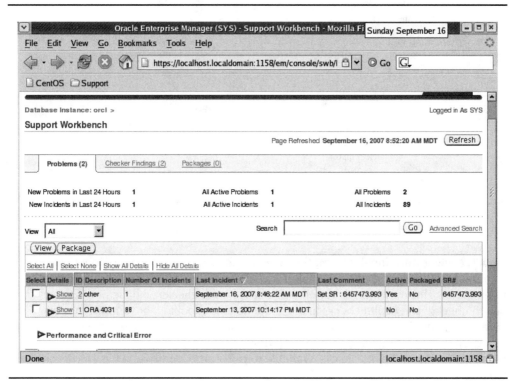

**FIGURE 3-4.** *OEM Support Workbench page*

These different health checks can be boiled down into the following categories:

- **Database Structure Integrity Check**   Verifies the integrity of database files, reporting on those that are inaccessible, corrupt, or inconsistent. When the database is mounted or open, then log files and data files listed in the control file are checked. When the database is in NOMOUNT mode, then only the control file integrity is checked.

- **Data Block Integrity Check**   Verifies that the disk image blocks are not corrupted. Checks include checksum failures, head/tail mismatch, and other logical inconsistencies. Many of the errors reported by this health check can be repaired using the Data Recovery Advisor. You can also view the V$DATABASE_BLOCK_CORRUPTION view to view information on data block corruption.

- **Redo Integrity Check**   Verifies the contents of the online redo log, ensuring accessibility and that corruption does not appear. Any archived redo logs will also be checked.

- **Undo Segment Integrity Check**   Verifies that logical undo corruption does not exist. If corruption exists, the health check will try to use Process Monitor (PMON) and System Monitor (SMON) to recover the corrupted transaction. If the Health Monitor cannot correct the problem, then information on the corruption will be stored in V$CORRUPT_XID_LIST for review.

- **Transaction Integrity Check**   Almost identical to the Undo Segment Integrity Check, this check examines undo corruption for specific transactions.

- **Dictionary Integrity Check**   Verifies that core dictionary objects are not subject to corruption.

A health check can be run in one of two modes. The first is *reactive mode.* In this mode, Oracle runs the health check automatically when a critical error occurs. The second mode is *manual mode.* In manual mode the DBA manually runs the health check using the **dbms_hm** PL/SQL package or you can choose to use the OEM interface. The results of the database health checks are stored in the ADR.

All of the health checks can be run with the database online or mounted. Some health checks can be run when the instance is available (NOMOUNT mode), including the Redo Integrity Check and the Database Structure Integrity Check.

To run the health check manually, you will want to first query the V$HM_ CHECK view to determine the name of the health check. Then simply call **dbms_ hm.run_check** to execute the health check as seen here:

```
BEGIN
    dbms_hm.run_check('Dictionary Integrity Check', 'my_run');
END;
/
```

We can see the results of the run by first finding the RUN_ID from the V$HM_RUN data dictionary view and then using the **dbms_hm.get_run_report** PL/SQL procedure as seen in this example:

```
select run_id, name from v$hm_run;
    RUN_ID NAME
---------- ----------------------------
         1 HM_RUN_1
        21 my_run

SET LONG 100000
SET LONGCHUNKSIZE 1000
SET PAGESIZE 1000
SET LINESIZE 512
DBMS_HM.GET_RUN_REPORT('MY_RUN')
----------------------------------------------------------------------------
SELECT DBMS_HM.GET_RUN_REPORT('my_run') FROM DUAL;
Basic Run Information
 Run Name                      : my_run
 Run Id                        : 101
 Check Name                    : Dictionary Integrity Check
 Mode                          : MANUAL
 Status                        : COMPLETED
 Start Time                    : 2007-09-16 08:00:39.883334 -06:00
 End Time                      : 2007-09-16 08:01:55.022851 -06:00
 Error Encountered             : 0
 Source Incident Id            : 0
 Number of Incidents Created   : 0

Input Paramters for the Run
 TABLE_NAME=ALL_CORE_TABLES
 CHECK_MASK=ALL

Run Findings And Recommendations
 Finding
 Finding Name : Dictionary Inconsistency
 Finding ID   : 102
 Type         : FAILURE
 Status       : OPEN
 Priority     : CRITICAL
 Message      : SQL dictionary health check: dependency$.dobj# fk 126 on
                object DEPENDENCY$ failed
 Message      : Damaged rowid is AAAABnAABAAAOiHABI - description: No further
                damage description available
 Finding
```

```
Finding Name  : Dictionary Inconsistency
Finding ID    : 105
Type          : FAILURE
Status        : OPEN
Priority      : CRITICAL
Message       : SQL dictionary health check: dependency$.dobj# fk 126 on
                object DEPENDENCY$ failed
Message       : Damaged rowid is AAAABnAABAAAQXqAA6 - description: No further
                damage description available
```

More and more DBAs are using OEM now, and Oracle allows you to run health checks (also called Checkers) from OEM, and check the results. To do so, click on the Advisor Central page link found at the bottom of the OEM Database home page. From there you will see a link titled Checkers near the top of the page. From there you will see a number of checkers, which represent the different kinds of database health checks you can run. Figure 3-5 provides an example of the OEM Advisor Central Checkers page.

Simply click on the checker you want to run, enter the requested parameter/ option values, and run the checker. After the checker runs, you will be returned to

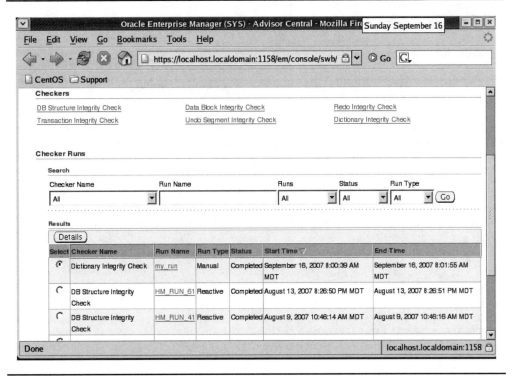

**FIGURE 3-5.**   *Oracle OEM Advisor Central Checkers page*

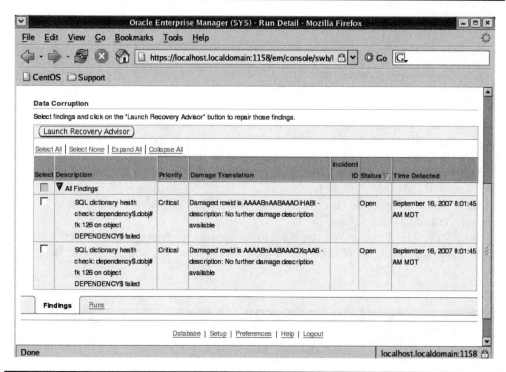

**FIGURE 3-6.** *Oracle OEM error found during data dictionary health check*

the Checkers page. From the Checkers page you can review the results of the Health Monitor check you executed. Figure 3-6 shows an example of an error that was discovered in my data dictionary when I ran a health check.

You can see from the OEM output that there is a problem with an object in my data dictionary. OEM offers me the ability to run the new Recovery Advisor in this case, which we will discuss later in this chapter.

Finally you can view the health check reports from the new **adrci** utility as seen in this example:

```
C:\>adrci
adrci> show homes
ADR Homes:
diag/tnslsnr/localhost/listener
diag/tnslsnr/localhost/listener_102
diag/clients/user_oracle/host_61728193_11
diag/clients/user_unknown/host_411310321_11
diag/asm/+asm/+ASM
diag/rdbms/orcl/orcl
diag/rdbms/robupg/robupg
```

```
diag/rdbms/dbua0/DBUA0
adrci> set homepath diag/rdbms/orcl/orcl
adrci>>show report hm_run my_run
<?xml version="1.0" encoding="US-ASCII"?>
<HM-REPORT REPORT_ID="my_run">
    <TITLE>HM Report: my_run</TITLE>
    <RUN_INFO>
        <CHECK_NAME>Database Dictionary Check</CHECK_NAME>
        <RUN_ID>21</RUN_ID>
        <RUN_NAME>my_run</RUN_NAME>
        <RUN_MODE>MANUAL</RUN_MODE>
        <RUN_STATUS>COMPLETED</RUN_STATUS>
        <RUN_ERROR_NUM>0</RUN_ERROR_NUM>
        <SOURCE_INCIDENT_ID>0</SOURCE_INCIDENT_ID>
        <NUM_INCIDENTS_CREATED>0</NUM_INCIDENTS_CREATED>
        <RUN_START_TIME>2007-06-02 11:18:05.672000 -06:00</RUN_START_TIME>
        <RUN_END_TIME>2007-06-02 11:18:16.062000 -06:00</RUN_END_TIME>
    </RUN_INFO>
```

You can also opt to review the report in your browser as seen in this example:

```
adrci>>set browser explorer
adrci>>show report hm_run my_run
```

Another way to view the reports from the health checks is to use the data dictionary views that Oracle provides. These views include the ones shown in the following table:

| View Name | Purpose |
| --- | --- |
| V$HM_RUN | Provides information on the various health check runs |
| V$HM_FINDING | Provides findings of the health check runs |
| V$HM_RECOMMENDATION | Provides recommendations from the health check runs |

Here are some examples of using these views. First, we can collect information on health checks that have been executed:

```
select run_id, name, check_name, status from v$hm_run;
    RUN_ID NAME        CHECK_NAME                                STATUS
---------- ---------- ----------------------------------------- ----------
         1 HM_RUN_1   Database Cross Check                       COMPLETED
        21 my_run     Database Dictionary Check                  COMPLETED
        41 Robert-OEM Database Dictionary Check                  COMPLETED
```

Now, let's look at the findings and recommendations:

```
select a.run_id, a.name, a.description desc_finding,
b.description desc_repair, b.repair_script
from v$hm_finding a, v$hm_recommendation b
where a.run_id=b.run_id (+);


 RUN_ID NAME       DESC_FINDING                     DESC_REPAI REPAIR_SCR
 ------- ---------- -------------------------------- ---------- ----------
     41 Dictionary SQL dictionary health check: d
        Inconsist  ependency$.dobj# fk 126 on obj
        ency       ect DEPENDENCY$ failed
```

Again we see my pesky data dictionary error.

### Step 4: Create a Service Request for a User-Reported Problem
**(If Applicable)** This step only applies if OEM does not display a problem, and you wish to track a problem that you are aware of and planning on requesting support for. If OEM displays the problem you are concerned with then proceed to step 5 to package the problem. After this step is complete, you will proceed to step 5 to package your user reported problem.

From the Support Workbench home page, you will find a link to create a user-reported problem. From the Create User-Reported Problem page, you will find a number of different issues that you can create a problem ticket for, including a generic "None of the Above" option that allows you to open a problem for just about anything. Many of these issues have advisors that you may want to run first.

If the advisors do not help, or if you are creating a problem that does not have an advisor available to help, you will then need to add details to allow OEM to track the problem. To enter these details, from the Create User-Reported Problem page, select the button that indicates that you wish to continue with the creation of the problem. An example of the Create User-Reported Problem OEM page can be seen in Figure 3-7.

Having determined that you want to continue with the creation of the problem, OEM will present the problem details page. From the problem details page, you will manually enter problem-related information.

The Problem Details page offers a number of options. If offers links to go to MetaLink, run the checkers, and then package the problem up for Oracle Support (more about packaging problems later in this chapter). Figure 3-8 provides a display of the Problem Details Page from OEM.

### Step 5: Oracle OEM Package and Upload Diagnostic Data to Oracle
**Support** OEM provides the ability to package the incident files associated with this problem. Packaging the problem will pull together the various files that Oracle will require to diagnose the problem at hand (one hopes). You can then submit the

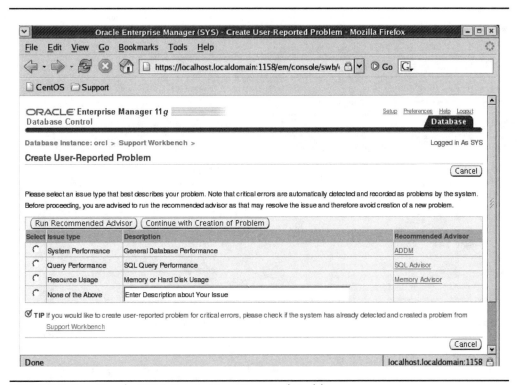

**FIGURE 3-7.** *Oracle OEM Create User-Reported Problem page*

package to Oracle. At that time an SR can be opened, or you can associate a package with an SR that has already been opened.

Packaging can be done in various ways. For example, we could create a package for our user generated incident created earlier in step 4 (using the quick package option you saw available in Figure 3-7). We can also create a package for a given problem from the Support Workbench page on OEM that you saw in Figure 3-7). In this case we would select the problem, and then click on the Package button to package the problem up.

So, what is a problem package anyway? A *problem package* is a logical structure stored in the ADR that points to the diagnostic files that will be required by Oracle to effectively support a given Oracle SR. Files in a given problem package may include trace files, dump files, alert logs and so on.

**NOTE**
*Problem packages are also sometimes called incident packages.*

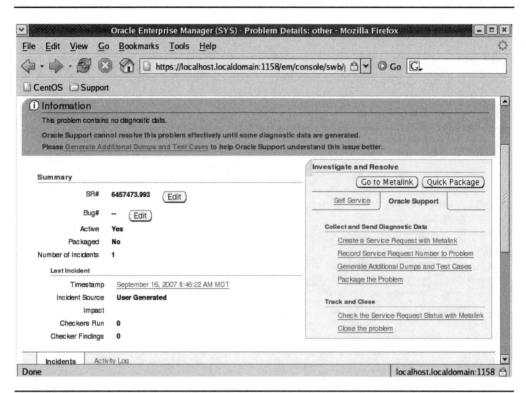

**FIGURE 3-8.** *Oracle OEM Problem Details page*

Problem packages can be customized. The DBA can add other files to the package or choose to remove files from the package. You can also edit the files in the package to remove any data that might be sensitive.

To package a problem and submit it to Oracle click on the problem and then on the package link. Oracle will give us an option to do quick packaging or custom packaging. Generally quick packaging will be sufficient, so we will select that. Oracle then provides a wizard that walks us through the packaging effort. Within this wizard we will enter a number of details such as:

■ Package description

■ SR number with Oracle if you already have one

■ Whether you want to actually send the package to Oracle

The wizard will allow you to preview the contents of the package before it gets shipped off to Oracle support. Additionally you can opt to send the upload immediately or later if you prefer.

You can also manually upload the incident package to Oracle by following the instructions that OEM will provide. You will find the new package to send in the incpkg directory in the $ORACLE_BASE/diag/rdbms/<dbname>/<instanceName>/incpkg/pkg_## directory, where ## is a sequence number that makes each package/incident unique. The location of the package is also available from OEM in the Package Details Page.

**NOTE**
*To successfully upload the problem package, you will need to have properly setup Oracle Configuration Manager.*

**Step 6: Track the Service Request and Implement Any Repairs** This is largely a manual process that simply means to keep up with the SR that you have created, and to add any new incidents to the package you have sent to Oracle. Additionally you may want to continue researching the problem through other sources, such as Google. As you discover information on the problem, or Oracle provides feedback, you can record comments that will be associated with the problem in the activity log of the problem via OEM.

**Step 7: Close the Incident** Once the incident has been resolved, you will want to close it from the OEM Support Workbench. To close an incident, go to the Problem Details page for the problem. Then from that page, select each incident that you wish to close and click on the Close button. OEM will close the incident at that time. Note that all incidents are automatically purged after 30 days. You can disable purging of a specific incident, from the Incident Detail page in OEM.

# RMAN New Features

RMAN offers a number of new features in Oracle Database 11*g*. These features include:

- Interfile backup parallelism
- Faster backup compression
- Better security
- Active database duplication
- Improved handling of long-term backups
- Backup failover for archived redo logs
- Archived redo log deletion policy enhancements
- Recovery catalog enhancements

- Undo backup optimization

- Block media performance improvements

- Block change support for standby databases

- Improved RMAN scripting

- Backup of read-only transportable tablespaces

**NOTE**
*See Chapter 4 for more information on the Data
Recovery Advisor (DRA), which is closely associated
with RMAN. DRA is a new advisor that takes
advantage of the fault Diagnosability infrastructure.*

## Interfile Backup Parallelism

When the bigfile tablespace first came out, the one question everyone asked is, *how*
are you going to back up a multi-terabyte database data file in serial? We should
have known that Oracle would address this problem, and they do in Oracle
Database 11*g*. Now RMAN can parallelize interfile backups. Parallel interfile
backups are known as *multisection backups*. With multisection backups Oracle will
allocate a channel for each section of the file to be backed up.

To enable multisection backups, you specify the section size parameter within
RMAN. RMAN will divide the files being backed up into file sections, which are just
logically divided, contiguous blocks in a file. RMAN will create a backup set with
one backupset piece for each file section. Here is an example of backing up a
bigfile tablespace called USER_DATA, chunking the backup into 300MB chunks.
Each 300MB chunk would be represented by a single backupset piece. If we
parallelized the backup into different channels, each channel would create a
separate backupset piece, in parallel:

```
backup section size 300m tablespace user_data;
```

One limitation here, as I see it, is that you cannot indicate that you want to skip
backing up a certain data file in a given backup. Thus if you issue the command
**backup database section size 300m**, then each data file of the database that is larger
than 300 megabytes will be chunked up. This can potentially slow down your
backups (there is somewhat more overhead in multisection backups than normal
backups). So, we recommend that your section size be large enough that you don't
inadvertently end up sectioning data files you don't really need to section.

**Arup Says...**

This is a great technique to parallelize backups on many spindles at the backup location. Typically most sites employ something similar to this backup strategy—first do an RMAN backup to a disk area; and then use a backup tool such as NetBackup, NetWorker, Tivoli and others, or even plain simple "tar" to move these backups from disk to the tape. Some of these tools work more efficiently if they get the data from the disk on many spindles, or at least on multiple filesystems or directories. This can be easily achieved now using the sectioning feature of RMAN. Suppose you have two filesystems, loc1 and loc2, and you want to spread the backup of tablespace SYSTEM over these two directories. You can write a query such as this:

```
RMAN> run {
2>      allocate channel c1 type disk format '/loc1/%U';
3>      allocate channel c2 type disk format '/loc2/%U';
4>      backup
5>      section size 300m
6>      tablespace system;
7> }
```

After this is completed, you can check the existence of the backup of the data file 1, that is, that of the SYSTEM tablespace.

```
RMAN> list backup of datafile 1;

... some more output ...

    List of Backup Pieces for backup set 6 Copy #1
    BP Key  Pc# Status       Piece Name
    ------- --- -----------  ----------
    10      1   AVAILABLE    /loc1/0eim19pd_1_1
    12      2   AVAILABLE    /loc2/0eim19pd_2_1
    11      3   AVAILABLE    /loc1/0eim19pd_3_1
```

Note how the backup was spread over the filesystems /loc1 and /loc2, in a round-robin fashion; so, even if the pieces were more than two, the distribution will be somewhat equal. Also note the column Pc#, which shows the Piece.

**TIP**
*Be careful not to section the backup of a large data file on a single disk or a small number of disks. The high cost to get the file due to disk head movements will most likely outweigh the potential benefits of this sectioned backup.*

## Faster Backup Compression

I think the addition of BZIP2 compression to RMAN in Oracle Database 10*g* was one of the best ideas that Oracle has ever had for that product. I love demonstrating in RMAN classes that I give how compression not only significantly reduces the size of your backup sets, but also can seriously speed up your backups (assuming you have sufficient CPU). Oracle Database has added a new compression option to the RMAN toolkit that you can use.

Oracle Database 11*g* introduces support for the ZLIB compression algorithm. The upside to ZLIB is that it is a faster zip algorithm than BZIP2. The downside is that ZLIB compression does not produce as compact an image as BZIP2, so your backup images will generally be larger. So it's speed versus space, the timeless conflict.

ZLIB compression is the default in Oracle Database 11*g*. You can use the RMAN **configure** command to define which type of compression you wish to utilize as seen in these examples:

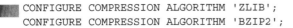
```
CONFIGURE COMPRESSION ALGORITHM 'ZLIB';
CONFIGURE COMPRESSION ALGORITHM 'BZIP2';
```

### NOTE
*This is an Oracle Database 11g upgrade issue, because the default compression method changes. You may find your backups taking more space after upgrading, because the ZLIB compression algorithm is suddenly being used. Unless your backups are just killing the CPU, I recommend that you configure RMAN to use BZIP2 after you upgrade.*

## Active Database Duplication

Prior to Oracle Database 11*g* if you were going to duplicate a database to another system via RMAN, you had to have either temporary storage location on that remote system for the backupset pieces or you had to have a shared network drive. Additionally you had to have a current backup in place in order to duplicate a database. With Oracle Database 11*g* you don't even need a current backup to duplicate your database, and you don't need to worry about having to move copies of your backups or shared drives! What makes this possible is a new feature called *active database duplication* (the old method, called *backup-based duplication*, is still available of course).

Active database duplication can occur on both the local box and over the network. Let's look at an example of using active database duplication over the network to duplicate our Oracle database. In this example, we will assume you want to use the same directory structure, so we first prepare the auxiliary database instance on a remote host. We then proceed to duplicate the source database to the auxiliary database on the remote host.

**NOTE**
*Active database duplication can also be used to create standby databases.*

## Prepare the Auxiliary Instance on the Remote Host

First, we need to create the auxiliary instance on the remote host to which we wish to duplicate our database. We assume you have already installed Oracle Database 11*g*, so the remaining steps are

1. Create the Oracle Database directory structures.

2. Create the password file for the auxiliary instance.

3. Configure networking for the auxiliary instance.

4. Create the parameter file for the auxiliary instance.

5. Start the auxiliary instance.

Let's look at each of these steps in some more detail as we execute them.

**Create the Oracle Database Directory Structures** Before we can duplicate the database we will need to create the directory structures that the duplicated database will be using. These include the directories for the data files and others as required. We assume you have already installed the Oracle database software and are generally familiar with duplicating a database using RMAN.

**Create the Password File for the Auxiliary Instance** Active database duplication requires that the auxiliary instance have a password file. This is because the source database will be connecting directly to the auxiliary database, requiring a password file. One other key is that you want to use the same SYSDBA password as the source database. You will also see, later in this example, that we use the **password file** option of the **duplicate** command. This will cause the duplication process to move the password file from the source to the target database during the duplication process. In this example, we create the password file for our remote database called REMOTE:

```
Cd %ORACLE_HOME%\database
Orapwd file=pwdremote.ora password=Robert
```

**Configure Networking for the Auxiliary Instance**   Duplication of databases requires that RMAN be able to connect to the auxiliary database instance via Oracle Networking. Because of this we will need to use the Oracle Network Configuration Assistant to configure networking to the auxiliary database instance. This is a typical DBA operation that you should already be familiar with. After configuring networking, ensure that you can connect to the auxiliary instance from the host system that you will be duplicating from.

NOTE
*You will have to hard-code the instance information into the listener.ora file to be able to facilitate the connection between the target and auxiliary database.*

**Create the Parameter File for the Auxiliary Instance**   There are different strategies for the creation of the parameter file when duplicating databases. In our example we will use the SPFILE technique, which only requires that we create an SPFILE for the auxiliary database with the database name set to some arbitrary value. During the duplicate process (and during an active database duplication), RMAN will create the SPFILE for the database being duplicated from a copy of the SPFILE for the source database. Parameters of the duplicate allow you to manipulate destination directories for the auxiliary/target database if this is required. In our temporary parameter file the **db_name** value is set to **dupdb** for the purposes of database duplication.

NOTE
*Other methods for creating the auxiliary parameter file exist (and they have not changed since Oracle Database 10g). Review the documentation if you need to use one of these alternative methods.*

**Start the Auxiliary Instance**   Having configured the auxiliary instance, we now **nomount** it in preparation for the duplication operation with RMAN. Simply log in to the database from SQL*Plus and issue the **startup nomount** command.

NOTE
*Some OSes might require other steps (for example, you might need to create the Oracle service for the instance with oradim). Please reference your platform-specific guide for instructions specific to your Operating System and platform.*

## Duplication over the Network

In this example, we assume RMAN is already configured with default channels (which have been a feature since Oracle 9*i*). To execute the duplication we need to start RMAN, connecting to the target database and the auxiliary database (we have chosen not to use a recovery catalog in this example):

```
Rman target=/ auxiliary=sys/Robert@mogo_destdb
```

Once successfully connected, we issue the **duplicate** command, and grab a cold cola from the machine down the hall as our database is effortlessly duplicated across the network. Note that we didn't need to have any current backups to perform this duplication, so the target database could be brand new and never backed up before. Here is our duplicate command:

```
DUPLICATE TARGET DATABASE TO auxdb FROM ACTIVE DATABASE
SPFILE NOFILENAMECHECK;
```

Note the use of the **from active database** clause, which is new in Oracle Database 11*g*. This parameter tells RMAN that you want this to be an active database duplication (obviously!). The **spfile** parameter indicates that you want to copy the SPFILE from the target database to the duplicated database for its use after the duplication process.

> **NOTE**
> *As I wrote this section, I did several active database duplications. One thing I noticed is that the method used to transport the data across the network did not seem to take full advantage of the bandwidth available. This seemed also to be true with regard to available CPU bandwidth and disk bandwidth. For example, I never saw my network bandwidth usage grow above 25 percent, and I never saw CPU usage grow beyond about 40 percent. Disk IO response was perhaps the worst, but it was far from overburdened. The point is that this would appear to be a slightly slower method of duplicating a database as opposed to a solution where you have made database backups available via some file-system-sharing protocol (for example, NFS).*
> *I also tested adding database load during the active database duplication and saw little performance impact on a two-CPU box.*

### End of the Line

After the duplication is complete, the newly duplicated database is renamed. If you are running Oracle on Windows, RMAN will also create a new service for you. The database can then be accessed. One final note is that RMAN does shut down the auxiliary instance but does not remove it. This makes it easy to do subsequent database duplications.

## Improved Handling of Long-Term Backups

Oracle Database 11*g* has changed some things with regard to archival backups (those using the **keep** option to override RMAN retention settings). The **logs** and **nologs** options of the **backup** command have now become obsolete. Instead, when you perform a backup with the **keep** option, Oracle will back up all database components required to ensure that a consistent version of the database can be restored:

1. The database backup is executed. This backup will include data files, the control file (regardless of autobackup settings), and the current SPFILE.

2. An archived redo log backup is executed.

3. Control file and server parameter files are backed up.

Note that each backup created with the keep option is assigned a unique tag that can be referenced during restore operations (I would recommend you assign it a tag with a naming convention that makes sense to you, instead).

The **keep** option also supports the creation of a restore point during the backup. This makes it easier to restore the archived backup. This is a normal restore point, but if you are using a recovery catalog this restore point will be retained for the lifetime of the backup. The **keep** option is also available (without the **restore point** option) when using the **change** command to modify existing backups.

Finally, be aware that an archived backup can be aged out of the control file if they are to be maintained for more than a year. It is recommended that if you wish to keep archived backups that you use a recovery catalog to prevent this from happening. In fact a recovery catalog is required when using the **keep forever** option. The **keep forever** option indicates the backup should be kept until it is deliberately removed by the DBA.

**NOTE**
*Of course, with offline backups, the database is already in a consistent state. No archive log backups are required for such a backup when using the **keep** option.*

## Backup Failover for Archived Redo Logs

Sometimes databases are actually archiving to multiple archive log destinations.
There may be times when an archived redo log is not in a particular destination
directory, or perhaps it is corrupt for some reason. Now in cases where RMAN
cannot back up an archived redo log in the flash recovery area, RMAN will fail
over to any other archived redo log destination directory and attempt to back up
the archived redo log from that location. For example, if Oracle is archiving to the
flash recovery area and another archived redo log destination directory is a
Network Attached Storage (NAS) drive, if an archived redo log backup fails in the
flash recovery area, RMAN will attempt to back up the archived redo log from the
NAS location.

## Archived Redo Log Deletion Policy Enhancements

In Oracle Database 11*g*, the archive log deletion policy configuration settings now
apply to all archived redo log destinations instead of just the flash recovery area.
While automatic deletion of archived redo logs will only occur in the flash recovery
area (FRA) as a matter of nominal FRA space management operations, other
archived redo logs will be made subject to the retention policy, and marked as
OBSOLETE. As such, commands such as **delete obsolete** will now impact archived
redo logs in all locations, removing them as required.

Also in Oracle Database 11*g* with the **all** option of the **to applied on [all] standby**
command, you can define the deletion policy as applying to all mandatory and
optional remote archive log destinations. Using the **all** option means that archived
redo logs on the primary database will not be marked for deletion until they are
consumed by all remote archived redo log destinations, mandatory or not.

You can also define a retention policy for archived redo logs that have been
backed up a predefined number of times. Use the **archivelog deletion policy
parameter** of the **configure** command with the **to backed up n times to device type**
command to indicate that archived redo logs should be removed after they have
been backed up **n** times on the same device. Note that any logs must have been
shipped to any required standby database locations before this command will be
successful.

## Recovery Catalog Enhancements

Two new recovery catalog enhancements are found in Oracle Database 11*g*. These
are the virtual private catalog, which is used to improve security, and the **import
catalog** command, which is used to merge one recovery catalog into another. Let's
look at each of these new features in a bit more detail.

## Better Catalog Security

In previous versions the owner of the catalog had compete access to the recovery catalog. It was an onerous task to grant access to the recovery catalog to other users, and even more difficult if you wanted to limit the ability of those users to see only specific data.

Oracle Database 11*g* now offers the virtual private catalog to make management of recovery catalog security easier. Now, the owner of the base recovery catalog can grant limited access (by database) to the recovery catalog views to other users. This is done though the new RMAN **grant** command (after some initial setup), which is used to grant privileges to a specific user and then to create the virtual catalog for that user. When granted privileges, the user can query the recovery catalog views of the databases to which they have been granted privileges. They can also store and execute local stored scripts; however, they will have read-only access to global stored scripts.

## Import Catalog Command

There may be cases where you have more than one recovery catalog and you wish to merge these disparate catalogs into one catalog. Oracle Database 11*g* makes this easy with the **import catalog** command. You can also move an existing recovery catalog between two databases using the **import catalog** command. All database RMAN backup metadata will be imported into the destination catalog schema by default; however, you can opt to define a list of databases that you want to import instead. Once the import is complete, the database will be unregistered from the source catalog schema by default (you can override this setting if you wish).

In the event that you are using global scripts in your recovery catalog, the **import catalog** command may run into a naming conflict if another global script is present in the destination catalog schema. In this case, RMAN will rename the global script.

Catalog imports are subject to RMAN compatibility restrictions with regard to the version of the recovery catalog schema, the RMAN executable, and the recovery catalog database. Check the Oracle documentation if you have any questions with regard to compatibility. You do not need to connect to the target database to import the catalog schema data, but you do need to connect to the destination catalog schema.

Here is an example of importing the recovery catalog. Here the source catalog service name is db_src and the destination catalog schema service name is db_dest:

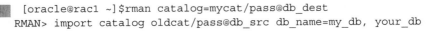

```
[oracle@rac1 ~]$rman catalog=mycat/pass@db_dest
RMAN> import catalog oldcat/pass@db_src db_name=my_db, your_db
```

**NOTE**
*If the import fails, the entire operation will be rolled back.*

## Undo Backup Optimization

A recovery does not require all undo capability available in the UNDO tablespace. For example, if a transaction has been committed, then the associated undo is not required. In an effort to reduce even further the time required to back up an Oracle database, Oracle will not backup unneeded UNDO if **backup optimization** is set to ON.

## Block Media Recovery Performance Improved

Oracle Database 10*g* introduced block media recovery, which allows you to restore specific corrupt blocks online, rather than the entire data file. This was a revolutionary step forward for Oracle. Oracle Database 11*g* enhances this feature by providing the ability to recover these blocks from the flashback logs (if flashback is enabled). This new feature can significantly reduce the time that it takes to perform block media recovery since RMAN will not have to restore backups from tape or disk. If RMAN cannot find the blocks in the flashback logs, it will then use RMAN backups (full or level-0 incremental) along with archived redo logs to recover the block.

## Other RMAN New Features

Oracle Database 11*g* comes with a number of new RMAN related features (you just knew a book from me would have some RMAN related stuff in it, didn't you!). These new features include:

- Block change support for standby databases
- Improved scripting
- Backup of read-only transportable tablespaces

### Block Change Support for Standby Databases

Support for the block change tracking file is now available on physical standby databases when performing incremental backups. This will make backups of standby databases potentially faster than with previous Oracle versions.

### Improved RMAN Scripting

Oracle Database 11*g* allows you to use substitution variables in your RMAN command files and stored scripts. The new **using** parameter of the RMAN command allows you to define the values associated with substitution variables contained within the stored script. To define the substitution variable, use the ampersand character followed by a number. For example, the following backup command uses two substitution variables &1 and &2:

```
Backup database tag '&1' keep until time 'sysdate+365' restore point
'&2' plus archivelog;
```

**Arup Says...**

One of the best things Oracle Database 9*i* offered was the block media recovery feature. In today's high-reliability storage area networks (SANs), the probability of failure of an entire array is very minimal, but the chance of isolated software or hardware corruption affecting one or more blocks is higher. That's where block media recovery really shone, allowing the repair to be really fast and targeting the high-likelihood events. This also allowed the possibility of repairing the disk instead of failing over to the standby database while still within the realm of the service level agreement (SLA).

Oracle Database 10*g* offered a new feature—flashback logs. The moment I heard about it and tested it, my first question to the Oracle PM was: why not make it part of the recovery process? Well, came the reply, there were many complications, understandably so since we are talking about complex software like Oracle. Now I am really excited to see these flashback logs being used for additional purposes. Running a database in flashback mode incurs some performance penalty, so now the penalty is somewhat justified by the more efficient recovery.

RMAN would them prompt us for the appropriate values to assign to &1 and &2. To execute this from a shell or batch script, we would call it as seen here:

```
Rman target=rman/pass @'/rman/script/myscript.rman' using $tag $rest_point
```

Or from the RMAN command line you could do this:

```
RMAN>@/rman/script/myscript.rman ROBERT RESTORE_AB
```

### Backup of Read-Only Transportable Tablespaces

If you use transportable tablespaces, you know that in Oracle Database 10*g* these tablespaces had to be made read/write in order to back them up. This is no longer the case and transportable tablespaces that are read-only will be backed up.

# Oracle Flashback-Related New Features

Oracle Database 11*g* introduces totally new Flashback-related features. First there is Oracle Flashback Transaction Backout, which allows you to back out transactions that are already committed. Then there is the Oracle Flashback Data Archives feature, which provides the ability to track changes to a table over its lifetime. Let's look at each of these features in some more detail.

# Oracle Flashback Transaction Backout

Oracle Database 11*g* adds a new feature to the Flashback toolkit, Oracle Flashback Transaction Backout. This feature allows you to back out a *committed* transaction and all dependent transactions while the database is still online. Only the selected transactions and dependent transactions will be backed out, other transactions will be untouched by the flashback transaction backout operation. This functionality is provided through the **dbms_flashback.transaction_backout** procedure or though an OEM interface into Flashback Transaction Backout.

## Setting Up for Flashback Transaction Backout

To use Flashback Transaction Backout, there are some prerequisites that your database must first meet. First you need to enable supplemental logging with primary key logging as seen in this example:

```
Alter database add supplemental log data;
Alter database add supplemental log data (primary key) columns;
```

Grant **execute** on **dbms_flashback** to the user who will be performing the Flashback Transaction Backout. Finally, **grant select any transaction** to the user who will be performing the Flashback Transaction Backout. One benefit of using OEM with Flashback Transaction Backout is that it checks for the correct permissions and will inform you if the user is not able to perform Flashback Transaction Backout, and OEM will also tell you what actions need to be performed to be able to execute a Flashback Transaction Backout.

## Executing a Flashback Transaction Backout via OEM

OEM is probably easier to use than manual commands when processing a Flashback Transaction Backout (we will just call this a transaction backout for the rest of this section). To start a transaction backout, go to the Schema tab on the top of the Database home page in OEM. Select tables from the Database Objects section of the Schema page. From the Tables page, select a table to execute the transaction backout operation on, and then select the Flashback Transaction action for the table you have selected.

OEM will proceed to take you to the Flashback Transaction: Perform Query page. This is where you can select the system change number (SCN) or time range of the query you wish to perform on your transaction. Once you have selected the needed information, Oracle will proceed to use Log Miner and mine all of the transactions on the selected table over the given period of time. It will then present the mined transactions on the next page for you to select. In Figure 3-9, Oracle found two transactions that we can back out.

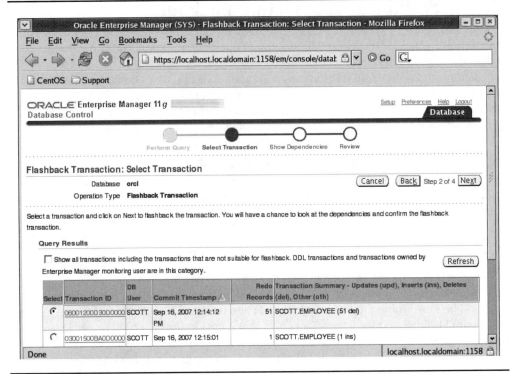

**FIGURE 3-9.** *Oracle OEM Flashback Transaction page*

**NOTE**
*Mining of the transactions is the Achilles heel of this whole process. It can take time if the start time and end time for mining is quite broad. Thankfully OEM does give you an estimate of how long the mining process should last, and an option to cancel the operation.*

You can click on any transaction ID and see the details of that transaction. This allows you to ensure that you have, in fact, found the correct transaction. Note that this information is collected from Log Miner, so the DML statement reported by Oracle may be presented somewhat differently than the one you actually executed. For example, a statement like the following: **insert into Robert values (10,10,10);** will be reported as **insert into "ROBERT"."TEST" values "ID" = 10, "ID2"= 10,**

**"DEF_ID" = 10;**. These statements used to back out the transaction are known as *compensating transactions.*

To continue the operation, we click on the radio button associated with the transaction we wish to back out and click on Next. Oracle will then generate a flashback transaction report that will provide you with the SQL required to undo that transaction. After reviewing the SQL, you can choose to run that SQL to remove the transaction. You can also choose to cancel the operation.

### Executing a Flashback Transaction Backout Manually

You can also manually execute a transaction backout. This is a much more complex and manual procedure, but available if you need to write an application with this capability or if you are just a DBA masochist and demand to be able to do it this way. To perform the backout, you will first need to know the transaction ID that you wish to deal with. The V$TRANSACTION view provides this for you with the XID column if you are in the middle of a transaction. Optionally you could use Log Miner to find the candidate transaction IDs. Here is an example of finding the transaction ID from V$TRANSACTION (in this case, we will cheat a little bit and assume it's a delete transaction):

```
select a.sql_text, b.xid
from v$open_cursor a, v$transaction b, v$session c
where a.sid=c.sid and c.taddr=b.addr
and a.sql_text like 'delete';

SQL_TEXT                                            XID
--------------------------------------------------- ----------------
delete from employee where empno=25                 03001800BC0D0000
```

Now we can simply use the **dbms_flashback.transaction_backout** procedure to back out the procedure. Note that this procedure is overloaded, and there are several different ways to generate the backed-out transaction. Review the documentation for more details on the variety of ways to perform the backout operation. Here is an example using the transaction ID:

```
Declare
    v_xid sys.xid_array;
begin
    v_xid := sys.xid_array('03001800BC0D0000');
    dbms_flashback.transaction_backout(numtxns=>1,
    xids=>v_xid, options=>dbms_flashback.cascade);
end;
/
```

When the transaction backout occurs, a report will be generated to the data dictionary, which you can review. These reports are generated to the following tables:

- **[DBA, USER]_FLASHBACK_TXN_STATE**   Any transaction that is shown in this view is backed out.

- **[DBA, USER]_FLASHBACK_TXN_REPORT**   Provides information about the compensating status of all transactions in the database.

## Oracle Flashback Data Archives

Oracle Flashback Data Archives provides the ability to track changes that occur on a table over the lifetime of the table. Until now many applications had to build in logging for this kind of transaction monitoring. You can use the Flashback Data Archives feature to satisfy security and compliance requirements. You can also use the data for data analysis and within a decision support system (DSS) environment. Let's look at how to set up Oracle Flashback Data Archives and then how it can be used.

### Set Up Oracle Flashback Data Archives

The user who will be defining any Flashback Data Archives will need to have the privilege **flashback archive administer** granted to them, as seen in this example:

```
Grant FLASHBACK ARCHIVE ADMINISTER to Robert;
```

We are now ready to create a flashback data archive (which we will call archives or an archive for the rest of this chapter). An *archive* contains all the data required to track and archive historical transactional data. Once the archive is

**Arup Says...**
With the days of regulations and mandates such as HIPAA, SOX, PCI, and an assortment of other hard-to-follow acronyms, comes an even more bitter pill— the need to store historical data for *legal* reasons. Note the stress on the word *legal*; the present requirement is not just slapping together a rag-tag homegrown set of scripts to record the changes to satisfy your own curiosity or do some debugging, but something that can hold up in a court of law, or at least in a formal inquiry. Flashback Data Archives come very handy in that respect. Combine that with low-cost storage such as NAS, and you've got yourself a great archive solution.

Note that the flashback archive is *not* based on triggers, so the performance penalty on queries is not substantial. The functionality of writing the archives is embedded in the code of the database. I have described more use cases of Flashback Data Archives in the Appendix.

created you can begin to track changes. To create the archive we use the **create flashback archive** SQL DDL command. When you create the archive, you will assign the archive to a tablespace and assign it a space quota and a retention period. Note that you may have many different archives. Each of these might be assigned different retention criterion (say one year, and two years). The records in each archive will be managed by Oracle, with records being purged after the retention criteria has expired.

**NOTE**
*Archives are likely to get quite large. Make sure you allocate enough space to the archive when you create it!*

In the following example of the creation of a flashback archive we create the archive with a retention period of one year. This archive is assigned to the **retention_archives** tablespace and is the default archive for the database (this command would fail if a default already existed). Note that since we defined this as the default archive, you must be logged in with **sysdba** privileges.

We have assigned a quota of 5G to this archive. By default the quota is unlimited. If an archive is assigned a quota and the archive fills up, you will not be having a good day. DML operations on the tables assigned to that archive will fail, you will get all sorts of nastygrams in the mail, and your boss will complain about irritating DBAs who always like to set up newfangled features when they come up. If you are still feeling brave, here is an example DDL to create an archive called archive_one_year :

```
Create flashback archive default archive_one_year
tablespace retention_archives
Quota 5g retention 1 year;
```

We might want to create another archive for two-year retention. This would not be the default archive of course. Here is the creation of the two-year archive (using a 24-month retention criteria instead of years). Note that in this case we do not have to be logged in as a **sysdba** user since we are not defining a default archive:

```
Create flashback archive archive_two_year
tablespace retention_archives
Quota 5g retention 24 month;
```

Retention can be in terms of years, months, or days and the quota can be expressed in megabytes (M), gigabytes (G), terabytes (T), and petabytes (P). Good luck to you if you are using petabytes of archival!! Please write to me and let me know how that goes! When an archive is created it can only be assigned to a single tablespace (or tablespace group). Archives can be assigned to other tablespaces using the **alter flashback archive** command discussed in the next section.

### Administer Oracle Flashback Data Archives

The **alter flashback archive** and **drop flashback archive** commands are used to manage existing archives. The **alter flashback archive** command can be used to make an existing archive the default archive (you can only have one default archive at a time) or change the current default archive to become a nondefault archive. You can also change the retention time of the archive and purge some or all of the archives data. Finally you can modify the tablespace assignment of the archive by adding, modifying, or removing tablespaces assigned to the archive. Here are some examples of using the **alter flashback archive** command:

```
-- Make Flashback Data Archive archive_two_year the default Archive:
-- Note that archive_one_year will no longer be the default!!
-- also note, you must be SYSDBA to execute this command.
ALTER FLASHBACK ARCHIVE archive_two_year SET DEFAULT;
-- To Flashback Data Archive archive_two_year,
-- Add to tablespace retention_one and make the quota 5g on that tablespace:
ALTER FLASHBACK ARCHIVE archive_two_year
ADD TABLESPACE retention_one QUOTA 5G;
-- Change the maximum space that Flashback Data Archive archive_two_year
-- can use in tablespace retention_one 20 G:
ALTER FLASHBACK ARCHIVE archive_two_year
MODIFY TABLESPACE retention_one QUOTA 20G;
-- Change the maximum space that Flashback Data Archive archive_two_year
-- can use in tablespace retention_one to unlimited:
ALTER FLASHBACK ARCHIVE archive_two_year
MODIFY TABLESPACE retention_one;
-- Change the retention time for Flashback Data Archive archive_two_year
-- to five years:
ALTER FLASHBACK ARCHIVE archive_two_year MODIFY RETENTION 5 YEAR;
-- Remove tablespace tbs2 from Flashback Data Archive archive_two_year:
-- Note that this will fail if archive_two_year is the last tablespace
-- assigned to this archive.
ALTER FLASHBACK ARCHIVE archive_two_year REMOVE TABLESPACE bad_tbs;
--Purge all historical data from Flashback Data Archive archive_two_year:
ALTER FLASHBACK ARCHIVE archive_two_year PURGE ALL;
-- Purge all historical data older than 30 days from Archive archive_two_year:
-- Note that an error will occur if you purge to a time before that archive
-- was created.
ALTER FLASHBACK ARCHIVE archive_two_year
PURGE BEFORE TIMESTAMP (SYSTIMESTAMP - INTERVAL '30' DAY);
-- Purge all historical data older than SCN 728969 from Archive archive_two_year:
ALTER FLASHBACK ARCHIVE archive_two_year PURGE BEFORE SCN 6443333;
```

As you might expect, the **drop flashback archive** command is used to drop a flashback archive. Of course, this does not drop the associated tablespace, which is probably a good thing since the tablespace might actually have some useful data still in it! Here is an example of the **drop flashback archive** command in use:

```
Drop flashback archive archive_two_year;
```

### Enable Oracle Flashback Data Archives

By default, archiving is disabled. You can enable archiving on specific tables when you create the table or you can alter the table to enable archiving. Here are examples of using the **create table** command and the **alter table** command to enable archiving:

```
-- Create the table, using the default archive location.
Create table test_arch (id number) tablespace users flashback archive;
-- Modify a table to use the default archive location.
Alter table other_test flashback archive;
-- Create a table to use a non-default archivelocation
Create table test_arch (id number) tablespace users
flashback archive archive_two_year;
-- Modify a table to use a non-default archive location.
-- Note that if you are archivng this table already, this command
-- will fail. You need to no flashback archive the table first.
-- So that archived data will be lost.
Alter table other_test flashback archive archive_two_year;
-- Modify a table to stop archiving.
Alter table other_test no flashback archive;
```

**NOTE**
*If you turn off archiving for a table, all the historical data for that table will be lost. If you drop a flashback archive, then all data contained in that archive is lost too.*

Note that when a table is being archived, certain DDL commands are disabled for that object. These include certain **alter table** commands and the **drop table**, **rename table**, and **truncate table** commands. Also commands that modify a column are not allowed. For example, after the creation of the **test_arch** table in the previous example, we cannot drop that table, as seen here:

```
SQL> drop table test_arch;
drop table test_arch
         *
ERROR at line 1:
ORA-55610: Invalid DDL statement on history-tracked table
```

Well, this is a fine predicament we find ourselves in! However, Oracle is smarter than that. All we need to do is disable archiving and then we can drop the object, as seen in this example:

```
SQL> Alter table test_arch no flashback archive;
Table altered.
SQL> Drop table test_arch;
Table dropped.
```

**NOTE**
*Because of the DDL restrictions associated with archiving, you need to use this feature cautiously with existing legacy systems.*

## Oracle Flashback Data Archives Views

Oracle provides views that you can use to administer Flashback Data Archives. These views include:

- **[DBA I USER]_FLASHBACK_ARCHIVE**   Provides information on all flashback archives contained in the database.

- **DBA_FLASHBACK_ARCHIVE_TS**   Provides information on all tablespaces that contain flashback archives.

- **[DBA I USER]_FLASHBACK_ARCHIVE_TABLES**   This view indicates which flashback archive a given table is assigned to. If a table is not assigned to a flashback archive, it will not appear in this view.

Here are some example queries against these views:

```
select * from dba_flashback_archive;
FLASHBACK_ARCHIVE_NA FLASHBACK_ARCHIVE# RETENTION_IN_DAYS  STATUS
-------------------- ------------------ -----------------  -------
ARCHIVE_ONE_YEAR                      1               365
ARCHIVE_TWO_YEAR                      2              1825  DEFAULT

 select * from dba_flashback_archive_ts;
FLASHBACK_ARCHIVE_NA FLASHBACK_ARCHIVE# TABLESPACE_NAME        QUOTA_IN_MB
-------------------- ------------------ --------------------   -----------
ARCHIVE_ONE_YEAR                      1 RETENTION_ARCHIVES     50
ARCHIVE_TWO_YEAR                      2 RETENTION_ARCHIVES     50
ARCHIVE_TWO_YEAR                      2 RETENTION_ONE

select table_name, owner_name, flashback_archive_name
from dba_flashback_archive_tables;
TABLE_NAME     OWNER_NAME                      FLASHBACK_ARCHIVE_NA
-------------- ------------------------------- --------------------
TEST           ROBERT                          ARCHIVE_TWO_YEAR
OTHER_TEST     ROBERT                          ARCHIVE_TWO_YEAR
```

## Using Oracle Flashback Data Archives

So, now that we have configured archiving, how do we use it? It's really quite simple, as the Flashback Data Archives feature is an extension of the existing Flashback technologies already in place. Before, we were subject to the availability of undo and its retention. If the undo was available, then we could flashback a table easily and see how it looked back in time; if the undo was not available, then the flashback efforts would fail. Guaranteed retention of undo helped to stabilize the availability of undo, but this was a global parameter, and could cause the whole database undo structure to become large and difficult to manage.

Oracle's Flashback Data Archives feature would make Mulder and Scully proud. It is a time machine, allowing you to preserve undo at a table level for as long as might be required. Because this feature is granular to the table as opposed to the database, the space impacts are reduced for long-term undo storage. Now, SQL queries using the **as of timestamp** parameter are no longer subject to limited undo storage, so queries such as the following are possible:

```
Select id from test as of timestamp (systimestamp - interval '6' month);
```

We can now also use the **flashback table** command to flashback the table to a much further back time in history, as seen in this example:

```
Flashback table test to timestamp (systimestamp - interval '6' month);
```

# Oracle Standby Database New Features

Oracle Database 11*g* offers new features for your standby database. These include lost-write detection, compression of archived redo logs, real-time query capabilities on physical standby databases, and snapshot databases. Let's look at these new features next!

## Lost-Write Detection

Oracle physical standby databases now provide lost-write detection. Typically, Oracle will make a write request to the IO subsystem and the IO subsystem will write the data and report that the write was successful (with an asynchronous write, the IO subsystem may actually report that the write was complete when in fact it is just queued to be written). Lost-writes occur when the IO subsystem actually does not write the data to the physical medium. This can cause data loss in the Oracle database.

If you are running a physical standby database in Oracle Database 11*g*, Oracle physical standby databases can detect the corruption. When this error is detected, Oracle recommends switching over to the physical standby database, making it the primary database. You can then re-create the primary database.

**NOTE**
*RMAN block-level recovery should also be possible in this case. This would require re-creation of your physical standby databases, however, you should determine your site's recovery strategy before such an event occurs!*

This new feature leads to quicker identification of problems and reduced down time. When the physical standby database detects the lost write, it will generate an error in the alert log of the standby database and managed recovery will be halted.

## Compression of Archived Redo Logs

Oracle will now compress archived redo logs when they are sent to a standby database site for gap resolution. This can significantly reduce the bandwidth required to get standby databases "caught up" in the case of gap resolution.

## Real-Time Query Capabilities from a Physical Standby Database

You can now query a physical standby database at the same time that the standby database is applying redo. This makes the physical standby database much more cost-effective and useful than before. You do not need to do anything special to enable this feature. Simply start redo, apply as you normally would, then open the standby database in read-only mode.

## Snapshot Databases

Oracle Database 11*g* introduces snapshot databases. These databases allow you to open a physical standby database, and change data and structures in that database, all while continuing to collect (but not apply) redo. You convert the physical

**Arup Says...**

Many organizations struggling with the need to maintain a true 99.999% uptime environment pondered over the question, should they invest in a redundant set of hardware in the physical standby database which is 99.999% idle? And they couldn't even run reports from it without sacrificing the ability to failover very quickly. Logical standby databases solved the issue somewhat, but they were not the answer, primarily because the logical standby database can't be used for backups. Physical standby database can offload the CPU cycles required for backups from the main database to itself, saving precious resources in the primary. These backups and archived logs could be applied to the main database as if they were taken on the primary.

The real-time query capability of the physical standby database solves the issue in the most logical way. It can be a physical standby and you can also run reports off it, in addition to running RMAN backups. Now, you can justify the high cost of the standby infrastructure. Who says you can't have your cake and eat it too?

standby database to a snapshot database by issuing the command **alter database convert to snapshot standby**. When this command is executed, Oracle will create a guaranteed restore point, which will be used later to flashback the standby database to the point at which it was converted, allowing Oracle to once again begin to apply redo to the standby database.

Once the standby database has been converted to a snapshot database, you can then open the database for read/write operations. You can then change the database as much as you like. Once you are ready to revert the database to a standby database. you issue the command **alter database convert to physical standby**.

**NOTE**
*Oracle flashback database is used to revert the snapshot database to a standby database. Any operation that might occur when the snapshot database is open in read/write mode that would prevent flashback operations, will prevent you from being able to reopen the database as a standby database.*

# Oracle Data Pump New Features

Oracle Data Pump was introduced in Oracle Database 10*g* and is further improved in Oracle Database 11*g*. In this section we will cover the following features:

- Export utility deprecation

- Compression of dump file sets

- Improvement in encryption

**Arup Says...**

The power of the snapshot standby database is somewhat clouded by all that razzmatazz in Oracle Database 11*g*. Imagine this: You are trying to figure out the best possible configuration of the database host, network, storage and all such systems. How can you do it? It's really simple. Create a snapshot standby database from the primary database, replay the workload captured from primary using the Database Replay feature and measure the performance. Then flashback the standby to the original state, change the parameters you want and replay the workload again. Repeat this cycle until you are satisfied with the changes you want to cast in stone. Then convert the snapshot standby database to a regular one.

- Data remapping

- Table renaming

- Data Pump and partitioned table operations

- Overwrite dump files

- The **data_options** parameter

- The **transportable** parameter

# Exp Utility Deprecated

I've got good news and bad news about the old exp utility. The bad news is that it's no longer supported by Oracle. If you find a bug, it's likely that you are not going to get it fixed in 11*g*. The good news is that the exp utility does still ship with Oracle Database 11*g*. So, your scripts that call exp will live to see yet one more version of the database. Fair warning though, there is no telling how much longer exp will be around. Besides, if you are reading this book, you are a hip kind of DBA! You don't go for the old-fashioned technologies. Finally, the imp utility is still supported.

# Compression of Dump File Sets

I'm sure that you get irritated at the size of dump file sets; I do. Oracle has heard our groans and now supports compression of Dump file sets. However, they missed the key word in our groans, and that word was "free." Availability of compression is a part of a new licensed product called the Advanced Compression option, which will be available for both standard and enterprise editions of Oracle Database. Let's all say *boo* together to see if they hear that sentiment as well.

Use of compression with Data Pump is facilitated through the use of the **compression** parameter of the **expdp** command, as seen in this example:

```
expdp Robert/robert DIRECTORY= data_pump_dir DUMPFILE=hr_comp.dmp
COMPRESSION=ALL
```

There are four options available for the **compression** parameter:

- **ALL**   Enables compression for the entire operation.

- **Metadata_only**   The default setting. Causes only the metadata to be compressed.

- **Data_only**   Only the data being written to the dump file set will be compressed.

- **None**   No compression will take place.

## Data Pump Encryption Enhancements

It seems to be in the news every week now, some company's data being compromised. If your data is sensitive, then encrypting the Data Pump dump files makes sense. Data Pump comes with new features associated with encryption:

- You can choose to encrypt metadata, data, or both via the use of the new **encryption** parameter.

- You can choose a specific encryption algorithm (AES128, AES192, or AES256) using the **encryption_algorithm** parameter.

- You can choose different encryption modes to be used on the export. (Dual, Password, and Transparent) via the **encryption_mode** parameter. This now allows you to use the Oracle Encryption Wallet with Data Pump.

Here is an example of using the new encryption parameters for a data pump export:

```
expdp Robert/robert DIRECTORY=data_pump_dir DUMPFILE=hr_comp.dmp
encryption=all encryption_password=Robert encryption_algorithm=AES128
encryption_mode=PASSWORD
```

## Data Pump Data Remapping (Obfuscation)

Oracle Data Pump now offers the ability to obfuscate data during an export or import operation. This functionality is supported with the use of the new **remap_data** parameter. With the **remap_data** parameter you define the schema table .column object(s) to be remapped, and you also define an associated function that will be called "remap" (or obfuscate) the column data. Oracle supports multiple remappings. Each remapping can use the same or a different remapping function.

As an example, we might have the following function that modifies input data:

```
Create or replace package my_package
as
function my_function (p_in_data varchar2)
return varchar2;
end;
/
Create or replace package body my_package
as
function my_function (p_in_data varchar2)
return varchar2
As
     v_return     varchar2(30);
```

```
begin
    v_return:=translate(p_in_data,
                        'abcdefghijklmnopqrstuvwxyz',
                        'bcdefghijklmnopqrstuvwxyza');
    dbms_output.put_line(v_return);
    return v_return;
end;
end;
/
```

Now, let's export a table and apply this function to modify a column's data. Here is our test table:

```
SQL> desc names
 Name                                      Null?    Type
 ----------------------------------------- -------- ----------------------------
 USER_NAME                                          VARCHAR2(30)
SQL> select * from names;
USER_NAME
-----------------------------
joe
```

And let's do the export:

```
expdp Robert/robert DIRECTORY=data_pump_dir DUMPFILE=remap.dmp
tables=Robert.names remap_data=Robert.names.user_name:Robert.my_package
.my_function
```

Let's reimport the data and see what it looks like (we dropped the table before we did the import):

```
impdp Robert/robert DIRECTORY=data_pump_dir DUMPFILE=remap.dmp
tables=ROBERT.NAMES remap_table=ROBERT.NAMES:COPY_NAMES
```

We could have also remapped the data during the import as in this example:

```
impdp Robert/robert DIRECTORY=data_pump_dir DUMPFILE=remap.dmp
tables=ROBERT.NAMES remap_table=ROBERT.NAMES:COPY_NAMES
remap_data=Robert.copy_names.user_name:Robert.my_package.my_function
```

### Arup Says...

One of the several requirements in today's regulated environments is to mask sensitive data such as credit card numbers, and so on, when moving production data to test systems. This is a hard requirement to satisfy, especially if you have a large database. It's about time Oracle came up with a facility to support it.

## Data Pump Rename Table

Oracle Data Pump allows you to rename a table during the import process with the **remap_table** parameter. With the **remap_table** parameter you define the original table schema and name, and then indicate the new name for the table. Here is an example where the table **robert.names** is renamed to **copy_names**:

```
impdp Robert/robert DIRECTORY=data_pump_dir DUMPFILE=remap.dmp
tables=ROBERT.NAMES remap_table=ROBERT.NAMES:COPY_NAMES
```

## Data Pump and Partitioned Tables

You can control partitioning of tables during a Oracle Data Pump import by using the new **partition_options** parameter of **impdp**. This parameter has the following options:

- **None**   Tables will be imported such that they will look like those on the system on which the export was created.

- **Departition**   Partitions will be created as individual tables rather than partitions of a partitioned table.

- **Merge**   Causes all partitions to be merged into one, unpartitioned table.

Here is an example of the use of the **partition_options** parameter. In this case we will take all partitions of the **names** table and combine them into one unpartitioned table on the destination side:

```
impdp Robert/robert DIRECTORY=data_pump_dir DUMPFILE=remap.dmp
tables=ROBERT.NAMES partition_options=merge
```

## Overwrite Dump Files

If you do lots of exports with Oracle Data Pump, you will be happy to know that you now have the option to overwrite any dump file that might already exist. To overwrite any pre-existing file, use the new **reuse_dumpfiles** parameter as seen in this example:

```
expdp Robert/robert DIRECTORY=data_pump_dir DUMPFILE=remap.dmp
tables=ROBERT.NAMES reuse_dumpfiles=Y
```

## Data Pump Data_Options Parameter

Oracle Data Pump has added the **data_options** parameter to provide for special handling of certain types of data-related issues. This includes handling of constraint-related issues during an import as well as how to handle **xml_clobs**.

The **xml_clobs** option of the **data_options** parameter of the Data Pump Export utility allows you to override the default behavior of Oracle Data Pump, which is to compress the format of the **xmltype clob**. To use this option, the XML schemas at the source and destination must be the same.

There may be times during an import that you will experience constraint violations during an Oracle Data Pump import. The **data_options** parameter, when set to **skip_constraint_errors**, will cause the import program to ignore errors generated by database constraints unless the constraint error is due to a deferred constraint. In the case of deferred constraints, imports will always be rolled back.

Here is an example of the use of the **data_options** parameter with **impdp**:

```
impdp Robert/robert DIRECTORY=data_pump_dir DUMPFILE=remap.dmp
tables=ROBERT.NAMES data_options=SKIP_CONSTRAINT_ERRORS
```

## The Transportable Parameter

The **transportable** parameter of Oracle Data Pump import and export extends the functionality of transportable tablespaces. Now, only the metadata associated with specific tables, partitions, or subpartitions will be extracted, rather than all metadata. You can then proceed to transport the associated data files as you normally would. You import the data with **impdp**.

```
expdp Robert/robert DIRECTORY=data_pump_dir DUMPFILE=remap.dmp
tables=ROBERT.NAMES transportable=always
```

You then copy the data files and the dump file set to the destination and plug in the database. You would use **impdp** as a part of this process to import the metadata into the database, as seen in this example:

```
impdp Robert/robert DIRECTORY=data_pump_dir DUMPFILE=remap.dmp
tables=ROBERT.NAMES remap_schema=Robert:new_Robert
```

# End of Line

Well, this has been another action packed chapter, hasn't it? Again, we have looked at a number of new and enhanced features in Oracle Database 11*g* that related to availability and recovery, and there is no doubt that there are a lot of them and that they are very useful. This has been perhaps one of my two favorite chapters to write, as these are my favorite topics. Arup's thoughts in this chapter are invaluable and quite useful. Thanks for participating in this work Arup!

# CHAPTER
## 4

# Oracle Database Advisors

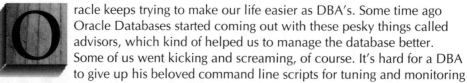racle keeps trying to make our life easier as DBA's. Some time ago Oracle Databases started coming out with these pesky things called advisors, which kind of helped us to manage the database better. Some of us went kicking and screaming, of course. It's hard for a DBA to give up his beloved command line scripts for tuning and monitoring (and honestly, there are still a number of cases when we have to break out those scripts). Oracle Database 11*g* continues the tradition of trying to help us do our jobs (the nerve!). Old Advisors are improved and new advisors have been added such as

- The Data Recovery Advisor

- SQL Repair Advisor

- Partition Advisor (SQL Access Advisor, or SAA)

- Streams Performance Advisor

In this chapter we will cover these advisors in some detail.

**NOTE**
*You will also want to review Chapter 9 and the Automatic SQL Tuning, which offers improvements on the SQL Tuning Advisor that was introduced in Oracle Database 10g.*

# The Data Recovery Advisor

The new Data Recovery Advisor is used to repair a number of different errors including data block corruption, undo corruption, and data dictionary corruption. The Recovery Advisor is integrated with OEM, the Health Monitor, and RMAN to help make dealing with data corruption problems as easy and seamless as possible. For the Data Recovery Advisor to function, Oracle must first detect an error. This can happen as a result of an error occurring naturally during the course of database operations (that is, some form of an ORA error) or if the DBA executed a health check that detects the error.

The Data Recovery Advisor will return the priority of the error (Critical, High, and Low) and its status (Open or Closed) and provides repair options available to you to correct the problem (such as perform media recovery). All information from the Data Recovery Advisor is stored in the ADR. The repair options presented may be automated or manual, or both options might be presented.

The Data Recovery Advisor can be reached within OEM from the OEM Database home page or by using RMAN. Let's look at both of these options in some more detail.

**NOTE**
*The Data Recovery Advisor (DRA) functions can only be run on a single-instance database (thus the RAC cluster must be brought now to single-instance mode). DRA also can not be used with a physical standby database.*

## Using the Data Recovery Advisor Through OEM

Simply click on the Availability link and then click on the Perform Recovery link (under the Manage Menu options), which will cause the Perform Recovery page to appear as seen in Figure 4-1 (note that our example has one datafile with an error appearing at the top of the page that needs to be corrected).

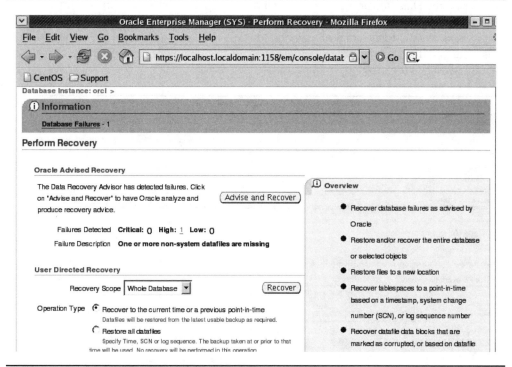

**Figure 4-1.** *The OEM Perform Recovery page*

**NOTE**
*Sometimes the Perform Recovery page will show a database failure at the top, but the Oracle Advised Recovery section will not show that there is a problem. This is because the database advisor has not completely "discovered" the failure. You can run the DB Structure Integrity Checker (we discussed checkers in Chapter 3) from Advisor Central and the failure will be discovered. You can also click on Database Failures, and proceed to correct the failure through a slightly different avenue. The later method is a bit more advanced, so you should be comfortable with RMAN in particular, and understand your failure well before you choose this method of recovery.*

To start the Data Repair Advisor, you will need to specify the host login credentials. Then under the Oracle Advanced Recovery section, click on the Advise and Recovery button. Oracle will proceed to the View and Manage Failures page shown in Figure 4-2. This page can display a number of different errors from data corruption, to loss of a datafile (which is the problem in our case).

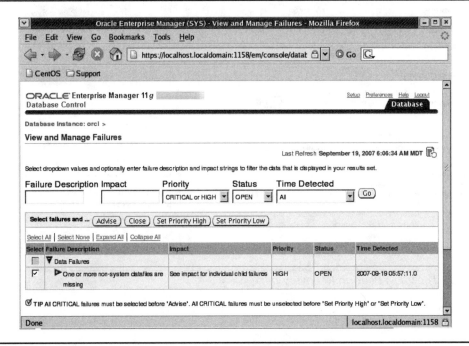

**Figure 4-2.** *The OEM View and Manage Failures page*

**NOTE**
*If you have any critical errors, they must be selected when you choose to click on Advise, or OEM will generate an error.*

From the OEM View and Manage Failures Page you select one or more failures that you want repair advice for. Having selected the failure, you click on Advise to start the appropriate advisor. In our case, this will take us to the next page, which provides suggestions on how you might manually correct the problem. Sometimes manual correction of the problem is the easiest thing to do. Figure 4-3 provides a look at the Manual Actions page that we received related to our missing datafile.

If the manual advice is insufficient to correct the problem, click on the Continue with Advise button. You will then find yourself on the Recovery Advice OEM page seen in Figure 4-4. Clicking on continue from this page takes you to a Review page where you can review the RMAN script that will be executed to perform your recovery. Click on the Submit Recovery Job button, and OEM will proceed to schedule the recovery.

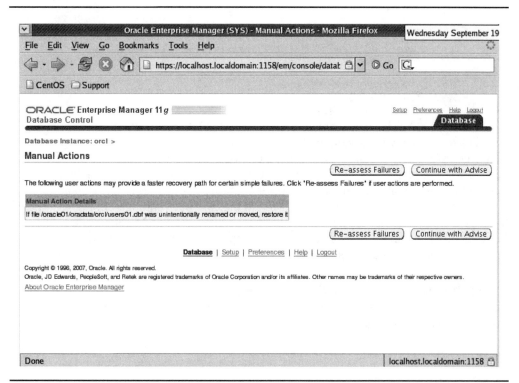

**Figure 4-3.**  *The OEM Manual Actions page*

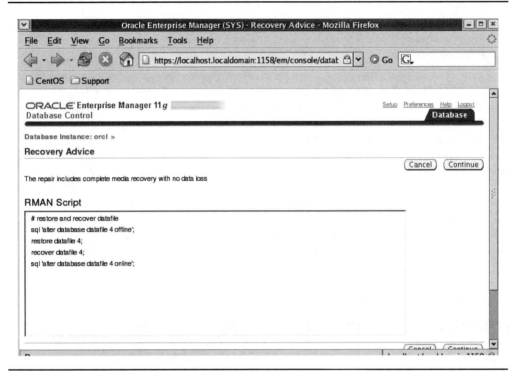

**Figure 4-4.** *The OEM Recovery Advice page*

Once the job has been scheduled, the Job Activity OEM page will appear. You can click on the View Results button to monitor the job while it is running. The Job Run page for a database restore is seen in Figure 4-5. Also note in Figure 4-6 that the page provides a breakdown of the work that the recovery operation will be doing. This includes information including the specific job steps, the status of that step and the time that the step either took, or has taken in the case of a running step. Refresh the page as required until the job status has changed from Running to Succeeded. Once the job is compete, you can click on the steps in the job breakdown to see the output from those steps and determine if the step was truly successful.

### Using the Data Recovery Advisor Through RMAN
Oracle has added new RMAN commands to allow you to execute the Data Recovery Advisor from the command line. These commands are

- List failure
- Advise failure

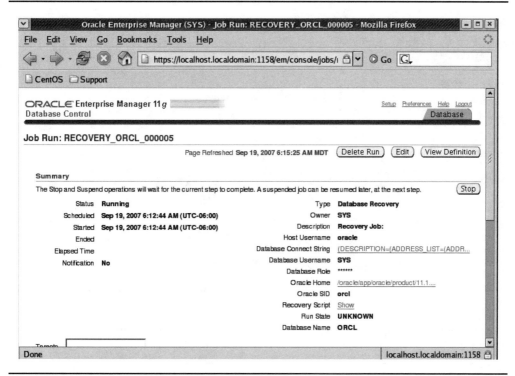

**FIGURE 4-5.** *The OEM Recovery Advice page*

- Repair failure

- Change failure

Typically, when dealing with a data corruption error, the workflow will be to use the **list failure** command, then the **advise failure** command and finally the **repair failure** command, in that order. Let's look at the use of these commands in a bit more detail.

**The List Failure Command**   The RMAN **list command** now has a new **failure** parameter that will list detected failures and their priorities (Critical, High, or Low), status (Open or Closed), the time when they occurred, and a summary of the failure. In this context, a failure is any persistent data corruption that currently exists on your system. Here is an example of the list failure command:

```
RMAN> list failure;
List of Database Failures
=========================
```

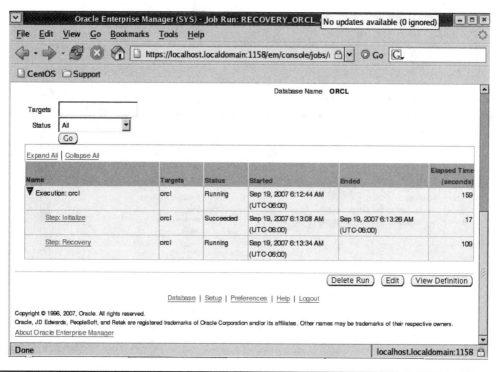

**Figure 4-6.** *The OEM Recovery Advice page (job breakdown)*

```
Failure ID Priority Status    Time Detected Summary
---------- -------- --------- ------------- -------
242        HIGH     OPEN      19-SEP-07     One or more non-system
                                            datafiles are missing
```

Note that in the preceding sample output, the data files that are missing are not listed. You can use the **list failure detail** command to generate additional details on the failure. Additionally the **list failure exclude failure *n*** command allows you to exclude specific failure numbers from the report output. Other options include listing only closed failures, only critical failures, only failures with high or low priorities, listing failures by failure ID, and excluding failures by failure ID. Here are some examples of the use of these options:

```
RMAN> list failure detail;
List of Database Failures
=========================
Failure ID Priority Status    Time Detected Summary
```

```
---------- -------- --------- ------------- -------
242        HIGH     OPEN      19-SEP-07     One or more non-system
                                            datafiles are missing
   Impact: See impact for individual child failures
   List of child failures for parent failure ID 242
   Failure ID Priority Status    Time Detected Summary
   ---------- -------- --------- ------------- -------
   470        HIGH     OPEN      19-SEP-07     Datafile 4:
'/oracle01/oradata/orcl/users01.dbf' is missing
      Impact: Some objects in tablespace USERS might be unavailable

-- Let's exclude failure_id 242… We should see no failures then.
RMAN> list failure exclude failure 242;
no failures found that match specification
```

**NOTE**
*The **list failure** command can only be run on a single-instance database (thus the RAC cluster must now be brought to single-instance mode). You also cannot use this command with a physical standby database.*

Note that the **list failure** command does not check for database errors in and of itself. The database is constantly checking for corruption issues, and those issues are recorded in the data dictionary on a regular basis (see more on the data dictionary and the recovery advisor later in this chapter). Therefore, it may be that some time will pass between when the corruption occurs (such as the loss of a data file) and the time it appears in the output of the **list failure** command. In our testing, this time lag has never been very long.

If an OPEN failure appears in the list, it will be linked to one or more repair actions that you can view via the new **advise failure** command. These options will help you to determine what repair options are available to correct the situation. Let's look at that command next.

**NOTE**
*If you just have a data file offline, then that data file will not be reported as a failure. If the offline data file is physically missing, then it will be reported as a failure.*

**The Advise Failure Command**   Once the **list failure** command displays an open failure, the **advise failure** command can be used to provide recommended actions that you can take to correct the failure. Here is an example of using the **advise failure** command:

```
RMAN> advise failure;
List of Database Failures
=========================
Failure ID Priority Status    Time Detected Summary
---------- -------- --------- ------------- -------
242        HIGH     OPEN      19-SEP-07     One or more non-system
                                            datafiles are missing
analyzing automatic repair options; this may take some time
allocated channel: ORA_DISK_1
channel ORA_DISK_1: SID=117 device type=DISK
analyzing automatic repair options complete

Mandatory Manual Actions
=========================
no manual actions available

Optional Manual Actions
=======================
1. If file /oracle01/oradata/orcl/users01.dbf was unintentionally renamed or
moved, restore it

Automated Repair Options
=========================
Option Repair Description
------ ------------------
1      Restore and recover datafile 4
  Strategy: The repair includes complete media recovery with no data loss
  Repair script: /oracle/app/oracle/diag/rdbms/orcl/orcl/hm/reco_2909488425.hm
```

You will notice from the output that RMAN provides both manual and automated repair options. The automated repair option contains RMAN commands (listed at the bottom of the report as the Repair Script) that can be used to correct the problem. Also note that repair options may involve data loss, and that the Data Recovery Advisor will indicate whether data loss will occur if a given recovery option is used. These commands are contained in a file within the ADR structure (discussed in Chapter 2). Here is an example of the recovery file:

```
# restore and recover datafile
sql 'alter database datafile 4 offline';
restore datafile 4;
recover datafile 4;
sql 'alter database datafile 4 online';
```

You can choose to run the recovery file manually or you can use the **repair failure** command, which is our next topic.

**The Repair Failure Command**   Now that we have detected a failure and determined the recovery actions recommended by Oracle, we can manually repair the failure, or allow Oracle to repair the failure automatically with the **repair failure** command.

To run the **repair failure** command the target database instance must at least be started. Some recovery operations (such as loss of an individual data file) will allow the database to be open. If multiple repairs are required, Oracle will try to consolidate them into one repair operation. Also, RMAN will double-check that the failures still exist, and will not perform a recovery operation if the failure has been corrected. Here is an example of using the **repair failure** command from RMAN (we have removed some RMAN output for brevity's sake):

```
RMAN> repair failure;
Strategy: The repair includes complete media recovery with no data loss
Repair script: /oracle/app/oracle/diag/rdbms/orcl/orcl/hm/reco_3113080068.hm
contents of repair script:
   # restore and recover datafile
   sql 'alter database datafile 4 offline';
   restore datafile 4;
   recover datafile 4;
   sql 'alter database datafile 4 online';
Do you really want to execute the above repair (enter YES or NO)? yes
executing repair script
Starting restore at 19-SEPT-07
using channel ORA_DISK_1
... Typical RMAN restore output is removed for brevity...
Starting recover at 19-SEPT-07
using channel ORA_DISK_1
... Typical RMAN recover output is removed for brevity...
media recovery complete, elapsed time: 00:00:03
Finished recover at 19-SEPT-07
sql statement: alter database datafile 4 online
repair failure complete
```

### NOTE
*Again, the **repair failure** command can only be run on a single-instance database (thus the RAC cluster must now be brought to single-instance mode). Note that this command will not repair failures such as data files that cannot be accessed by a specific node in an RAC cluster.*

If you wish to preview a failure action, you can use the **repair failure preview** command. This command will display the repair actions to be applied, but not execute the repair itself.

**The Change Failure Command**    The RMAN **change** command now has a new **failure** keyword that allows you to change the status of failures detected by the Oracle database. For example, you can change the priority of a specific failure, or all failures from high to low. You can also opt to close one or more failures. By default RMAN will prompt you to ensure that you wish to make the change. You can use the **noprompt** clause of the **change** command to force the change to occur without prompting. Here is an example where we changed the priority of failure 187 to LOW:

```
RMAN> Change failure 187 priority low;
List of Database Failures
=========================
Failure ID Priority Status    Time Detected Summary
---------- -------- --------- ------------- -------
187        HIGH     OPEN      09-JUN-07     One or more non-system
                                            datafiles are missing
Do you really want to change the above failures (enter YES or NO)? yes
changed 1 failures to LOW priority
```

**NOTE**
*You can not switch the status of a CLOSED failure to OPEN.*

### Arup Says...

How much value does the Data Recovery Advisor add in real-life situations?

Plenty. Imagine a sort of robotic DBA that analyzes and advises but never takes any action. Consider a scenario like this: It's New Year's Eve; everyone is incommunicado except the lowly, very green, junior DBA who is holding down the fort. And now he gets the alert—datablock corruption. Well, there is a time and place for everything, and hitting the manuals to understand the error is not the right thing to do at that time. The DBA needs advice: solid, practical, and actionable advice he can use at that moment, not hours spent in analysis. DRA comes in very handy here. Perhaps it does not help a seasoned DBA in understanding the issue any more than the DBA would have independently without help, but for a nonseasoned average DBA, that could translate to the difference between days and minutes to get back into operation.

The other advantage comes in the aid of RMAN commands. It's no secret that RMAN commands are cryptic and daunting even for the most seasoned DBAs. The DRA builds out the RMAN scripts to perform the necessary action, which is a great timesaver in my opinion.

### Data Recovery Advisor Data Dictionary Views

Several new views have been added to Oracle Database 11*g* to support the Data Recovery Advisor. These views start with V$IR as seen in the following table.

| View Name | Description |
| --- | --- |
| V$IR_FAILURE | Provides information on the failure. Note that records in this view can have parent records within this view. |
| V$IR_FAILURE_SET | This table provides a list of the various advice records associated with the failure. This allows you to join the view V$IR_FAILURE to the V$IR_MANUAL_ CHECKLIST view. |
| V$IR_ MANUAL_CHECKLIST | This view provides detailed informational messages related to the failure. These messages provide information on how to manually correct the problem. |
| V$IR_REPAIR | This view, when joined with V$IR_FAILURE and V$IR_FAILURE_SET, provides a pointer to the physical file created by Oracle that contains the repair steps required to correct a detected error. |

Here are some example queries:

```
-- Do we have an open error reported?
select failure_id, time_detected, description from v$ir_failure
Where status='OPEN';

FAILURE_ID TIME_DETE DESCRIPTION
---------- --------- ------------------------------------
       242 19-SEP-07 One or more non-system datafiles are mis
                     sing
       605 19-SEP-07 Datafile 4: '/oracle01/oradata/orcl/user
                     s01.dbf' is missing
```

# The SQL Repair Advisor

There is a Monty Python sketch called "The Office." In it, two office workers observe several persons jumping from higher levels of the building, apparently to their death. In the sketch, they make it appear that these are executives. After some investigation, we found out that in fact, they were SQL developers jumping to their death.

Why? Because SQL statements can be maddeningly frustrating to write. Often just getting the **where** clause just right can be a time-consuming process. Then comes, the inevitable ORA-0600 errors (or other ORA errors). In the end, it's clear that SQL was the inspiration of the "Office" sketch.

So, how do we make things better? ORA-0600s are going to happen. ORA-7445s are going to happen, Daleks are going to happen (oh, wait...wrong tool... just need a sonic screwdriver for them, sorry about that!). Enter the SQL Repair Advisor. When a SQL statement has failed, you can run the SQL Repair Advisor. The SQL Repair Advisor will analyze the statement and will provide a recommendation. This recommendation can sometimes be in the form of a patch, which you can implement. You should test the patch if you choose to implement it.

The SQL Repair Advisor is run from the Oracle Support Workbench (see Chapter 3 for more information on the Support Workbench). An instance of an ORA-0600 will create a problem within the Workbench. Select the ORA-0600 problem that is associated with your SQL statement. From the Problem Details page you can then choose to start the SQL Repair Advisor. After the SQL Repair Advisor has completed executing, it will provide you with an option to review the suggested recommendation and provide you with the ability to implement that feature. You can also view, disable, and remove patches from the SQL Workbench.

## The SQL Access Advisor

**NOTE**
*We have not covered manually running the SQL Access Advisor in this chapter rather on purpose. The process is largely unchanged. If you are manually running SQL Access Advisor tasks in 10g, you will still use the **dbms_advisor.execute_task** procedure to generate the SQL Access Advisor recommendations.*

The SQL Access Advisor (SAA) has been improved to provide advice on partitioning tables (including materialized views) and indexes to provide better performance of SQL statements. Also, the indexing and materialized view recommendations of the SQL Access Advisor may now include partitioning recommendations for those new objects. As in previous versions of the Oracle database you can access the SQL Access Advisor from OEM or from the use of the **dbms_advisor** PL/SQL Oracle-supplied package. Note that if you are using the SQL Access Advisor from OEM, by default the analysis that includes recommendations for the use of materialized views is not selected.

**NOTE**
*The advisors in Oracle Database 10g used SQL workloads, which contained the workload data that would be used for Oracle Advisor analysis. In Oracle Database 11g you should create SQL Tuning Sets, which replace the SQL workloads, instead. You can still use SQL workloads, but SQL Tuning Sets are the recommended means of defining workloads for the advisors.*

You should already be familiar with the SQL Access Advisor, it's not new to Oracle Database 11g. To start the SQL Access Advisor you will go to the Advisor Central page from the OEM home page. From there click on the SQL Advisors link. On the SQL Advisors OEM page you will see the SQL Access Advisor link. Click on that link and you will find yourself taken to the first page of the SQL Access Advisor. From this page you can instruct the SQL Access advisor to either verify the use of various access structures, or you can have it recommend new structures, which is what we are interested in. Simply click on the continue button to proceed.

The next page is the SQL Access Advisor Workload Source page. This page provides us with a number of different ways of executing the SQL Access Advisor. We can have it analyze existing workloads in the shared pool. We can have it analyze a given SQL Tuning Set, or we can have it generate a hypothetical workload from an existing schema and tables within that schema. This page has not really changed since Oracle Database 10g.

Having selected our workload, we click on next and find ourselves on the SQL Access Advisor: Recommendation Options page. While this page is not new, there is a new structure option that we can ask the SQL Access Advisor to recommend, partitioning. If we wish the SQL Access Advisor to make recommendations for partitioning existing objects, click on the partitioning box as seen in Figure 4-7.

Clicking on Next, the rest of the SQL Access Advisor workflow is pretty much unchanged since Oracle Database 10g. You will be taken to a page to schedule the execution of the advisor (use the blindfold option before scheduling the execution please), and following the scheduling page will be the SQL Access Advisor Review page.

From this later page, you click on the Submit button and the SQL Access Advisor will start doing it's job. OEM will take you to the Advisor Central page where you can monitor the execution of the SQL Access Advisor analysis, and wait for it to complete.

Once the analysis is complete, you can view the results of the SQL Access Advisor Task by clicking on the name of the task on the Advisor Central page. The resulting page that is presented in OEM is the summary result for the SQL Access Advisor which is somewhat large so it's presented in Figures 4-8 and 4-9. In Figure 4-8 we

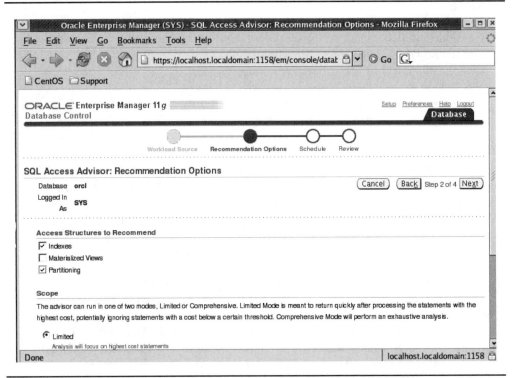

**FIGURE 4-7.** *OEM SQL Access Advisor Recommendation Options page*

have a summary of information about the completed SQL Access Advisor task. We also see four different tabs that we can select from (Summary, Recommendations, SQL Statements and Details). Each tab provides us with different information that has been gathered by the SQL Access Advisor task that was executed.

In Figure 4-9 we see a graphical representation of the positive effects that Oracle expects you will see when you implement it's recommendations. You can see the old workload I/O cost and estimated Workload I/O cost (in our case, it seems to be a pretty big I/O savings). Further we can see that there is an expected 8x query execution time improvement expected, a big plus in my books for sure! Finally on Figure 4-9 we can see the number of recommendations (1 in this case) that were made by the SQL Access advisor.

We can click on the Recommendations link of the Result page and see more specifics with regards to the recommendation. Of most interest here is the lower portion of the page as seen in Figure 4-10. Here we see each individual recommendation. These recommendations are color coded so you can easily see what they are. In our case, we have an index recommendation and a partitioning recommendation (ah, our

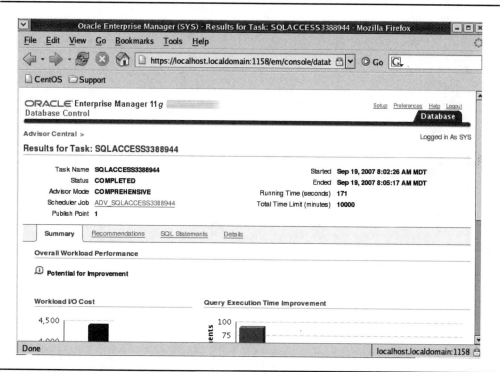

**FIGURE 4-8.** *OEM Summary Results page for SQL Access Advisor Task*

new feature there!). It is from this page that you can schedule the implementation of any recommendations. Simply check (or uncheck) any recommendations you wish to implement and then click on the schedule implementation button. Oracle will proceed to implement the recommendations for you,

If you want to check Oracle's work before you implement it's recommendations, or if you wish to implement them manually, you can click on the Show SQL button and see the detailed SQL statements that the advisor is recommending that you execute. In this example here are the recommendations that the Advisor made and would implement if we instructed it to do so (we have cut some of the SQL generated out for brevity):

```
Rem SQL Access Advisor: Version 11.1.0.6.0 - Production
Rem Repartitioning table "SCOTT"."MY_TAB"
SET SERVEROUTPUT ON
SET ECHO ON
Rem Creating new partitioned table
Rem
```

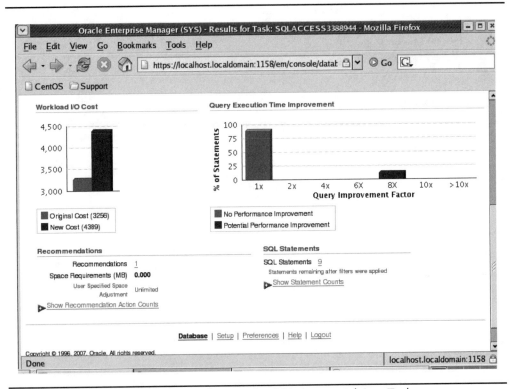

**FIGURE 4-9.** *OEM Summary Results page for SQL Access Advisor Task*

```
CREATE TABLE "SCOTT"."MY_TAB1"
(    "THE_DATE" DATE,
     "THE_COL" VARCHAR2(100),
     "SEQUENCE" NUMBER
) PCTFREE 10 PCTUSED 40 INITRANS 1 MAXTRANS 255 NOCOMPRESS LOGGING
TABLESPACE "USERS"
PARTITION BY RANGE ("THE_DATE") INTERVAL( NUMTOYMINTERVAL( 3, 'MONTH'))
(PARTITION VALUES LESS THAN
(TO_DATE(' 2007-12-01 00:00:00', 'SYYYY-MM-DD HH24:MI:SS'
, 'NLS_CALENDAR=GREGORIAN')) );


Rem Copying constraints to new partitioned table
Rem
ALTER TABLE "SCOTT"."MY_TAB1" ADD CONSTRAINT "PK_MY_TAB1"
PRIMARY KEY ("THE_DATE", "SEQUENCE")
USING INDEX PCTFREE 10 INITRANS 2 MAXTRANS 255 COMPUTE STATISTICS
```

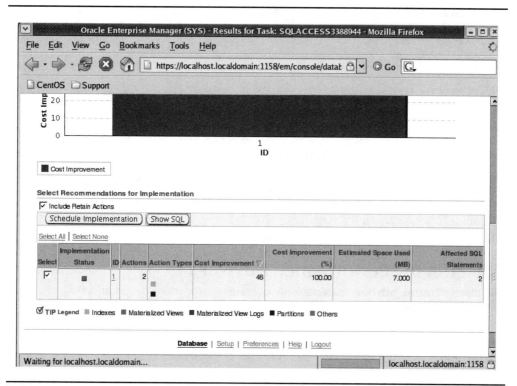

**FIGURE 4-10.** *OEM Recommendations page for SQL Access Advisor Task*

```
TABLESPACE "USERS" ENABLE;
Rem Copying indexes to new partitioned table
Rem
CREATE UNIQUE INDEX "SCOTT"."PK_MY_TAB1" ON "SCOTT"."MY_TAB1"
("THE_DATE", "SEQUENCE")
PCTFREE 10 INITRANS 2 MAXTRANS 255 COMPUTE STATISTICS
TABLESPACE "USERS" ;
Rem Populating new partitioned table with data from original table
Rem
INSERT /*+ APPEND */ INTO "SCOTT"."MY_TAB1"
SELECT * FROM "SCOTT"."MY_TAB";
COMMIT;
begin
dbms_stats.gather_table_stats('"SCOTT"', '"MY_TAB1"', NULL,
dbms_stats.auto_sample_size);
end;
/
```

```
Rem Renaming tables to give new partitioned table the original table name
Rem
ALTER TABLE "SCOTT"."MY_TAB" RENAME TO "MY_TAB11";
ALTER TABLE "SCOTT"."MY_TAB1" RENAME TO "MY_TAB";
/* RETAIN INDEX "SCOTT"."PK_MY_TAB" */
```

**NOTE**
*For the SQL Access Advisor to work properly, you need to ensure that the objects you wish it to make recommendations on are properly analyzed.*

The SQL Statements tab will provide you with details on the SQL statements that will be impacted by the recommended changes. The Details tab will provide you with specific details about the specific execution of the SQL access advisor, the options that were used and any filtering that was used.

## The Streams Performance Advisor

The **dbms_streams_advisor_adm** package contains a procedure called **analyze_current_performance**. This procedure will gather information about your Oracle streams components and analyze the performance of those components. To use this package you run the **analyze_current_performance** procedure from the streams administration account of a given system in your streams configuration.

**Arup Says...**

Partitioning has been one of the most valuable tools in the arsenal of the DBAs to manage objects—large and small alike—but more of the large types. It's effective in cases of canned software as well, where the code can't be changed. However, ask an average DBA about partitioning and you will draw a blank. Fear of the unknown combined with the general lack of understanding of where to start looking for partitioning strategies plays a big role in not taking advantage of this great tool.

SQL Access Advisor's Partition Advisor changes all that. It analyzes the real workload from your apps and makes partitioning recommendations. Granted, the recommendations pale compared to those coming from a seasoned DBA or architect, but it's a start and a step in the right direction. I suggest you run the SAA (with the partitioning option turned on) for the full workload and examine the reports coming out of it, especially the partitioning recommendations. You may be surprised to find one or two recommendations you can use, or at least they will boost your thought process.

Typically you will want to run this procedure two or three times before you review the results. After each run, determine the ADVISOR_RUN_ID from the DBA_STREAMS_TP_COMPONENT_STAT view. You can then use the ADVISOR_RUN_ID to query various views that contain the related advisor output including DBA_STREAMS_TP_PATH_BOTTLENECK, DBA_STREAMS_TP_COMPONENT_STAT, and others. Here is an example of using the Streams Performance Advisor:

```
-- First, run the advisor
SQL>exec DBMS_STREAMS_ADVISOR_ADM.ANALYZE_CURRENT_PERFORMANCE;
SQL>exec DBMS_STREAMS_ADVISOR_ADM.ANALYZE_CURRENT_PERFORMANCE;
SQL> SELECT DISTINCT ADVISOR_RUN_ID
  2  FROM DBA_STREAMS_TP_COMPONENT_STAT
  3  ORDER BY ADVISOR_RUN_ID;
ADVISOR_RUN_ID
--------------
            11
            12
-- Now query advisor views. We could lookup the components via the
-- DBA_STREAMS_TP_COMPONENT view… This view gives us a list of
-- bottlenecked components.
SELECT PATH_ID, COMPONENT_ID, COMPONENT_NAME, COMPONENT_TYPE,
       COMPONENT_DB
FROM DBA_STREAMS_TP_PATH_BOTTLENECK
   WHERE BOTTLENECK_IDENTIFIED='YES' AND ADVISOR_RUN_ID=12
   ORDER BY PATH_ID, COMPONENT_ID;
Path ID Component ID Name                 Type                 Database
------- ------------ -------------------- -------------------- -------
--------
      1            8 CAPTURE_MML          CAPTURE              DODO.NET
      2            8 CAPTURE_MML          CAPTURE              DODO.NET
      3            6 APPLY_PROC1          APPLY                DODO.NET
      5            7 APPLY_PROC2          APPLY                DODO.NET
```

# Oracle Database 10*g* Database Advisor Views

A number of new views are available in Oracle Database 11*g* to assist you with SQL tuning. These new views include the following:

■ DBA_ADVISOR_DIR_DEFINITIONS

■ DBA_ADVISOR_DIR_INSTANCES

■ [DBA|USER]_ADVISOR_DIR_TASK_INST

■ [DBA|USER]_ADVISOR_EXECUTIONS

■ DBA_ADVISOR_EXECUTION_TYPES

- [DBA|USER]_ADVISOR_EXEC_PARAMETERS

- [DBA|USER]_ADVISOR_FDG_BREAKDOWN

- DBA_ADVISOR_FINDING_NAMES

- DBA_ADVISOR_PARAMETERS_PROJ

- [DBA|USER]_ADVISOR_SQLA_COLVOL

- [DBA|USER]_ADVISOR_SQLA_TABLES

- [DBA|USER]_ADVISOR_SQLA_TABVOL

- [DBA|USER]_ADVISOR_SQLA_WK_SUM

- [DBA|USER]_ADVISOR_SQLPLANS

- [DBA|USER]_ADVISOR_SQLSTATS

# End of Line

The Oracle Advisors are there to help make our lives as DBA's better. New DBA's benefit immensely from the Advisors, as they reduce the impact of the DBA learning curve on the Enterprise. Even the old hand DBA's are finding the advisors to be a powerful ally, speeding up work and reducing the amount of typing of SQL commands that we have to do.

The data recovery advisor introduced in Oracle Database 11*g* has such potential to eliminate disaster. I don't know how many times I've seen junior DBA's attempt a recovery, only to get it wrong. Now, we simply let Oracle figure things out and viola, we are back in business.

The ability of the SQL Access Advisor to suggest partitioning is likewise a powerful new feature, and one that will be very helpful to the DBA. The SQL Advisors are designed to make administering the Oracle Database easier, so perhaps someday, Junior DBA's will not need to be hiding behind the sofa in fear of this powerful database called Oracle.

# CHAPTER
## 5

# Oracle Database Change
# Management

his chapter is about new features related to change management in Oracle Database 11*g*. With the new functionality that we introduce you to in this chapter, you will find that you can reliably determine the impact of a change to your systems. This allows you to be proactive about change-related problems, rather than reacting after the change has occurred. In this chapter we will discuss Database Replay and SQL Performance Analyzer.

# Database Replay

When you make changes that can impact your database, how do you gauge the impact of those changes on that database and the users of that database? For example, when you upgrade hardware or software, how do you quantify the impacts of those changes on your user community? I've been involved in many cases where what seemed like a simple patch set upgrade of the RDBMS software version wreaked havoc with system performance. Customers want to avoid this problem, of course, so they demand testing before you go live. The problem is that testing can take time and be very expensive, and therefore, upgrades and changes that can have a very positive impact on your system are delayed or not performed simply because of the time and costs involved. What we need is a way to quantify the impacts of these changes on the system.

Oracle Database 11*g* introduces Database Replay to address this very problem. Database Replay has the potential to be the one new feature in Oracle Database 11*g* that will change the way you as a DBA do things, and potentially will make your life easier. In the following sections we will look at Database Replay, how it works, and how to put it to work for you.

**NOTE**
*Database Replay will not solve all your testing problems. For example, it will not address network slowness issues that might occur between the client and the server as a result of a network router issue, but it's a major improvement over what was previously available and will help reduce database finger-pointing since you can quantitatively state that your database performance has not changed, or if it has, how much it has changed.*

## Using Oracle Database Replay

Oracle Database Replay addresses the issues associated with environmental changes by providing the ability to test the impact of those changes on a test system. Thus, you can gauge the impacts of these changes before you move them to production.

The testing takes a sample workload that you record during a given period of time and "replays" it on your test system. Important workload attributes such as concurrency and transactional dependencies are maintained to make the testing as real-world as possible. What kinds of changes might you test? Such changes include:

■   Database upgrades

■   Database patch installs

■   RAC-related changes (adding nodes, interconnect changes, and so on)

■   OS platform changes and upgrades

■   Hardware changes (CPU, memory, or storage)

Once the testing is complete, you can analyze the test results and determine whether there are any issues that need to be addressed. Issues that might come up in testing include errors that might appear (perhaps you will discover a bug in the new version of Oracle you intend to install); you might find that there is some form of data divergence due to a bug that was either in the old system or in the new system. You might also find some significant performance issues that need to be addressed before you go into production. The potential number of problems you might find is significant, and anyone would agree that finding them before you move into production is a worthwhile result. The end result, then, is that when you move these changes to production, you will be confident in the success of those changes.

Of course, this begs an important issue of the configuration of the test system to be used for Database Replay. If your test system diverges from your production system in any meaningful way, then the reliability of the resulting testing will be questionable. It is therefore important to ensure that the test environments mimic the production environments as closely as possible.

## Database Replay—Overview

Oracle has added a new shadow capture process that records the transactions occurring on the database into log files. All database-related requests are captured by this shadow processing in a way that has a minimal impact on the database (Oracle reports that the TCP overhead is ~4.5 percent). Each session requires 64k of additional overhead during flashback workload capture. Additional disk space is also required for the shadow files, and this should be located on a different set of physical disks than your database disks to ensure that the resulting disk IO does not impact the database disks.

If you are running on RAC, you will have a separate shadow recording process and shadow files on each node of the cluster. During replay these separate files will need to be relocated on shared drives so all nodes will have access to them.

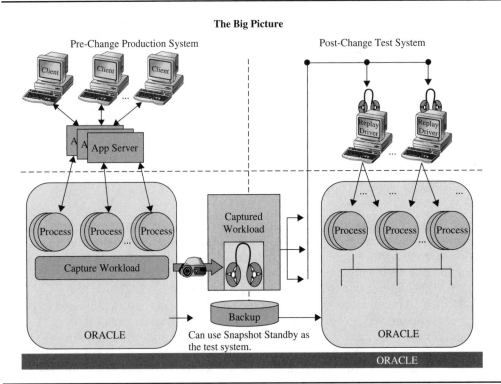

**FIGURE 5-1.** *Graphic of Database Replay*

After the workload is captured, it will need to be preprocessed before it can be used for replay. This preprocessing is a one-time action. It must occur on a database that is the same version as the database that captured the workload, but it can be performed on any Oracle database of the same version.

During replay, replay clients are used to consume the workload recording from the shadow files and replay the workload on the database. To the database, the replay clients look like normal external clients making requests to the database. The overall architecture of Database Replay can be seen in Figure 5-1.

## Database Replay Workload Support and Limitations

Database Replay supports most common workloads. This includes:

■ All SQL operations including most with binds

■ All long object (LOB) operations

- Local transactions

- Login and logoff

- Session switching

- Some PL/SQL remote procedure calls

The following operations are not supported:

- Direct path load operations

- Oracle call-level interface (OCI)-based object navigation and REF binds

- Streams and non-PL/SQL-based Advanced Querying (AQ)

- Distributed transactions

- Flashback operations

- Shared server operations

# Database Replay—Capture Workload

The first step in replaying a workload is to actually capture the workload you want to replay. Kind of makes sense, doesn't it? In this section we will discuss preparing to capture the workload and then actually capturing the workload. You can use OEM or manual means to start workload capture. We will finish off this section with additional information on workload capture, such as how to remove captures from the system, and we will discuss data dictionary views that you can use to manage workload capture.

## Database Replay—Capture Workload Setup

When planning for the workload capture, ensure that you have sufficient disk space for the captured workload. You will need to make sure that the directories that will be used are accessible by the Oracle owning account. The account that is used to manage the workload capture is known as the *recording user*. The account used to manage the replay of the captured workload is called the *replay user*. Each of these user accounts should have SYSDBA privileges. This is because these accounts may need to shut down the database as a part of the capture or replay processes.

You will want to back up your database (or set a restore point if you want to use Flashback Database) before the capture process begins so that you can restore this backup to the test system. During the database replay, you will need to be able to restore the test system to the SCN where the workload capture started. I recommend that you use RMAN for your backup and recovery operations.

Another thing to consider is whether you will want to recycle your database before starting the capture process. Why would you want to recycle the database, you ask? Problems with Database Replay can occur if you start workload capture in the middle of an in-flight transaction that has certain dependencies. For example, if the in-flight transaction has added a parent record, after which you start workload capture, and then the transaction attempts to add a child record, guess what happens during replay? The replay process will try to add the child record and an error will be recorded. Since this is an in-flight (incomplete) transaction, the backup will not restore the parent record. This ultimately will lead to data divergence, which is not what you want to see happen in your testing.

If you know your workload and you know that in-flight transactions will not be a problem, then you will not need to shut down your database. If you can't control your transactions and in-flight transactions are a possibility, then you will need to shut down your database. Of course, this may not be possible in a 24/7/365 production environment. In such cases, you will just need to be aware of the possibility and impact of in-flight transactions and be prepared to deal with them when analyzing the replay results.

One other setup note is that you will want to create a directory within Oracle to assign to the capture processes. This is done with the **create directory** command from the SQL prompt. The capture process will put all capture-related files in this directory.

To summarize the steps to preparing for workload setup:

1. Make sure the database is in ARCHIVELOG mode and back it up.

2. Ensure there is enough disk space for the shadow logs to hold the captured workload.

3. Determine whether you need to recycle the database.

**NOTE**
*Depending on how much you use the capture process, you will probably want to create a new directory for each use. I recommend that you use a smart naming convention on your directories that includes the date of the capture. This will help you manage these directories over time.*

## Database Replay—Capture the Workload

Workload capture can be accomplished through OEM or manually. In the following sections we will look at managing workload capture via OEM and then we will address management of workload capture via manual means.

**The Workload Capture Shadow Files**  The workload capture process creates files as it captures the workload. These files are stored in an Oracle directory that you first create with the **create directory** SQL command. On the OSes on which I tested, various files were created including:

- A wcr_rec* file with a .start extension.

- A wcr_capture.wmd file.

- Various wcr_(transaction_id}.rec files. It appears that there is one file each per transaction.

During my testing I did a **create table as select** (CTAS) operation on a table that had 800k rows and an average row length of 23, and the resulting shadow file for that transaction was a bit over 3k. I also did some timing tests. During workload capture the CTAS operation took 10 seconds; with workload capture turned off, the CTAS operation took 7 seconds, so there was about a 30 percent impact on that test. Of course, your results might be different (and probably will be, since my test system was not all that fast, nor did it have lots of memory allocated to it).

**Workload Capture with OEM**  Oracle Database 11*g* OEM has support for workload capture and replay. To navigate to the proper page from the OEM home page, click on the Software and Support tab. From there you will find a link to Database Replay under the Software Assurance section of the page. On this page, seen in Figure 5-2, you will find the Database Replay workflow listed (Capture, Preprocess, and Reply) and an option to execute each of these tasks. In our case, we will click on the Capture Workload link. This takes us to the first page with the workflow to implement workload capture, as seen in Figure 5-3.

You will need to complete each step and acknowledge its completion before you can proceed to the next step. We have listed these steps in the previous section, "Database Replay—Capture Workload Setup".

After clicking on Next, we find ourselves on the OEM Capture Workload Options page. The following step allows you to configure options for the workload capture process. First, you can define whether you do or do not want to restart the database prior to the start of the capture process. Second, you can apply workload filters to the capture process. With filters you can choose to exclude a workload based on session attributes such as a given user. This is very handy if you have a utility database with many schemas in it, and only one schema is undergoing changes that might impact the database. You can then exclude the other schemas to reduce the size of the shadow capture files. Figure 5-4 provides an example of the OEM Capture Workload Options page on OEM.

**NOTE**
*Oracle's recommendation is to restart the database to minimize data divergence during replay.*

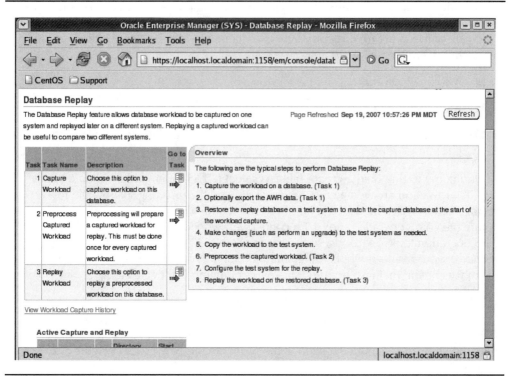

**FIGURE 5-2.** *OEM Database Replay page*

The next page is the Capture Workload: Parameters page. It is here that we can set various parameters for workload capture including the name of the capture process. We can also select the Oracle directory from a drop-down list; this is a directory (defined in Oracle via the **create directory** command and visible in the DBA_DIRECTORIES view) in which the shadow capture files will be created. If we opted to shut down the database, then we are given various shutdown options (abort, immediate, or transactional). You can also choose to restart the database with the **default initialization** parameter file, or you can use a different parameter file if you wish. Figure 5-5 provides an example of the Capture Workload Parameters page.

Clicking Next takes us to the Capture Workload: Schedule page. This simply allows us to schedule when we want to start the workload capture process. Typically this will be immediately, but you can do it on a scheduled basis. Note that this page requires that you enter both the host credentials (the Oracle account user ID on the OS) and the database account credentials (with SYSDBA privileges) in order to schedule the job. Figure 5-6 provides an example of the Capture Workload Schedule page.

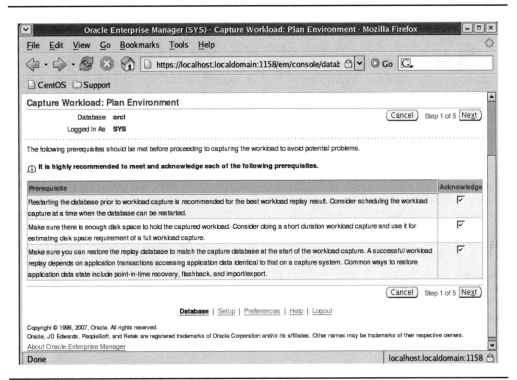

**FIGURE 5-3.** *Capture Workload main page*

Now it's time to run this baby! We click on Next and we find the Capture Workload: Review page. This page provides a summary of the actions to be taken and allows you to begin the workload capture process by selecting the Next button. Simply click on Next and the workload capture process should fire right off! If you opted to restart the database, OEM will ask you if you are sure you want to restart the database and it will proceed to do so. Figure 5-7 provides an example of the Capture Workload Review page.

After the database capture process has started (or if you decided to restart the database, after the shutdown process begins), you will be presented with an informational page on OEM that instructs you on the next steps to complete.

If you rebooted the system the Oracle will log you back into OEM once the restart has completed. Having started the workload (and optionally rebooting) you will find yourself at the View Workload Capture page ready to monitor workload capture. From this page you can view a number of attributes associated with the workload capture process that is running, including how long it has been running, the average number of active sessions, and the number of errors that have occurred. Figure 5-8 provides a screenshot of the View Workload Capture page.

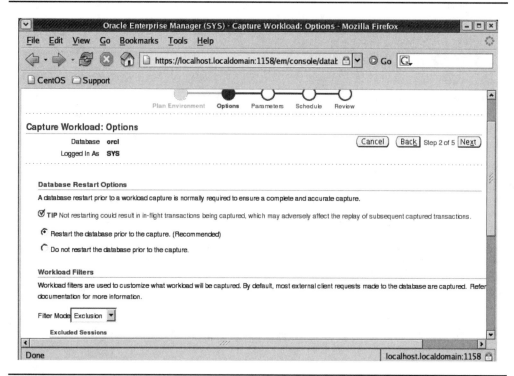

**FIGURE 5-4.** *Capture Workload Options page*

Clicking on the OK button on this page will return you to the Database Replay workflow page. From this page you can view the active capture process from the Active Capture and Replay screen seen in Figure 5-9.

You have now successfully started workload capture. We will discuss the next steps shortly, but first we need to first discuss how to manually enable workload capture. We will also talk about the various views that you can use to monitor your workload and discuss some of the underlying things that occur during the capture process.

**Manual Workload Capture**   To configure and start workload capture, Oracle Database 11*g* provides a new PL/SQL supplied procedure, **dbms_workload_capture**. To manually start the capture process you will need to

1.   Define and configure any filters you wish to reply.

2.   Start the workload capture.

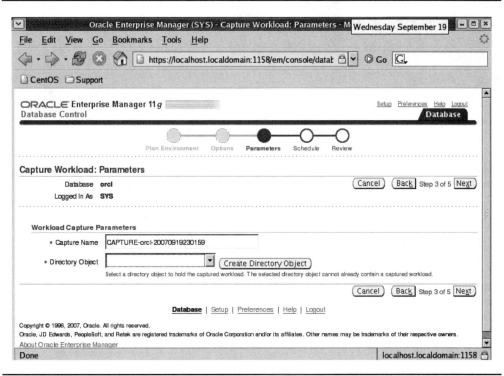

**FIGURE 5-5.**   *Capture Workload Parameters page*

Filters allow you to control what the workload capture process captures. The **dbms_workload_capture.add_filter** procedure is used to add various filters to the capture process. In our example, we are going to create a filter called CAPTURE_FILTER. We will define in this filter in such a way as to capture only the user called SCOTT:

```
BEGIN
   DBMS_WORKLOAD_CAPTURE.ADD_FILTER (fname => 'capture_filter',
                                     fattribute => 'USER',
                                     fvalue => 'SCOTT');
END;
/
```

Valid filter attributes (**fattribute**) include **program**, **module**, **action**, **service**, **instance_number**, **and user**. Note that the attribute needs to be in single quotes.

If you need to remove a filter, simply use the **dbms_workload_capture.delete_filter** supplied PL/SQL procedure as shown here:

```
EXEC DBMS_WORKLOAD_CAPTURE.DELETE_FILTER (fname => 'capture_filter');
```

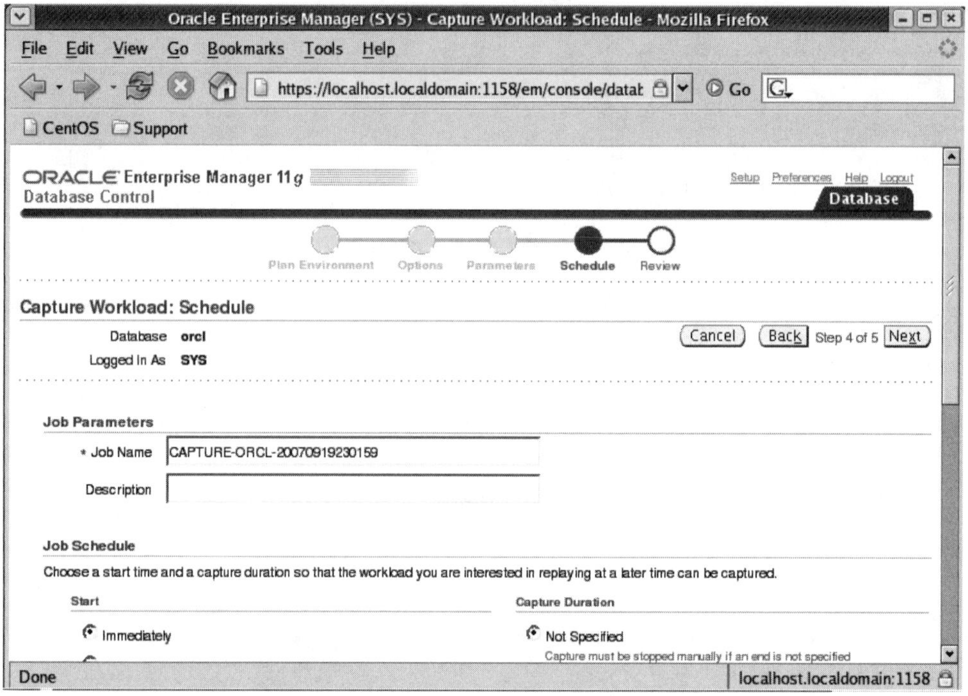

**FIGURE 5-6.** *Capture Workload Schedule page*

Now that you have created (or deleted) your filters, you are ready to start your workload capture. To start the workload capture, use the **dbms_workload_capture.start_capture** supplied PL/SQL procedure. When calling this procedure, you will give the capture process a name, and you will define the directory to be used (again, this directory is created with the SQL **create directory** command) and the duration of the capture. Here is an example of a call to start our capture process, which we will call Pre_Upgrade_capture_070107_01. We use the MY_CAPTURE directory, which we will have already created, and the duration of this capture will be 1200 seconds. If we did not define the **duration** parameter, then capture would continue until we stopped it manually. Here is our **start_capture** command:

```
BEGIN
    DBMS_WORKLOAD_CAPTURE.START_CAPTURE (name => 'Pre_Upgrade_Capture_092507_01',
                        dir => 'Workload_Capture', duration => 1200);
END;
/
```

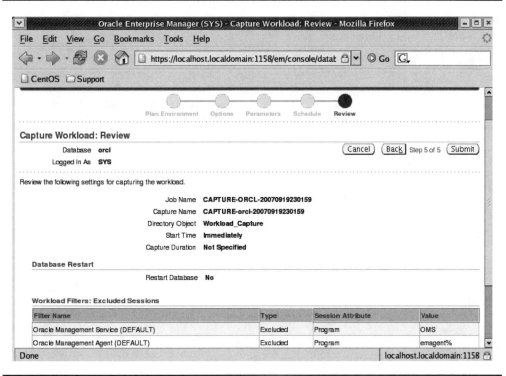

FIGURE 5-7.    *Capture Workload Review page*

 **NOTE**
*Naming conventions including the date and even the time (or a sequence number) are always a good idea when using Database Capture.*

Once the **start_capture** procedure is successful, Oracle will return you to the SQL prompt. Other parameters available for use with the **start_capture** procedure are the **default_action** and **auto_unrestrict** parameters. The **default_action** parameter allows you to define whether filters defined earlier are considered INCLUDE (the default) or EXCLUDE filters. Note that all filters that you define will be applied to any capture process. The **auto_unrestrict** parameter will cause the capture process to take the database out of restricted mode if set to TRUE. Often during capture you will want to shut down and start up the database in restricted mode to ensure that the capture process is not capturing any in-flight transactions. Restarting the database in restricted session and setting the **auto_unrestrict** parameter to TRUE allows the capture process to start at a known state. The default for this parameter is TRUE.

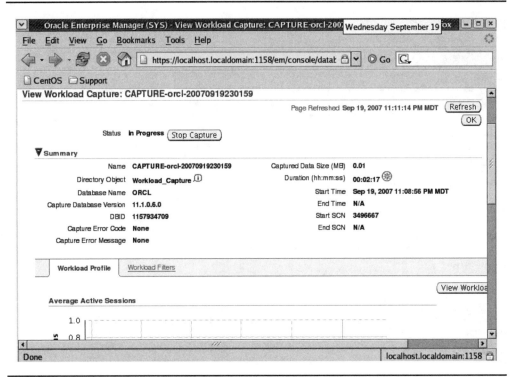

**FIGURE 5-8.** *View Workload Capture page*

You can monitor the capture process by querying the DBA_WORKLOAD_ CAPTURES view, as seen in this example:

```
select id, name, status from dba_workload_captures;
        ID NAME                            STATUS
---------- ------------------------------- ------------------------
        12 Pre_Upgrade_Capture_092507_01   IN PROGRESS
```

## Database Replay—Stop Workload Capture

When you are done capturing the workload, you will want to stop the capture process. In this section we will discuss how you stop the capture process. First we will look at stopping the capture process using OEM. We will then look at how to stop the capture process if you are doing a manual database capture.

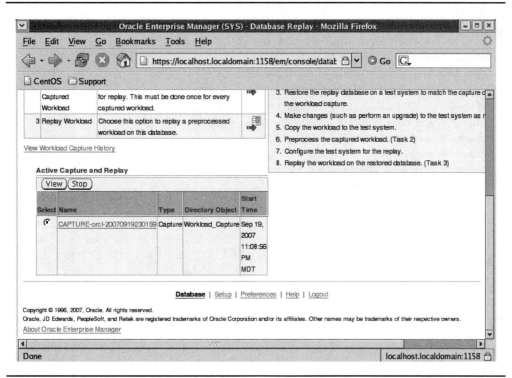

**FIGURE 5-9.**   *OEM Database Replay Workflow – Active Capture and Replay page*

**The OEM Method to Stop Workload Capture**   You can stop the workload capture by clicking on the Stop button on the OEM Database Replay page; or, from the detail page associated with the workload capture, click the Stop Capture button. Shutting down the database will also serve to stop workload capture.

**The Manual Method to Stop Workload Capture**   You can use the **dbms_workload_capture.finish_capture** procedure to stop workload capture. Here is an example of stopping the workload capture process:

```
Exec dbms_workload_capture.finish_capture;
```

By default, the **finish_capture** procedure will wait 30 seconds and then shut down the capture process. An optional **timeout** parameter allows you to define a shorter or longer timeout. You could use this if you need to shut down some processes before the capture process terminates. Another parameter called **reason** lets you define the reason you are stopping the capture process.

**NOTE**
*In some cases I would terminate the capture process (or if an error occurred and it self-terminated). In some of these cases, I tried to restart the capture job only to find that there was a job in the scheduler called WRR$_AUTO_STOP_CAPTURE_nn. This job is used to automatically stop the capture process once it is started. I found that you have to wait until this job is executed from the scheduler, or remove it manually, before you can restart the capture process. You will also need to clear the directory of any files before you can restart the capture process.*

## Database Replay—Delete a Capture

Of course you will want to remove captures from time to time. This section discusses how to remove metadata related to workload capture from the Oracle Database. First we will talk about removing capture workload information using OEM, and then we will discuss manually removing workload capture metadata.

**The OEM Method to Delete a Workload Capture**   You can delete a workload capture by clicking on the View Workload Capture History link in OEM from the main Database Replay home page. From here you can view existing workload captures and choose to delete them.

**The Manual Method to Delete a Workload Capture**   To delete a workload capture completely from the capture site, use the PL/SQL supplied procedure **dbms_workload_capture.delete_capture_info**. This will remove all capture-related information from the database. This will not remove physical files created during the capture process; you will need to perform this action.

To delete the workload, you will need to get the CAPTURE_ID of the capture process from the DBA_WORKLOAD_CAPTURES table. Once you have gotten the CAPTURE_ID, you call the procedure as seen here:

```
-- Get the ID and name of the captures
select id, name from dba_workload_captures;
        ID NAME
---------- ----------------------------------------
         1 CAPTURE-orcl-20070919230159
-- Remove capture ID 1
exec dbms_workload_capture.delete_capture_info(1);
PL/SQL procedure successfully completed.
```

### Database Replay—Workload Capture Data Dictionary Views

New data dictionary views are available for use with workload capture. They include:

- **DBA_WORKLOAD_CAPTURES**  Provides information on workload capture operations, both ongoing and historical. Important information in this view is the name of the capture process (**name**) and the starting SCN (START_SCN).

- **DBA_WORKLOAD_FILTERS**  This view provides information on the filters that will be applied to any workload capture process.

## Database Replay—PreProcess the Captured Workload

After you have stopped collection, you will need to preprocess the shadow collection files. To do so, we start at the Database Replay OEM home page, which we introduced you to earlier in this section (we will cover the manual steps of this process later in this section). From the workflow we will select Step 2, with a task name labeled as preprocess captured workload.

### Preprocessing the Workload from OEM

To start the preprocess of our workload shadow files from OEM, we start with the Database Replay home page. You then select the Preprocess Captured Workload option from the task list. This will bring up the Preprocess Captured Workload page. From here, you select the directory object that we chose earlier to store the workload capture shadow files. Once you select the directory, information about the capture files contained in that directory is listed. Click on the Preprocess Workload button to preprocess the capture workload. OEM will confirm that you intend to preprocess the workload that has been captured. Confirm by following the wizard as it moves you through scheduling the preprocessing by selecting Next. Figure 5-10 provides an example of the Preprocess Captured Workload page. Once the job is scheduled, OEM will return you to the Database Reply OEM page.

**NOTE**
*To check on the overall success of the pre-processing of the captured workload you will need to go to the job scheduler page in OEM and click on the pre-process job to see the details of that job execution. The Preprocess job may fail, but you will receive no notification of that failure unless you check the status of that job.*

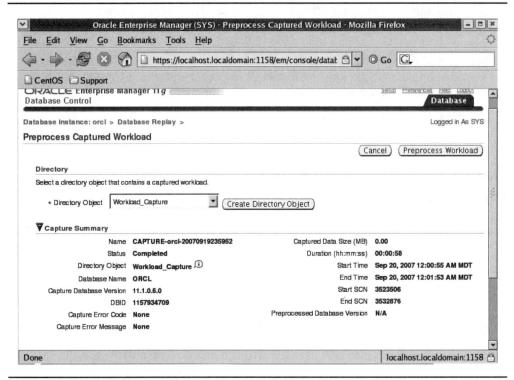

**FIGURE 5-10.** *OEM Preprocess Captured Workload*

## Manual Workload Preprocessing

To preprocess the workload manually you use the PL/SQL procedure **dbms_workload_replay.process_capture**. Use the **capture_dir** parameter to indicate the directory that your workload capture shadow files were created in, as seen in this example:

```
BEGIN
    DBMS_WORKLOAD_REPLAY.PROCESS_CAPTURE (capture_dir => 'MY_CAPTURE');
END;
/
```

The result of the **process_capture** procedure will be additional files in the MY_CAPTURE directory. These include:

- A WCR_CONN_DATA.EXTB file

- A wcr_login.pp file

- A wcr_process.wmd file

- A WCR_SCN_ORDER.EXTB file

- A WCR_SEQ_DATA.EXTB file

## Database Replay—Workload Capture History

You can report on existing captures and their status from OEM and by producing a manual report. In this section we will first look at how to generate the report from OEM and then we will look at how to manually generate a report on a workload capture from the SQL*Plus command line.

**Generate a Workload Capture History Report via OEM**   You can view the history of workload captures from OEM. From the Database Replay home page on OEM, click on the View Workload Capture History link. This will take you to the the OEM View Workload Capture History page seen in Figure 5-11.

From this page, you will find links to the various captures stored in the Oracle Database. You can click on an individual capture for more detailed information on that capture. Additionally, when you click on the individual capture, you can produce a Workload Capture report that will provide statistical information captured during the workload capture.

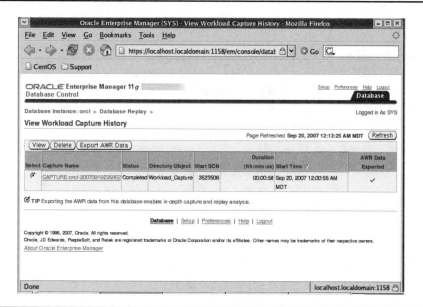

**FIGURE 5-11.**   *OEM View Workload Capture History page*

**Generate a Workload Capture Report Manually**   The Workload Capture Report
produced by OEM can also be replicated manually. To generate the report you use
the **get_capture_info** and **report** functions in the **dbms_workload_capture** PL/SQL
package, and then display the output, as seen in this example:

```
DECLARE
   cap_id        NUMBER;
   cap_rpt       CLOB;
BEGIN
   cap_id  := DBMS_WORKLOAD_CAPTURE.GET_CAPTURE_INFO(dir => 'Workload_Capture');
   cap_rpt := DBMS_WORKLOAD_CAPTURE.REPORT(capture_id => cap_id,
                          format => 'TEXT');
   dbms_output.put_line(cap_rpt);
END;
/
```

The output of the Workload Capture Report can give you an idea if the workload
you have captured represents the workload you want to use in your replay testing.

# Database Replay—Replay Workload

Ok, time to make the doughnuts. It's time to actually replay our workload,
simulating what happened on our database at some time in the past. In this section
we will discuss setting up for database replay, the different options available during
replay, and then we will hold our breath as we fire up this monster and watch it
actually replay our database transactions!

### Database Replay—Set Up the Replay Database

Once the workload has been captured and preprocessed, we can prepare the test
database to replay it. First we need to re-create the test database, restoring it to
the SCN where the capture process was started. This SCN is listed in the
DBA_WORKLOAD_CAPTURES view, as seen in this example:

```
select name, start_scn from dba_workload_captures;

NAME                               START_SCN
-------------------------------- ----------
Pre_Upgrade_Capture_070107_01      7445674
```

**NOTE**
*Restoring the database to the SCN listed in
DBA_WORKLOAD_CAPTURES is not technically
required, but it makes sense so you can mimic the
production database as closely as possible.*

You can use any accepted database restore method to create the replay database. RMAN, Data Pump, or manual backup and recovery methods are all acceptable. In our case, we would probably use Active Database Duplication, which is RMAN's new ability to duplicate databases live, over the network, without a backup. See Chapter 3 for more on this exciting new RMAN feature. Here is an example of the command we used to create our replay database:

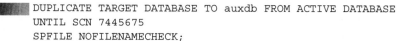

```
DUPLICATE TARGET DATABASE TO auxdb FROM ACTIVE DATABASE
UNTIL SCN 7445675
SPFILE NOFILENAMECHECK;
```

**NOTE**
*You may need to do a log switch and wait for the redo log to be archived before your point-in-time duplication will be successful.*

Once you have restored the test database, you will want to protect it from any inadvertent changes. You may want to leave the database in restricted mode until you are ready to start the replay operations, and you might want to disable any automated jobs that might make changes within the database. Also, to reduce data divergence, Oracle recommends (but does not require) that you reset the system clock just before you start Database Replay to the time/date where the workload capture was started.

## Database Replay—Consider Replay Options

There are three different options to consider when performing Database Replay:

- Synchronization mode
- Connection time scale
- Think time scale

You will set these options before you begin the Database Replay. They are set via OEM or via a call to the **dbms_workload_replay.prepare_replay** PL/SQL supplied procedure. Together these options control the overall time it will take to complete a database replay. If the defaults are left as is, on two systems that are completely identical, the run times of the Replay should equate to the run time of the capture process. Let's look at each of these options in a bit more detail.

**Synchronization Mode**   You can use this option to disable SCN-based synchronization of the replay. When SCN-based synchronization is enabled (**true**), then the commit order of the transactions within the workload being replayed will be preserved.

When you disable synchronization, then transactions will be replayed without synchronization, and data divergence may occur. This attribute is supported by the **synchronization** parameter and can be **true** or **false**. **true** is the default value.

**Connection Time Scale**   You can use the connection time scale to manage the timeframe between the start of the replay and when each session connection is made, contrasted to the timeframe of the start of the workload capture and the connection. Thus, you can scale up the work volume slower or faster as your testing dictates. This attribute is supported by the **connect_time_scale** parameter, which defaults to a value of 100. This number is represented as a percentage of the time between each connection experienced by the capture process. Thus, if this number is set to 50, the time between the start of the replay and the first user connection would be slowed by 50 percent.

**Think Time Scale**   The think time scale attribute represents the adjustment of user think time during Database Replay. Adjust the think time as required to manage the correct think time between database calls during Database Replay. This attribute is supported by the **think_time_scale** parameter, which defaults to 100 percent. This number is represented as a percentage of the think time experienced by the capture process. Thus, if this number is set to 50, the time between the start of the replay and the first user connection would be slowed by 50 percent.

An optional related parameter, **think_time_auto_correct**, will adjust the think time between transactions, should a transaction run longer during replay. For example, assume that a transaction takes 30 seconds on the capture system with a think time between that and the next transaction of 10 seconds (so 40 seconds total elapsed). If the same transaction on the replay system takes 33 seconds on the capture system, the adjusted think time would be 7 seconds so as to maintain the integrity of the overall think time of the replay process.

## Database Replay—Stage for Database Replay

In this section we will discuss preparing for Database Replay. In this section we will discuss:

- Moving the capture files to the replay system
- Using flashback database/standby database

**Move the Capture Files to the Replay System**   Prior to being able to run Database Replay you will first need to configure the directory for the database replay files created when you performed your database capture. You will then need to move the preprocessed files (we discussed preprocessing earlier in this chapter) in the capture directory on the host system to the replay directory on the test system.

Just as with the capture system, you will need to create a directory in the replay system with the **create directory** command.

**Consider Using Flashback Database/Standby Database**  Another recommendation that I have for you relates to the use of Oracle Database's flashback technologies. I would recommend that you configure flashback database on the replay system and then set a guaranteed restore point immediately before you start your database replay. This will allow you to flashback the database after you execute a replay operation, allowing you to execute the replay many times. You can also use a snapshot standby database (see Chapter 3 for more on snapshot databases) for this kind of operation if you like. This allows you to use the database as a standby database once your testing is complete. When using a snapshot standby database, you don't need to worry about setting the restore point, because you simply revert the database to the original standby configuration.

**Deal with External References**  External references such as database links, external tables, and the like need to be addressed on the test system. Of course, many sites have rules that disallow production database links on test systems. For example, if you have a database link on your production system, that same database link name needs to be present on the test system. For security purposes, though, that link might point to a completely different distributed system. If the links do point to different systems, you need to make sure the data on those systems properly represents the data form and structure on the source system that the original database link pointed to. Any data divergence on remote systems can result in errors during replay operations.

You can use the **dbms_workload_replay.remap_connection** PL/SQL supplied procedure to remap any external databases that might be required during workload replay. The DBA_WORKLOAD_CONNECTION_MAP view on the capture system will be helpful in providing a list of external connections that were used during the workload capture.

## Execute Database Replay—OEM

At this point, the OEM and manual database replay processes diverge. First we will address replaying the workload from OEM, and then we will look at manual database replay. We start the OEM replay from the Database Replay Home Page that we have already introduced you to. Here you will find that Step 3 on the database replay workflow is titled Replay Workload. Click on the Go to Task button to proceed with replaying the workload.

Next we see the OEM ReplayWorkload page. This page prompts you for the directory object that contains the workload you wish to process. Select the directory that the workload is contained in, and the page will update with a summary of the capture that is contained in that directory as seen in Figure 5-12. You can review

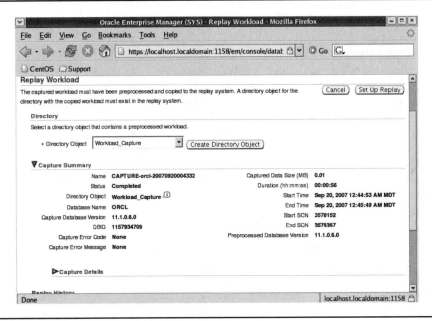

**FIGURE 5-12.** *OEM View Workload Capture History page*

the capture summary and details to ensure that this is the capture you wish to replay. If so, click on the Set Up Replay button to continue.

The next page contains a list of actions that you will need to take before you can execute the replay. With the exception of the setup of the database clients, we have covered these items earlier, but to summarize they are

1. Restore the database for replay.

2. Perform any system changes that you wish to test (parameter changes, software changes, and so on).

3. Resolve any references to external systems (for example, database links).

4. Set up the replay clients; these should already be installed when you install the database software. So there should be no initial setup required.

Once all these steps are completed, then you may click on Continue to proceed to the next page.

The next page provides the opportunity for you to review any external system references such as database links and directory objects. You should have already dealt with these issues, and therefore you should be able to click on Continue to move past this page.

Next we have the Replay Workload Choose Initial Options page. This page allows you to choose the initial options with regards to replay. Truthfully, there are not many options to pick from on this page, and typically you will just click on Next to proceed to the next page.

You will now find yourself on the Replay Workload Customize Options page. Here you review the connection strings found in the workload. You should review these and make sure you have mapped them correctly. You can also review the different replay parameters (discussed earlier in this chapter) such as **synchronization**, **connect_time_scale**, and **think_time_scale**. Click on Next to continue to the next page.

The Prepare Replay Clients page is the next page and it indicates that we are ready to start the replay process. This is the last stop, your last opportunity to make sure everything is setup correctly. Verify everything is ready, and click on Next and hold your breath.

As the reply is scheduled, we are taken to the Wait for Client Connections page. It is now time to start the workload clients. See the next section, titled "The Replay Clients," for details on this operation. OEM will detect that the replay clients have been started. It will list each of the clients that it detects has been started, and the page refreshes quite frequently. Once all the clients have been started, click on Next. Note that even after replay has started, you can start additional replay clients if you choose. Figure 5-13 shows an example of the Replay Workload: Wait for Client Connections Page indicating that a replay client has started.

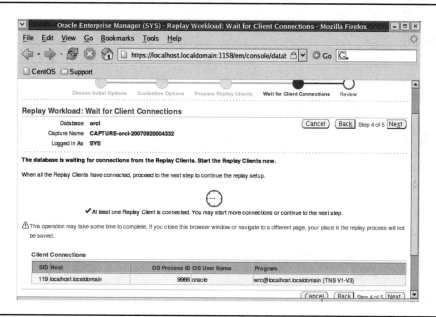

**FIGURE 5-13.**   *OEM View Workload Capture History page*

**NOTE**
*Replay will not start just because you have started the replay clients.*

The next page is the replay workload review, which really is your last gasp, make-sure-I'm-doing-the-right-thing page. This page reviews the capture information that you are about to replay one more time. An example is seen in Figure 5-14.

Click on Submit to execute the capture process and be prepared to be amazed! Figure 5-15 provides an example of the View Workload Replay page.

This page provides information on the progress of the workload replay, such as the total duration of the replay and how far into the replay you are. You can stop the replay if you choose, monitor its progress, get information on errors, and so on. The page refreshes every 60 seconds during the replay process or you can refresh it more frequently.

Once the workload has completed, the workload clients will automatically stop and the status line on the page will indicate that the workload replay has completed. You can then review the replay report (we discuss this report later in this section) for errors and other information.

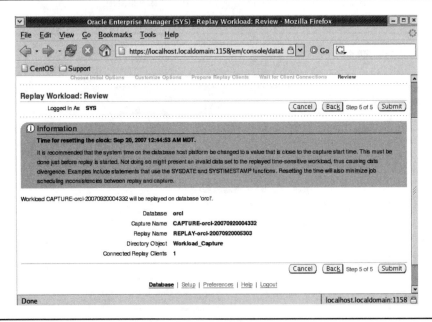

**FIGURE 5-14.** *OEM View Workload Capture History page*

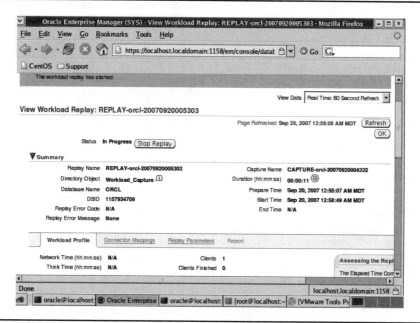

**FIGURE 5-15.** *OEM View Workload Capture History page*

### The Replay Clients

The replay clients are started from the command line by starting the **wrc** executable. There is no OEM interface available to start the clients for you. To start the clients, you start a command-line session and set the Oracle environment as appropriate for your operating system. You can either change to the directory where the replay files are contained, or you can define the location of that directory using the **replaydir** parameter. Here is an example of the startup of the **wrc** executable:

```
C:\oracle\product\admin\rob11gr4\test_dir>wrc mode=replay
userid=system password=Robert
```

In your testing you may want to have a number of replay clients, depending on the workload of the system and the level of concurrency.

The **wrc** executable comes with a number of options. First it comes with three modes:

- **Replay (Default)**   Causes the replay client to replay the workload.

- **Calibrate**   Used to estimate the number of replay clients and CPUs that will be needed to replay the workload. The following code listing provides an example of using the calibrate mode to determine how many **wrc** clients you will need to run. In this case we just need one:

```
[oracle@localhost ~]$ wrc mode=calibrate replaydir=/oracle01/capture
Workload Replay Client: Release 11.1.0.6.0 -
Production on Thu Sep 20 19:39:12 2 007
Copyright (c) 1982, 2007, Oracle.  All rights reserved.

Report for Workload in: /oracle01/capture
----------------------
Recommendation:
Consider using at least 1 clients divided among 1 CPU(s).
Workload Characteristics:
- max concurrency: 1 sessions
- total number of sessions: 1
Assumptions:
- 1 client process per 50 concurrent sessions
- 4 client process per CPU
- think time scale = 100
- connect time scale = 100
- synchronization = TRUE
```

■ **List_hosts**    Lists the hosts that were used during the capture or the replay.

There are also a number of different keywords that you can use when calling **wrc**. These keywords define various attributes associated with that execution of **wrc** such as the username, the password, and the replay directory. You can see a list of all the valid keywords for the various modes that wrc operates in by typing in wrc –help.

## Execute Database Replay—Manual

We will now address replaying the workload manually. First we will look at manually initializing the replay data. This is required if you are moving the workload to another system. We will then prepare the database for replay and then we will finally start the replay process.

**Initialize the Replay Data**    Once you have moved the workload capture files to the replay system, you will need to initialize those files. To do this, log in to the database and use the PL/SQL stored procedure **dbms_workload_replay.initialize_replay** to initialize the workload in the database. Here is an example:

```
BEGIN
   DBMS_WORKLOAD_REPLAY.INITIALIZE_REPLAY (
                        replay_name => 'Pre_Upgrade_Capture_070107_01',
                        replay_dir => 'MY_REPLAY_DIR');
END;
/
```

One of the things that this procedure does is populate the DBA view **dba_workload_replays**. There may be cases where you will need to remove a replay record from the system. You can use the **dbms_workload_replay.delete_replay_info** procedure to perform this action, as seen in this example:

```
select id, name from dba_workload_replays;
        ID NAME
---------- ----------------------------------------
         3 REPLAY-rob11gr4-20070712204202

SQL> exec dbms_workload_replay.delete_replay_info(3);
```

**Prepare for Database Replay**   Having initialized the workload and mapped any external connections (we discuss remapping connections earlier in this chapter), we are ready to prepare for the replay operation. For this we use the **dbms_workload_replay.prepare_replay** PL/SQL procedure. It is here that we determine the various replay options discussed earlier (such as synchronization) that will be used. We pass in the various options that we want to utilize and Oracle will prepare the workload for replay. Here is an example where we set the synchronization parameter to **false**:

```
BEGIN
   DBMS_WORKLOAD_REPLAY.PREPARE_REPLAY (
      synchronization=>FALSE);
END;
/
```

In this example we have accepted the defaults for the remaining parameters, **connect_time_scale**, **think_time_scale**, and **think_time_auto_correct**. We are now ready to start the workload replay!

**Initiate Database Replay**   After all this work, it's almost anticlimactic to start the replay. First, you will need to start one or more **wrc** replay clients (discussed earlier in this chapter) and then you simply use the PL/SQL procedure **dbms_workload_replay.start_replay** to begin the workload replay, as seen in this example:

```
Exec dbms_workload_replay.start_replay;
```

Oracle will start the replay process. Once replay has started, the call to the **start_replay** procedure will complete and you will be returned to the SQL prompt to monitor the replay operation. When the workload replay is complete, the replay clients will disconnect.

**Arup Says...**

Thank you very much, Robert, for showing how to use the manual, command-line way as well as the OEM path. When OEM provides such a nice interface to execute database capture and replay, why should we consider the command-line path?

The most obvious reason may be that some of us eschew the idea of running a GUI tool. As trivial as it may sound, it may actually be true in some cases. In OEM, there are two flavors—the Database Control (or DB Control), the one that comes with the database software and runs on the database server as a web browser; and Grid Control, the one that you install centrally communicating to all databases via agents. In the latter case, the web browser runs on the server separate from the database server. In many production databases, it may be unacceptable to run a web server on the same server as the database. Grid Control is acceptable in that case, but DB Control, which runs on the same server as the database, is not. Grid Control is always behind schedule on Oracle databases. So, it might be a while before it appears for Oracle 11*g*, and so you may not have the OEM for the production database until that time. In that case your options are limited to the command line.

Second, you may want to automate the process via a script that makes the parameter change, runs the replay, and iterates it several times. So, thank you, Robert, for showing how to use this feature by command line.

**Monitoring Replay**    You can monitor the replay process using the following views:

■ **dba_workload_replays**

■ **dba_workload_replay_divergence**

■ **v$workload_replay_thread**

**Stop Workload Replay**    Again, a somewhat anticlimactic procedure, **dbms_workload_replay.cancel**, is used to cancel workload replay, as seen in this example:

```
Exec dbms_workload_replay.cancel_replay;
```

**Arup Says...**

Although Oracle suggests that you replay the workload on a *different* database, there is no technical restriction on doing so. You can replay the workload on the same database where it was captured. In many cases, that may prove very useful, if you can find the outage for the duration of the test. For example, suppose you are assessing the impact of changing parameters on the test system; it will be an apple-to-apple comparison if you capture and replay the workload on the same test database. All you have to do is set a restore point prior to the replay, and then flashback to that restore point after the replay. Take a snapshot before and after each replay so that you can compare the effects. Your tasks will be somewhat like this:

1. Capture workload. This will create a set of two AWR snapshots.

2. Preprocess the captured files.

3. Create a restore point:

   ```
   SQL> create restore point pre_replay;
   ```

4. Change parameters or other variables as needed.

5. Start replay. This will create a set of two AWR snapshots.

6. Flashback database to the restore point (of course, your database should be configured for flashback operations!):

   ```
   SQL> shutdown immediate
   SQL> startup mount
   SQL> flashback database to restore point pre_replay;
   SQL> alter database open resetlogs;
   ```

7. Repeat Steps 4 through 6 as many times you want. Now, using OEM or the command line, generate a period comparison report between the snapshots collected in different iterations. That will tell you how each run impacted the database.

Another use case may be the choice of the standby database. Suppose you are planning to migrate to a new environment. You can leverage the Database Replay and the snapshot standby features to get to the best configuration. The steps will be roughly as follows:

1. Create a snapshot standby on the new environment.

2. Replay and check results.

3. Change parameters.

4. Repeat Steps 2 and 3 until you get the best performance.

5. When ready, convert the snapshot standby to regular standby and then activate the standby as primary.

## Generate a Workload Replay Report

The Workload Replay Report provides information on the replay process. To generate the report you use the **get_replay_info** and **report** functions in the **dbms_workload_replay** PL/SQL package, and then display the output, as seen in this example:

```
DECLARE
  rep_rpt        CLOB;
BEGIN
  rep_id  := DBMS_WORKLOAD_REPLAY.GET_REPLAY_INFO(dir => 'Workload_Capture');
  rep_rpt := DBMS_WORKLOAD_REPLAY.REPORT(replay_id => rep_id, format =>
'TEXT');
    dbms_output.put_line(rep_rpt);
END;
/
```

The output of the Workload Replay Report will provide you with a wealth of information on the replay session.

### Arup Says...

The Database Replay feature in this release, in my opinion, is the best thing Oracle introduced since partitioning option in Oracle 8, and this alone is worth upgrading to Oracle 11*g*. Why is this feature so attractive?

When QA people test the systems or application, what do they do? Hopefully, they get some sample SQL statements from the shared pool (most likely they just write them up as they think the code must look, instead of checking it in the shared pool) and run the statements over and over again using some load generator tool. This is not an entirely invalid test, but definitely not representative of the system. When testing for new apps, this may be the only choice because there is no actual statement to pull from the shared pool; but consider the case when you want to migrate to a new hardware or move from filesystems to ASM and want to gauge the impact of the changes. You would want to run exactly the same statements and in the same format against the database running on the new system, wouldn't you? In those cases, the synthetic statements cooked up by QA testers will just not cut it; you need actual statements as they happened and that's what Database Replay delivers. This is also why Oracle calls this feature a part of a suite called *Real* Application Testing (RAT). The rather interesting name aside, RAT allows you to test the changes yourself, without involving the testing group, to assess the impact of a lot of changes—database parameter changes, changes to the OS, patch applications, storage changes, hardware changes, and many others. Changes are inevitable; but with RAT (I really wish they had used a different name!), it will be possible to predict the changes somewhat more accurately.

# The SQL Performance Analyzer

If you have done more than a few upgrades of the Oracle database, you might well have experienced a problem where the execution plans change. This can be a frustrating part of the upgrade process. Other changes to the Oracle database can cause execution plans to change too, such as the addition or removal of schema objects (indexes, materialized views), collection of statistics, changes to the OS such as upgrades, and hardware changes such as the addition or removal of physical disks. Oracle Database 10*g* introduces the SQL Performance Analyzer to deal with these problems. The SQL Performance Analyzer will analyze a given change and identify SQL statements impacted by that change and measure the performance improvement or degradation resulting from that change.

Oracle provides two interfaces to the SQL Performance Analyzer. The first is through OEM and the second is through PL/SQL using the **dbms_sqlpa** supplied package. In the following sections we will review how to use the SQL Performance Analyzer.

## Overview of SQL Performance Analyzer

This is an overview of the steps followed when using the SQL Performance Analyzer. Some of these steps are automated in OEM, and others you will perform when doing a manual or OEM analysis. The basic workflow is

- Capture the SQL workload in the form of a SQL Tuning Set.

- If you are using a test system, set up the test system and move the SQL tuning set to the test system.

- Measure the SQL workload performance before the change.

- Make the change.

- Measure the SQL workload performance after the change.

- Compare the performance results.

## SQL Performance Analyzer via OEM

OEM provides an easy workflow that will walk you through the use of the SQL Performance Analyzer. In this section we will provide a quick overview on accessing the SQL Performance Analyzer through OEM and then discuss the three workflows that OEM provides to ease the use of the SQL Performance Analyzer:

- The Optimizer Upgrade Simulation workflow

- The Parameter Change workflow

- The Guided workflow

## Overview of OEM and the SQL Performance Analyzer

OEM provides access to the SQL Performance Analyzer from the software and support link on the OEM home page. From there simply click on the link to the SQL Performance Analyzer which is under the Real Application Testing section of the page. On the SQL Performance Analyzer (see Figure 5-16) page you will find the three different workflows available for you to choose from (we will discuss these in more detail in the following sections). These options are:

- Optimizer Upgrade Simulation

- Parameter Change

- Guided Workflow

Additionally you can see any existing SQL Performance Analyzer tasks listed on this page.

## The Optimizer Upgrade Simulation OEM Page

If you choose the Optimizer Upgrade Simulation link on the SQL Performance Analyzer page, you will be taken to the Optimizer Upgrade Simulation page seen on Figure 5-17. This page will prompt you for information that Oracle will require

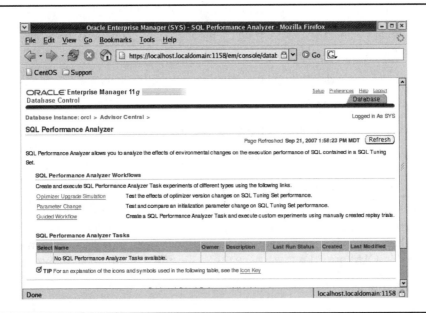

**FIGURE 5-16.** *OEM SQL Performance Analyzer page*

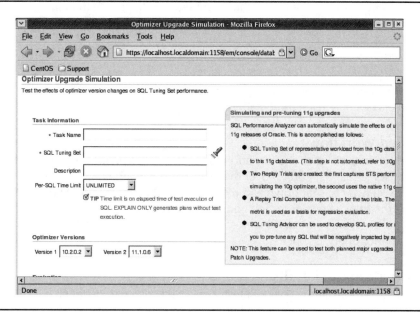

**FIGURE 5-17.**  *OEM Optimizer Upgrade Simulation page*

to perform the analysis. Using this function you can test the impacts of your upgrade from 10g to 11g, and how that upgrade will impact performance.

To perform this test you will need to create a SQL Tuning Set on the 10g system that is representative of the workload on your system. You will then move that SQL Tuning Set to the Oracle Database 11g database for analysis. See Chapter 4 for more on creating SQL Tuning Sets and. Later in this section we discuss Transporting SQL tuning sets to other databases.

Before you start the test, you will need to define the old optimizer version and the new optimizer version number that you will be testing in the optimizer version section. You will also need to determine what metric you wish to use to compare the two optimizers. By default Execute Elapsed Time is chosen for you, but several other choices are available. Finally, you can control when the analysis will take place. When you are ready to schedule the analysis, simply click on Submit and OEM will take care of the rest for you. OEM will then return you to the SQL Performance Analyzer home page.

## The Parameter Change OEM Page

The Parameter Change OEM Page is much the same as the Optimizer Upgrade Simulation OEM page, except that you will enter the name of the parameter you wish to test and the baseline value and the changed value for that parameter (thus, you can baseline against a parameter that is configured differently than in your own system).

> **NOTE**
> *The list of parameters to be tested only includes certain dynamic parameters. Some dynamic parameters, such as **sga_target**, cannot be tested.*

## The Guided Workflow

The guided workflow allows you to perform the SQL performance analysis, while maintaining some manual control over the process. This might be required, for example, if you need to shut down and restart the database as a part of your testing, as might be the case if you are testing nondynamic parameter setting changes. The guided workflow gives you individual steps to follow as you proceed through the SQL performance analysis process.

## An Example and the Results

Let's look at a quick example. We will test the impacts of a parameter change on a givent SQL Tuning Set. From the SQL Performance Analyzer OEM Page (Figure 5-16) we select the Parameter Change link. On the top portion of the Parameter Change OEM Page (Figure 5-18) you can see that I've given the SQL Performance Analyzer

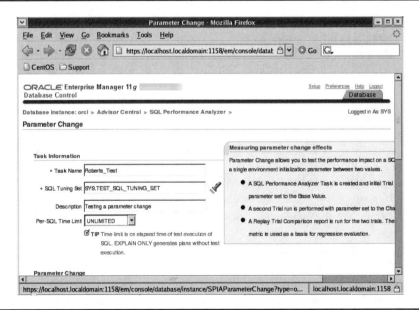

**FIGURE 5-18.** *Example OEM Parameter Change page (top half)*

task a name of Roberts_Test. I've assigned the SQL Tuning set SYS.TEST_SQL_
TUNING_SET to the task, along with a description. I've left the Per-SQL Time Limit
set to unlimited. I could set it to EXPLAIN_ONLY and just generate execution plans
to compare. By default the SQL Performance Analyzer will compare both execution
times and plans.

In Figure 5-19 we see the bottom half of the Parameter Change OEM Page. Here
we define the parameter (just one) we want to test the change on. In our case, we
have chosen to determine the impact that changing **db_file_multiblock_read_count**
from 14 to 32 will have on our SQL Tuning Set. We also set the evaluation metric.
The default is elapsed time, but we can choose from a number of different metrics
such as CPU Time, Buffer Gets, Disk Reads, Direct Writes, or Optimizer Cost.
Finally we can define when the task should execute (we have selected immediate
execution). We then click on the X button to begin the analysis.

OEM will return us to the SQL Performance Analyzer home page. We will now find
our parameter change task listed in the SQL Performance Analyzer Tasks window as
seen in Figure 5-20. Note that a box in the Last Run Status column indicates that the task
is currently running. This will turn into a checkmark once the task has successfully run.

We can view the results of the analysis from the SQL Performance Analyzer
home page. Simply click on the completed task for which you wish to review
results. From this page, you can click on the task name (in our case ROBERTS_TEST)
to bring more detail on the specific SQL Performance Analyzer Task. Figure 5-21

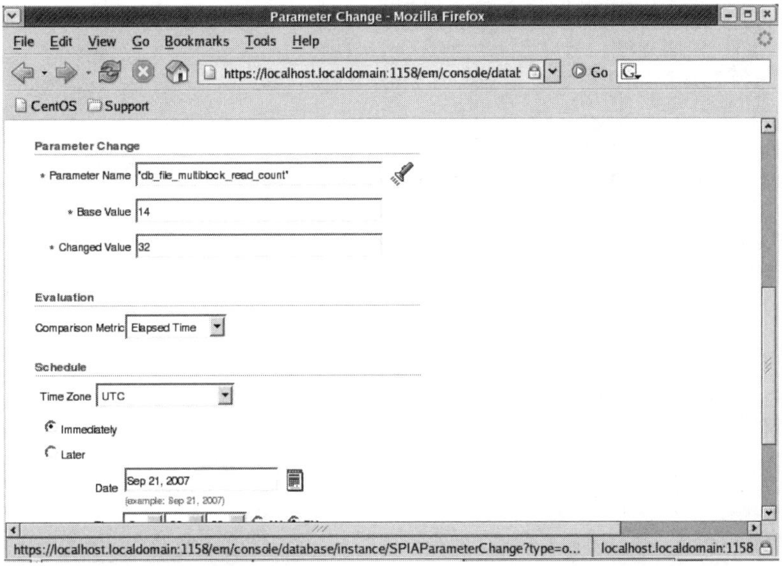

**FIGURE 5-19.**   *Example OEM Parameter Change page (bottom half)*

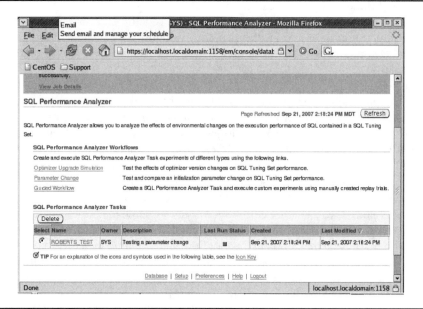

**FIGURE 5-20.** *SQL Performance Analyzer window with task*

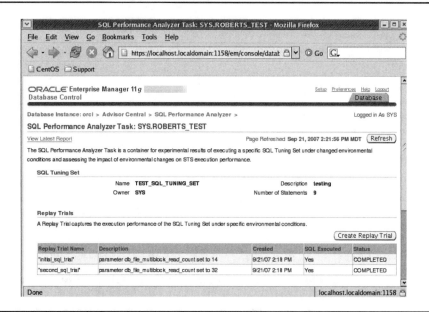

**FIGURE 5-21.** *SQL Performance Analyzer Task window*

provides a look at the SQL Performance Analyzer Task Page with details of our **roberts_test** task.

From this page we can see details about the task. You can replay the trail if you wish by clicking on the replay trail button (for example, perhaps you changed some OS parameter and you want to see if that makes a difference). You can also compare different trials if you like from the Replay Trial Comparisons region of the SQL Performance Analyzer Task Page.

You can view the report from the task by clicking on the View Latest Report link at the top of the page (or click on the icon in the comparison report column in the Replay Trial Comparisons region of the page). The resulting report, shown in Figure 5-22, provides a graphical representation of the positive or negative benefits of our test. For example, in my test, the elapsed time of the second SQL trial (the new parameter setting) was less than that of the first trial (the old parameter setting). We also see the number of SQL statements that were improved, regressed or stayed the same. Lower on the page is a list of the statements that are impacted by the change and if the impact was positive or negative.

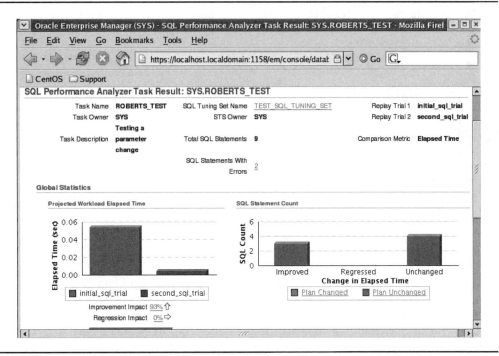

**FIGURE 5-22.**   *SQL Performance Analyzer Task page*

For additional information on impacted plans, simply click on the improved, regressed, or unchanged graphs, and you will be taken to a detail screen highlighting the plans that fit within the given category. Each plan allows you to drill further down into the individual SQL statements to compare statistics and execution plans. Also you can run the SQL Tuning Advisor on a specific plan to see if there is anything that can be done to improve the performance of that plan.

Based on this test, it appears that I should reset **db_file_multiblock_read_count** to 32 instead of 16 on my system.

# SQL Performance Analyzer via PL/SQL

The following sections address the use of the SQL Performance Analyzer via PL/SQL. We will cover the following steps:

- Create a SQL Tuning Set with the correct workload.

- Transport the SQL workload to a test system (optional).

- Configure the baseline environment.

- Execute the SQL Performance Analyzer task.

- Make the change.

- Execute the SQL Performance Analyzer task.

- Compare the results.

**NOTE**
*The SQL Performance Analyzer can be used cross-platform. So you can use this tool to test your old hardware against new hardware that you are trying to decide to buy, or to compare performance among several hardware vendors.*

## Create a SQL Tuning Set with the Correct Workload

SQL Performance Analyzer uses SQL Tuning Sets to determine which SQL statements it should analyze. We discussed the creation of a SQL Tuning Set in Chapter 4. Create a SQL Tuning Set that contains the SQL statements/workload that might be impacted by the change you are going to make. In some cases, you may not know all of the SQL statements that would be impacted, so it's a good idea to capture a typical workload for the SQL Performance Analyzer to use.

### Transport the SQL Workload to a Test System (Optional)

If you will be doing your testing on a system other than the one that you generated the workload on, then you will need to transport the SQL Tuning Set to that test system. To do so you will need to follow these steps:

1.  From a user other than the SYS user, create the staging table for the SQL Tuning Set.

    Use the **dbms_sqltune.create_stgtab_sqlset** procedure to create the staging table, as seen in this example:

    ```
    Exec dbms_sqltune.create_stgtab_sqlset(table_name=>'STAGE_TABLE');
    ```

2.  Move the SQL Tuning Set into the Staging table.

    Use the **dbms_sqltune.pack_stgtab_sqlset** procedure to move the tuning set you created into the staging table. In this example, we have already created a SQL Tuning Set called MY_SQL_TUNE_SET and we are moving it into STAGE_TABLE:

    ```
    begin
        dbms_sqltune.pack_segtab_sqlset(
            sqlset_name=>'MY_SQL_TUNE_SET',
            staging_table_name=>'STAGE_TABLE');
    end;
    /
    ```

3.  Move the table from the source database to the test database.

    There are a number of ways to do this. You can use Data Pump to export and import the table, or you could move the data across a database link if you prefer.

4.  Unpack the SQL Tuning Set into the test database.

    On the test database to which you have moved the table, use the **dbms_sqltune.unpack_stgtab_sqlset** procedure to load the SQL Tuning Set from the table into the test database. In this example we are moving the MY_SQL_TUNE_SET set into a table called STAGE_TABLE, replacing any duplicate records:

    ```
    begin
        dbms_sqltune.unpack_segtab_sqlset(
            sqlset_name=>'MY_SQL_TUNE_SET',
            replace=>TRUE,
            staging_table_name=>'STAGE_TABLE');
    end;
    /
    ```

**NOTE**
*Of course, your test system should replicate the production system as closely as possible. Even a small difference between the production system and the test system can make a difference.*

## Configure the Baseline Environment

Before you start your first analysis, you may wish to configure your database differently to represent the baseline. For example, you may wish to configure a specific database parameter differently before you perform the analysis. For example, we might change the setting of **db_file_multiblock_read_count**, as seen in this example:

```
Alter system set db_file_multiblock_read_count=32;
```

## Create the SQL Tuning Task

Before we can run the analysis we need to create the SQL Tuning task. This is done with the **dbms_sqltune.create_tuning_task** procedure. This task (available in Oracle Database 10*g*) has many different options. In this example we will create a tuning task called MY_PARAMETER_TEST_001, using the SQL Tuning Set we used earlier called TEST_SQL_TUNING_SET:

```
Declare
      retval     varchar2(200);
begin
      retval:=dbms_sqltune.create_tuning_task(
      sqlset_name=>'TEST_SQL_TUNING_SET',
      sqlset_owner=>'SYS',
      task_name => 'MY_PARAMETER_TEST_001');
end;
/
```

## Execute the SQL Performance Analyzer Task

To start the SQL Performance Analyzer we use the **dbms_sqltune.execute_tuning_task** procedure, as seen in this example:

```
begin
dbms_sqltune.execute_tuning_task(
            task_name => 'MY_PARAMETER_TEST_001',
            execution_name => 'initial_sql_trial');
end;
/
-- check the status of the task to make sure it is completed.
select status from dba_advisor_tasks where task_name = 'MY_PARAMETER_TEST_001';
STATUS
-----------
COMPLETED
```

In this example we have created a SQL Performance Analyzer task called **my_parameter_test_001**. After the task ran, we checked the **dba_advisor_tasks** view to make sure that it was completed.

### Reconfigure the Environment

Now we are ready to make our environment change. This might be a change to a parameter or an addition of an index or some other item of interest. For example, we might change the setting of **db_file_multiblock_read_count**, as seen in this example:

```
Alter system set db_file_multiblock_read_count=32;
```

### Analyze the Changed Environment

Now that you have made your environmental change(s), we need to rerun the analysis, as seen in the following example. It's essentially the same as the previous analysis run, except that we change the **execution_name** parameter:

```
begin
dbms_sqltune.execute_tuning_task(
            task_name => 'MY_PARAMETER_TEST_001',
            execution_name => 'post_change_sql_trial');
end;
/
-- check the status of the task to make sure it is completed.
select status from dba_advisor_tasks where task_name = 'MY_PARAMETER_TEST_001'
and last_execution='post_change_sql_trial';

STATUS
-----------
COMPLETED
```

**NOTE**
*In the initial cut of Oracle Database 11g, we found these tests to be pretty slow. Be careful when you execute these tuning tasks, considering the impact they might have on the system. We fully expect that as these features mature, performance will be less of an issue.*

In this example, we ran the same tuning task that we ran previously, giving it a different execution name so we could distinguish the two tasks. We also checked to make sure the task ran successfully by querying **dba_advisor_tasks** again.

**NOTE**
*Of course, this feature is not available in Oracle Database 10*g*. So, how do you test whether an upgrade to 11*g* will have a negative impact on your SQL statements performance? First you go ahead and do the upgrade in a test environment. Then you make sure that the parameter **optimizer_features_ enable** is set to the version of your Oracle 10*g* Database (for example, it might be set to 10.2.0.0) and run the pre-change analysis with that parameter set. You can then set **optimizer_features_enable** to 11.0.0.0 and run the analysis again. Comparing the results will give you some indication of the positive or negative impact of your upgrade to Oracle Database 11*g*.*

## Compare the Results

Once the before-and-after analysis has been executed, you need to compare the results of the before-and-after performance analysis. This is done with the PL/SQL procedure **dbms_sqltune.execute_analysis_task**, as seen in this example:

```
begin
     dbms_sqltune.execute_tuning_task(task_name=>'MY_PARAMETER_TEST_001',
         execution_params=>dbms_advisor.arglist('RANK_MEASURE1',
                          'buffer_gets'));
end;
/
```

In the previous example we started a compare analysis on the MY_PARAMETER_ TEST_001 task. We have indicated with the **execution_params** parameter that we want to compare the performance of the two sets of execution data (the **rank_measure1** parameter) based on the **buffer_gets** parameter.

## Generate the Analysis Report

After running the comparison, you will want to review the results of the comparison and determine whether any performance impacts are introduced by the change (and you hope that the change helps performance). The analysis report can be run using the PL/SQL supplied procedure **dbms_sqlpa.report_analysis_task.** In this example, we have run the summary report for the tuning task. The procedure provides for varying levels of reporting.

```
VAR rep CLOB;
EXEC :rep := DBMS_SQLTUNE.REPORT_TUNING_TASK('MY_PARAMETER_TEST_001', -
'text');
```

```
SET LONG 100000 LONGCHUNKSIZE 100000 LINESIZE 120
PRINT :rep
```

## Data Dictionary Views of Interest

As you use the SQL Performance Analyzer you may have to use a few views including:

- **[DBA | USER]_ADVISOR_EXECUTIONS**   Provides information on the executions of the SQL Performance Analyzer

- **[DBA | USER]_ADVISOR_TASKS**   Provides information on SQL Performance Analyzer tasks

- **[DBA | USER]_ADVISOR_FINDINGS**   Provides information on the SQL Performance Analyzer findings

- **[DBA | USER]_ADVISOR_SQLPLANS**   Provides a list of all execution plans associated with the analysis

- **[DBA | USER]_ADVISOR_SQLSTATS**   Provides statistics on all the SQL statements

### Arup Says...

The second member of the RAT family (Real Application Testing, as Oracle calls it; not the rodents)—SQL Performance Analyzer (SPA)—deserves some special attention. You might be wondering how this is any different from the Database Replay feature explained earlier in the chapter.

On the surface both do the same things—replay something and compare the results. But they are different. The first important difference is that SPA allows you to examine which SQL statements you want to replay. You can even create your own SQL statements that you have put in the application and replay them against the database after changing parameters. This is not possible in Database Replay. The second difference is the mode of execution. SPA executes the SQL statements sequentially, not concurrently. Therefore you will see the impact on the SQL statements independently but not the contention among themselves. Database Replay can play them concurrently and hence you can see the effect of contention.

Another major difference is the link between SPA and SQL Tuning Optimizer (STO). You can launch the STO from the SPA page for the SQL statements, check the recommendations made by STO, and then replay them to see the impact.

# End of Line

Change management in Oracle has perhaps been one of the last of the uncharted frontiers. In Oracle Database 11*g* Oracle has started to introduce new features that will help to reduce the overall impacts of change to the database. Be it change as a result of an upgrade to a new version of the database or a parameter change, we can now be better prepared to understand the impacts of those changes before we unleash it out to the community. Being pro-active about change, what a concept!

# CHAPTER
## 6

# Oracle Database 11g
# Security

ecurity has become a prominent theme in many a database these days, and it's no wonder. With hackers, terrorists, corporate data theft, and loss of backup tapes on their way to storage facilities, DBAs need to watch out for the security of the data in their charge. In this chapter we will discuss features and enhancements in Oracle Database 11*g* including:

- Auditing

- Passwords

- Fine-Grained Access Control (FGAC)

- Tablespace encryption with Transparent Data Encryption (TDE)

- Other TDE-related enhancements

- Oracle SECUREFILE LOBS

# Auditing

If you create an Oracle database using the Oracle Database Configuration Assistant in Oracle Database 11*g*, or if you upgrade a database using the Database Upgrade Assistant, you will have the option of enabling the Oracle Database 11*g* auditing defaults. If you accept the Oracle Database 11*g* auditing defaults then database auditing will be enabled for certain database operations. These operations are listed in the following table:

| | | |
|---|---|---|
| Alter any procedure | Create any job | Drop any table |
| Alter any table | Create any library | Drop profile |
| Alter database | Create any procedure | Drop user |
| Alter profile | Create any table | Exempt access policy |
| Alter system | Create external job | Grant any object privilege |
| Alter user | Create public database link | Grant any privilege |
| Audit role by access | Create session | Grant any role |
| Audit system | Create user | |
| Audit system by access | Drop any procedure | |

You can disable auditing by changing the **audit_trail** parameter to NONE or using the **noaudit** SQL command to stop auditing specific statements. If you enable auditing during an upgrade, the already existing auditing will not be removed, however, the new auditing will be added to all existing schemas. You should be aware that if you use default auditing, there is no automatic cleanup of the AUD$ table where the underlying audit records are stored. You will need to maintain this table yourself.

**NOTE**
*Oracle Database 10g still puts the AUD$ table in the SYSTEM tablespace. Many DBAs move AUD$ to its own tablespace. However, Oracle does not officially support moving AUD$ outside the SYSTEM tablespace. In any event you need to make sure you manage the tablespace space consumed by the records in AUD$.*

# Password-Related Features

Several new password-related features are present in Oracle Database 11*g*. These include:

- Password settings related to the default profile
- Password complexity
- Password case sensitivity
- Hacking prevention with failed logon delays
- Password hashing changes
- Default password usage

Let's look at these features in a bit more detail.

## Password Settings and the Default Profile

Oracle Database 11*g* has changed various password setting defaults in the **default** profile. In the following table we provide the resource name, the Oracle

Database 10*g* default value, and the Oracle Database 11*g* default value for the default profile:

| Resource Name | Oracle Database 10*g* Default | Oracle Database 11*g* Default |
|---|---|---|
| Failed_login_attempts | 10 | 10 |
| Password_grace_time | Unlimited | 7 (days) |
| Password_life_time | Unlimited | 180 |
| Password_lock_time | Unlimited | 1 (days) |
| Password_reuse_max | Unlimited | Unlimited |
| Password_reuse_time | Unlimited | Unlimited |

Note that this can have implications when you upgrade to Oracle Database 11*g*. In particular the change to **password_life_time** means that your users will now have to change their passwords every 180 days by default.

## Password Complexity

You may have used the Oracle password verification routine contained in the $ORACLE_HOME/rdbms/admin/utlpwdmg.sql script. Oracle Database 11*g* has improved this functionality, making the password complexity verification routine better. In the new version of utlpwdmg.sql you will find two different copies of the password verification routine. The first is a new version of the password verify routine called **verify_function_11G**. The old version of the password verify function is still available in utlpwdmg.sql, except that it's commented out.

The new verify function offers the following password checks:

1. The password must be a minimum of eight characters in length.

2. The password cannot be the same as the username.

3. The password cannot be the same length as the username.

4. The password cannot be the username spelled backwards.

5. The password cannot be the same as the server name or the server name with digits from 1 to 100 appended.

6. Simple passwords will be rejected.

7. The password must include one digit and one alpha character.

## Password Case Sensitivity

Password case sensitivity has been introduced in Oracle Database 11*g*. By default case sensitivity is enabled. The **sec_case_sensitive_login** parameter controls case sensitivity. To enable case sensitivity the **sec_case_sensitive_login** parameter should be set to TRUE. To disable case sensitivity set the parameter to FALSE.

During upgrades or imports from previous versions of Oracle Database, existing user passwords will remain case-insensitive until the passwords are changed. You can determine if a password is case-sensitive by referencing the PASSWORD_ VERSIONS columns of the DBA_USERS view. Valid values in the PASSWORD_ VERSIONS column would be 10G for passwords assigned in 10*g* that are not case sensitive yet in 11*g* (because they have not been changed). 10G 11G indicate a password assigned to an account in 10*g* but then upgraded to 11*g* or an account created in 11G that is case sensitive.

The **orapwd** program, which is used to create the password file, has also been modified to allow or disallow case-sensitive passwords. A new parameter, **ignorecase**, has been added to the command line. **Ignorecase** must be set to Y to enable password case sensitivity for SYS and SYSDBA connections.

> **NOTE**
> *Because Oracle Database versions prior to Oracle Database 11*g* would always uppercase all passwords (even when presented in lowercase), you must consider the impacts of enabling case sensitivity when upgrading to Oracle Database 11*g*. Enabling case sensitivity can impact a great many things, for example, scripts with passwords stored in lowercase (where in fact the password is an uppercase password) and database links. Test carefully if you are upgrading and intend to use this new feature.*

## Hacking Prevention with Failed Logon Delays

Oracle Database 11*g* has introduced a logon delay that will take effect after the third failed password entry attempt. Oracle will incrementally delay the next logon or password prompt after the third failed attempt, up to a maximum of 10 seconds. This only delays the time between login prompts and does not delay an actually successful logon.

Oracle passwords can now contain multibyte characters without quoting. Also the characters $, _, and # are allowed within a password without quoting when you use the SQL*Plus **connect** command, or if you enter the password from the SQL*Plus password prompt. As of this writing there were still places where these characters did not work without being quoted, such as the SQL*Plus command line in UNIX and

**Arup Says...**

This is one of those thorny areas that show up painfully during upgrades from 10*g* to 11*g*. Most applications developed under 10*g* probably did not consider password case sensitivity, so they may be passing passwords in any case, especially from user input. A web app, for instance, accepts the user's password (which may have been entered in any case) from a form and tries to connect to the database. In 10*g* this wouldn't have posed a problem with the case-insensitive password, but in 11*g* it will fail if the correct case is not used. Of course, the best option is the apps changing their code to make the password given in the connect string either lower- or uppercase, but that could be more easily said than done. So, what can you do, as a DBA, if you want to avoid one of those upgrade-broke-my-system moments?

Simple. Just issue the following command:

```
alter system set sec_case_sensitive_logon = false;
```

The passwords will be case-insensitive now (just like the 10*g* behavior). Later, the developers can fix their apps to pass the passwords in a consistent case and then you can change the parameter to TRUE.

when using the **create user** and **alter user** commands. (Applications may also handle these characters differently, so test carefully.)

Oracle has also added new parameters to help protect against various Internet attacks including DOS attacks and brute force attacks. These parameters are

- **Sec_protocol_error_further_action** Defines what actions should be taken if a bad packet is received from a remote system. Options with respect to the client connection are as follows:

  - **CONTINUE** Do not disconnect the client session. This is the default setting.

  - **DROP** Drop the client connection after a specific number of bad packets. This parameter takes an integer argument that defines the number of bad packets that are acceptable.

  - **DELAY** Delay accepting client requests after a bad packet is requested. This parameter takes an integer argument that defines the delay time in seconds.

- **Sec_protocol_error_trace_action** Defines the level of tracing that should occur. Options include:

  - **NONE** No logging occurs.

- **TRACE**   A trace file is generated when bad packets are received. This is the default setting.

- **LOG**   A small logging message is entered in the database alert log.

- **ALERT**   An alert message is sent to the DBA via OEM.

- **Sec_max_failed_login_attempts**   Defines the number of authentication attempts that a given client connection can make on the server before the client process is dropped. The default value is 10.

- **Sec_return_server_release_banner**   Determines if the server banner will be returned to a client connection. Not returning the banner will make hacking a database more difficult since the user will not know which version of the database they are trying to hack.

## Password Hashing Changes

Oracle passwords are now hashed using SHA1 encryption. The SHA1 algorithm produces a 160-bit hashed output of the database password. Additionally, hashed passwords are "salted," which ensures that the resulting hash value for each hashed password is different, even if the password is the same.

## Default Password Use

In previous versions of the Oracle database various accounts might be assigned default passwords, which can be a security risk. Oracle Database 11*g* introduces a new data dictionary view, DBA_USERS_WITH_DEFPWD, that you can query to determine whether a given user account is using one of these default passwords. Here is an example of an 11*g* database that has a few too many accounts using default passwords (okay, these are also likely to be locked too):

```
SQL> SELECT * FROM DBA_USERS_WITH_DEFPWD;
USERNAME
------------------------------
DIP
MDSYS
WK_TEST
CTXSYS
OLAPSYS
OUTLN
EXFSYS
SCOTT
```

# Fine-Grained Access Control on Network Services

Oracle supplied PL/SQL utility packages such as **utl_tcp**, **utl_smtp**, **utl_mail**, **utl_http**, and **utl_inaddr** that provide access to network services now have enhanced security available. Rather than PUBLIC being granted execute privileges on these packages, Oracle now has you create an access control list (ACL) in order to use these packages.

**NOTE**
*This is a potential upgrade issue if you are using these packages. If you are using any of the network service PL/SQL packages, you may get ORA-24247 errors after upgrading if you do not create an ACL for the PL/SQL packages you are using.*

Creating the ACL takes two steps. First you create the ACL and define the privileges. Then you assign the ACL to one or more network hosts. Let's look at these steps in a bit more detail.

## Create the ACL and Define the Associated Privileges

To create the ACL list, you use the **dbms_network_acl_admin.create_acl** PL/SQL package. In the call to the package you will assign a name to the ACL list, give it a description, and assign a user account or a role that is being granted or denied permissions. In the call you will also define whether this is a grant or a revoke of a privilege, and what privilege you are granting or revoking. Finally you can optionally enter start and end dates that the grant should be subject to. Here is an example of a call to the **dbms_network_acl_admin.create_acl** package:

```
Begin
  Dbms_network_acl_admin.create_acl(
       acl=>'myweb-site-com-permissions.xml',
       description=>'Test ACL',
       principal=>'ROBERT',
       is_grant=>TRUE,
       privilege=>'connect');
end;
/
```

In the preceding example, we have created an ACL called myweb-site-com-permissions.xml. We have given the grant **connect** (it's case-sensitive) to the user ROBERT. There are two privilege options, connect and resolve. You must have the **connect** privilege to connect to an external network with the UTL* utility packages. The **resolve** privilege provides rights to use UTL_INADDR to resolve hostname issues.

Once the ACL is created, you can add additional users or privileges using the **dbms_network_acl_admin.add_privilege** procedure as seen here:

```
Begin
    dbms_network_acl_admin.add_privilege(
        acl=>'myweb-site-com-permissions.xml',
        principal=>'SCOTT',
        is_grant=>TRUE,
        privilege=>'connect');
end;
/
```

You can also use the **dbms_network_acl_admin.delete_privilege** procedure to drop privileges and the **dbms_network_acl_admin.drop_acl** procedure to drop ACLs.

## Assign the ACL to Network Hosts

Once you have created the ACL, you will need to assign that ACL to a network host.computer using the **dbms_network_acl_admin.assign_acl** procedure. Here is an example of the use of this procedure:

```
Begin
    dbms_network_acl_admin.assign_acl(
        acl=>'myweb-site-com-permissions.xml',
        host=>'RobertsDellXPS');
end;
/
```

### Arup Says...

This is one of those *wow* features. Remember the Voyager worm that crawled the Oracle databases all over the world about a year ago? The worm spread by contacting a remote host using the **utl_tcp** package, even though the two databases have no db links between them. The solution, in many cases, was to shut off all access to **utl_tcp**. Although it worked for most, some users legitimately needed access to **utl_tcp**. Using the ACL feature, you can now create a very fine-grained ACL that allows access to only specific hosts, not all. So anyone can have access to **utl_tcp**, but it's ineffective unless the target port exists in the ACL.

## ACL-Related Data Dictionary Views

Oracle provides views that you can use to check ACL-related privilege assignments. These views include:

- DBA_NETWORK_ACLS

- [DBA/USER]_NETWORK_ACL_PRIVILEGES

# Tablespace Encryption

Oracle Database 11*g* now supports tablespace-level encryption of data. In this section we will discuss the following aspects of this new feature:

- Overview of Oracle tablespace encryption

- Preparing the database for encryption

- Creating an encrypted tablespace

- Encrypted tablespace performance

## Overview of Oracle Tablespace Encryption

Oracle Database 10*g* introduced Transparent Data Encryption (TDE), allowing you to encrypt data within specific columns of a table. Oracle Database 11*g* enhances Transparent Data Encryption by providing for the encryption of all contents of a given tablespace. Any permanent tablespace can be encrypted. Undo and temporary tablespaces cannot be encrypted; however, all blocks and data created in these tablespace types will be encrypted if they originate from an encrypted tablespace. Additionally the redo log stream will be encrypted. Partitioning allows you to mix and match encryption. One partition can be encrypted, and another may not be encrypted, simply by virtue of which tablespace they are in.

Most Oracle features are available with encrypted tablespaces. There are some restrictions on transporting encrypted tablespaces (cross-endianness transport is not supported, and there are wallet-related restrictions if you are using wallets in the destination database). Binary files (BFILES) and external tables are not encrypted in Oracle (which makes sense as neither of these are stored in tablespaces!). Finally, you cannot change the key of an encrypted tablespace once it has been set.

**NOTE**
*Caution, if you lose the key, you lose your data.*
*Not a good thing. Protect your key from theft, but*
*also from loss! Lose your key and even Harry Potter*
*cannot save you.*

# Preparing the Database for Tablespace Encryption

If you are already using Transparent Data Encryption in Oracle Database 10*g* to encrypt columns, then you will be set up to use tablespace encryption. If you are not using TDE, then to use tablespace encryption you must configure the database. This includes:

- Configuring the **compatible** parameter correctly

- Configuring an Oracle wallet

- Opening the Oracle wallet

- Determine which encryption algorithm you wish to use

Let's look at each of these preparatory steps in more detail next.

### Configuring the Compatible Parameter Correctly

To use tablespace-level encryption, you must have the **compatible** parameter configured to a value of 11.1.0 or greater. Note that changing the **compatible** parameter may impact other functionality in the database, so make sure you test carefully after changing the **compatible** parameter. Note that the **compatible** parameter is not a dynamic parameter, and you will have to cycle the database before the new setting will take effect.

Here is an example of changing the **compatible** parameter (as you might do after a database upgrade from Oracle Database 10*g* to Oracle Database 11*g*):

```
Alter system set compatible='11.1.0.0.0' scope=spfile;
```

### Configuring and Opening Your Oracle Wallet

If you have already used Oracle's Transparent Data Encryption features, then you will have already configured your database's Oracle wallet. All operations using Transparent Data Encryption will require that you create and open a wallet. If you have not configured your Oracle wallet, fear not; that is the topic of this section and it's fairly simple. First we need to create an entry for our wallet in the database sqlnet.ora file. Then we will need to open the wallet and set the master encryption key. Let's look at these steps in more detail:

**Configure the Sqlnet.ora File (Optional)**   Oracle will, by default, create the wallet in the directory $ORACLE_BASE/admin/$ORACLE_SID/wallet (you will need to create this directory if it does not already exist). If you wish to use a location other than the default location, then configure the **encryption_wallet_location** parameter in the sqlnet.ora file of our database. Here is an example of such an entry:

```
Encryption_wallet_location=
(source=(method=file)
(method_data=(directory=/mywallet)))
```

**NOTE**
*You can locate the directory for the wallet in any location. However, Oracle recommends that you not use the same directory where the standard obfuscated wallet (cwallet.sso) is located. This is typically in the $ORACLE_HOME/sysman/config/ monwallet directory.*

**Open the Wallet and Create the Master Encryption Key**    Having determined where the wallet will be stored, we need to create the master encryption key and open the wallet. We use the following **alter system** command to perform this action (note this creates the wallet in the default directory):

```
Alter system set encryption key authenticated by "robert";
```

Note that you will only run this command once, and that the result is the creation of the wallet using the password of robert, which is case-sensitive. Also note the double quotes in the command instead of single quotes. The wallet will be opened after it's created.

The wallet is closed each time the database is shut down. You will need to reopen the wallet each time you cycle the database, and the database will not open until you open the wallet (which implies you have to nomount or mount the database, open the wallet, and then open the database). The command is slightly different to open an existing wallet:

```
Alter system set encryption wallet open authenticated by "robert";
```

While it might be an unusual operation, you can also close the wallet with the **alter system** command as seen here:

```
Alter system set encryption wallet close;
```

**NOTE**
*The password for the wallet is case-sensitive.*

## Determine Which Encryption Algorithm You Wish to Use

Oracle Database 11*g* supports four different encryption algorithms:

- 3DES168

- AES128 (Default)

- AES192

- AES256

From a purely secure point of view the AES256 algorithm would appear to be the most secure since it's a 256-key encryption algorithm.

## Creating Encrypted Tablespaces

You use the **create tablespace** command to create an encrypted tablespace, just as you would any other tablespace. To indicate the encryption algorithm to be used, you use the **encryption using** keyword. You must also include the keyword **encrypt** in the **storage** clause to actually cause the tablespace to be encrypted. Here is an example:

```
Create tablespace my_secure_tbs
datafile '/oracle01/oradata/orcl/my_secure_tbs_01.dbf' size 100m
encryption using '3DES168' default storage (encrypt);
```

You can also encrypt a tablespace using the default encryption algorithm by just using the encryption keyword as seen here:

```
Create tablespace my_second_secure_tbs
datafile '/oracle01/oradata/orcl/my_second_secure_tbs_01.dbf' size 100m
encryption default storage (encrypt);
```

The [DBA|ALL|USER]_TABLESPACES views have a new ENCRYPTED column added that indicates whether the tablespace has been encrypted or not.

There is no provision for enabling encryption of existing tablespaces in Oracle Database 11*g*. Therefore if you wish to do such a thing you will need to create the encrypted tablespace and then move the data into that tablespace using Oracle Data Pump or a SQL command like **alter table move**. The same applies for decryption of a tablespace; you simply have to move objects from an encrypted tablespace to one that is not encrypted to de-encrypt the data.

**NOTE**
*Tablespace encryption is not subject to the same column-length restrictions that column-level encryption is. For example, if you try to encrypt a VARCHAR2(4000) column, you will get the following results:*

```
create table test_table_two (test_name
varchar2(4000) encrypt)
ERROR at line 1:
ORA-28331: encrypted column size too long
for its data type
```

*You will not get this error if you create this table in an encrypted tablespace.*

## Encryption and Database Performance

Encryption can have impacts on database performance, sometimes significant. Unlike compression, which serves to reduce the number of blocks read at the cost of CPU, encryption does nothing to reduce the IO overhead, while adding CPU overhead for encryption/de-encryption. Performance testing with tablespaces configured for 3DES and AES encryption showed marked reduction in database response times in both DML and SQL query operations. For example on my system (an Intel dual-CPU system that is admittedly not in the running for fastest system of the year), loading a table with 1,752,000 rows of data (119MB) took 21:30.39 minutes when unencrypted. Using 3DES encryption the same data took 28:30.24 minutes and AES took 28:54.13 minutes. In some cases where performance is a consideration, it may make sense to just encrypt the columns you need to protect rather than the entire object.

**NOTE**
*If you have used encrypted columns before, you will be aware that Oracle offers a NOSALT option. NOSALT is not available with tablespace encryption.*

### Arup Says...

If you have used Transparent Data Encryption (TDE), introduced in 10*g* R2, earlier, you might be wondering how this feature—Transparent Tablespace Encryption (TTE)—adds any significant value. At first blush, they both appear to do the same thing—transparently encrypting data; but with a major difference: TDE applies to a column while TTE applies to a whole tablespace for all objects within it and all columns of those objects. Well, why would you really care about all the columns being encrypted, anyway? So, what additional value does TTE provide?

The biggest disadvantage of TDE was performance; you couldn't take advantage of the index range scans or pattern matching on encrypted columns. For instance, suppose you have an index on the column Social Security Number (SSN), which is encrypted by TDE. If you want to select all SSNs starting with 123, you issue **select * from accounts where ssn like '123%'**. Since the column is encrypted, the index on SSN will not be used by this query, which, of course, affects performance.

That is exactly where TTE excels. It encrypts everything it has inside it, *but only on the disk*. When the data goes into the cache, the values are decrypted. Index matching occurs in the cache, where the values are in cleartext anyway; so performance is not affected. This feature is unique in any non-Oracle encryption solution and makes it so attractive.

# TDE and Log Miner, Logical Standby, and Streams

TDE is now fully supported by Oracle Log Miner. As a result, logical standby databases now also support the use of TDE. Note that the wallet that contains the keys must be opened so that Log Miner can decrypt the encrypted data. You will also note that the V$LOGMNR_CONTENTS view is populated with unencrypted data. This is a fully expected result, according to Oracle. On the standby database the wallet must be a copy of the wallet that is on the primary database. You can change the table key and the table encryption algorithm on the standby database. Oracle Streams now also supports TDE.

# Oracle SECUREFILE LOBS

Oracle Database 10*g* provides for two different ways of storing LOBs in the database. The previous way is now known as BASICFILE (which is still the default). The new way is known as SECUREFILE. SECUREFILE LOBS offer several new features.

First, Oracle Database 11*g* reduces data redundancy by creating a secure hash index and using that index to detect duplication. Identical LOBs are then coalesced into a single image. The result is a reduction in storage and easier management.

SECUREFILE LOBS can also be compressed. This compression is separate from any table or index compression. Two means of compression are supported, medium and high.

Finally, SECUREFILE LOB data can be encrypted or stored in clear text. Each LOB encryption specification is independent of the others. Several encryption algorithms are supported including 3DES168, AES128, AES192, and AES256.

When you create a LOB, Oracle will by default create the old style of LOB, which is known as a BASICFILE. If you wish to have SECUREFILE be the default, you can set the **db_securefile** parameter to either of the following values:

- **ALWAYS**  Attempt to create as a SECUREFILE if possible. If not possible, then revert to BASICFILE.

- **FORCE**  Always create as a SECUREFILE. If unable, then generate an error.

SECUREFILE LOBS must be created in tablespaces using Automatic Segment Space Management (ASSM), and you must have your wallet open in order to use SECUREFILE.

Here is an example of the creation of a table with a SECUREFILE LOB:

```
create table notes (note_doc clob
encrypt using 'AES128')
lob(note_doc) store as securefile
(cache nologging);
```

# End of Line

Security becomes more and more important as time goes on. Oracle Database 11*g* has made some great strides in security as you can see from the pages in this chapter. What remains for the DBA is to figure out how to best implement these features. Sometimes it's easy, and sometimes it's hard but in the end, it's our job to protect these databases.

# CHAPTER
# 7

# Oracle Database BI and Data Warehousing New Features

racle Database 11g offers a wealth of new features that relate to business intelligence (BI) and the Oracle Data Warehouse. Several new partitioning features are introduced, in addition to virtual columns and features related to statistics collection. Additionally Oracle Data Pump is improved, as are materialized views. The **pivot** and **unpivot** clauses are introduced, and finally, table compression is much improved. In this chapter, we will cover all these features in much more detail.

# Partitioning

New partitioning features introduced in Oracle Database 11g include:

- Interval partitioning

- Extended composite partitioning

- Reference partitioning

- System partitioning

- System-managed domain indexes

Let's look at each of these new features in more detail next.

## Interval Partitioning

Until now range-based partitioning often required some ongoing maintenance. For example, if you were using date-based range partitioning with each partition storing data for a particular month, you would need to create new partitions as new months arrived. Now interval partitioning will create these partitions on demand for you.

### Create Interval-Partitioned Tables

When you create a interval-partitioned table, you use the new **interval** keyword in the **create table** statement to indicate the interval that you want each partition to represent. For example, if you wanted to partition your DAILY_SALES table by month using interval partitioning, then you would use this **create table** command (forgive our minimal syntax in this chapter, of course things like PCTFREE and PCTUSED are important!):

```
create table daily_sales
( product_id number not null
, customer_id number not null
, sale_dt date not null
```

```
, quantity_sold number(3) not null
, unit_sale_price number(10,2) not null
, total_sale_price number(10,2) not null
, total_discount    number(10,2) not null)
partition by range (sale_dt)
interval (numtoyminterval(1,'MONTH'))
( partition p_before_1_jan_2007 values
 less than (to_date('01-01-2007','dd-mm-yyyy')));
```

In this example the DAILY_SALES table will be created with one initial partition (partition P_BEFORE_1_JAN_2007). This partition is known as the *transition point*. If you include multiple partitions in the **create table** statement, then the last partition defined will be the transition point. Oracle will create other partitions based on the transition point. We can see the initial partition if we query against a data dictionary:

```
select partition_name, high_value
from user_tab_partitions
where table_name = 'DAILY_SALES'
order by partition_position;


PARTITION_NAME                  HIGH_VALUE
----------------------------    ----------------------------------------
P_BEFORE_1_JAN_2007             TO_DATE(' 2007-01-01 00:00:00', 'SYYYY-M
                                M-DD HH24:MI:SS', 'NLS_CALENDAR=GREGORIA
```

Oracle Database 11*g* will automatically create new partitions in the table as new data is entered into the table that requires a new partition. For example, if we enter data for sales in February of 2007, we will need a new partition and the database obliges, as seen here:

```
Insert into daily_sales values
(1,100,to_date('02-01-2007','mm-dd-yyyy'),100,10.00,1000.00,0);
commit;

select partition_name, high_value
from user_tab_partitions
where table_name = 'DAILY_SALES'
order by partition_position;


PARTITION_NAME                  HIGH_VALUE
----------------------------    ----------------------------------------
P_BEFORE_1_JAN_2007             TO_DATE(' 2007-01-01 00:00:00', 'SYYYY-M
                                M-DD HH24:MI:SS', 'NLS_CALENDAR=GREGORIA
SYS_P41                         TO_DATE(' 2007-03-01 00:00:00', 'SYYYY-M
                                M-DD HH24:MI:SS', 'NLS_CALENDAR=GREGORIA
```

**NOTE**
*The partition is created regardless of the commit operation. A rollback operation will not remove the new partition.*

Note the call to the **numtoyminterval** function in the **interval** statement. This function converts the number passed into a valid interval year-to-month literal. You would use **numtoyminterval** if you wanted partitions created automatically based on a given span of months. For example, our **create table** statement will create a new partition for every month. If we wanted to create a partition for every quarter, we might change the interval command to **interval (numtoyminterval(3,'MONTH'))**, making sure that the first partition was created at the end of a given quarter, such as:

```
( partition p_before_1_jan_2007 values
  less than (to_date('12-31-2007','dd-mm-yyyy')));
```

You might also use the **numtodsinterval** function if you need to convert to a valid day-to-second literal. This function can be used if you want partitions created on a smaller scale like daily, hourly, per minute, or even down to the second. Use of the **store in** clause is allowed so you can define which tablespaces partitions should be created in.

**Arup Says...**
Interval partitioning puts one more "auto" into automated management in Oracle Database. How many times have you received visits from irate customers or angry emails about an error, "inserted value does not map to any partition"? Well, all that is past now with interval partitioning. Oracle adds the partitions as needed; not you.

However, there is a little annoying aftereffect: The partitions generated by the system are not named by you; their names are system-generated—SYS_P41, in this example. So, how can a developer target a specific partition by name without querying the data dictionary all the time?

There is a great new syntax in Oracle 11*g* in SQL to address partitions by values, not by name. Here is how you will use it:

```
select * from daily_sales partition for (to_date('31-dec-2007',
'dd-mon-yyyy'));
```

This will automatically choose the partition where 2-JAN-07 data resides, even though the SQL did not specify the name. In Oracle 11*g*, developers should be encouraged to use this syntax instead of using partition names. In that case, when you change the name of the partition, the SQL statements will not be affected.

## Interval-Partitioned Table Restrictions

Restrictions that you need to be aware of with regard to interval-partitioned tables include the following:

- The interval-partitioned table can only have one partitioning key column, and it must be of type NUMBER or DATE.

- Index-organized tables are not supported.

- You cannot create a domain index on an interval-partitioned table.

- Interval partitioning does not support subpartitions. Thus, you can create an interval partition on the main partition of a composite partitioned table, but the subpartition cannot be interval-partitioned. Here is an example of creating a composite interval-partitioned table using range-list partitioning:

```
create table daily_sales
( product_id number not null
, customer_id varchar2(2) not null
, sale_dt date not null
, quantity_sold number(3) not null
, ship_dt date not null
, unit_sale_price number(10,2) not null
, total_sale_price number(10,2) not null
, total_discount   number(10,2) not null)
partition by range (sale_dt)
interval (numtoyminterval(1,'MONTH')) store in (tbs_1, tbs_2)
subpartition by list(customer_id)
  ( partition p_before_1_jan_2007 values
 less than (to_date('01-01-2007','dd-mm-yyyy'))
 (subpartition sub_zero_three values('AA','AB','AC','AD'),
  subpartition sub_four_seven values('AE','AF','AG','AH')));
```

In this example, if we add a record outside the 01-01-2007 partition boundaries, a new partition will be added, but only one subpartition will be created, as seen here:

```
select table_name, partition_name, subpartition_count subpart_count
from user_tab_partitions where table_name='DAILY_SALES';
```

| TABLE_NAME | PARTITION_NAME | SUBPART_COUNT |
|---|---|---|
| DAILY_SALES | P_BEFORE_1_JAN_2007 | 2 |
| DAILY_SALES | SYS_P42 | 1 |

We can also see from the next query that the one partition will accept any value:

```
select table_name, partition_name, subpartition_name, high_value
from dba_tab_subpartitions
```

```
where table_name='DAILY_SALES';
TABLE_NAME     PARTITION_NAME        SUBPARTITION_NAME
------------   -------------------   --------------------
HIGH_VALUE
-------------------------------------------------------
DAILY_SALES   P_BEFORE_1_JAN_2007   SUB_FOUR_SEVEN
'AE', 'AF', 'AG', 'AH'
DAILY_SALES   P_BEFORE_1_JAN_2007   SUB_ZERO_THREE
'AA', 'AB', 'AC', 'AD'
DAILY_SALES   SYS_P42               SYS_SUBP41
DEFAULT
```

- The **values** clause does not allow the use of **maxvalue**, and the partitioning key column cannot specify NULL values.

### Maintain Interval-Partitioned Tables

Interval-partitioned tables are maintained the same way you maintain any other kind of range-partitioned table. For example, if you like you can merge partitions, as seen here:

```
alter table daily_sales
merge partitions for(to_date('01-JAN-2007','dd-MON-yyyy'))
, for(to_date('01-FEB-2007','dd-MON-yyyy'))
into partition p_31_2007;
```

You might have noticed that the partition names are system-generated names, which I hate personally. You can use the **alter table rename partition** command to rename these partition names if you like. Here is an example:

```
alter table daily_sales rename partition sys_p41 to p_Jan_2007;
```

You can also migrate existing range-partitioned tables to use interval partitioning. You simply use the **alter table** command, as seen in this example where we create a new partition every month:

```
alter table employee_compensation
set interval (numtoyminterval(1,'MONTH'));
```

You may wish to see what the current interval setting for a given table is. You can use the [DBA|ALL|USER}_PART_TABLES view to query this information. In the following example we see that the interval for the DAILY_SALES table is monthly:

```
select  table_name, interval from user_part_tables
where table_name='DAILY_SALES';

TABLE_NAME                     INTERVAL
----------------------------   -------------------------
DAILY_SALES                    NUMTOYMINTERVAL(1,'MONTH')
```

# Extended Composite Partitioning

Composite partitioning has been around in one form or another for some time, so you should be familiar with the basic concept behind composite partitioning. Oracle Database 11g extends composite partitioning, adding the following composite partitioning methods:

- **Composite range-range partitioning**   This partitioning method will partition data using the range method. Then for each partition, subpartitions are created using the range method.

- **Composite list-range partitioning**   This partitioning method will partition data using the list method. Then for each partition, subpartitions are created using the range method.

- **Composite list-hash partitioning**   This partitioning method will partition data using the list method. Then for each partition, subpartitions are created using the hash method.

- **Composite list-list partitioning**   This partitioning method will partition data using the list method. Then for each partition, subpartitions are created using the list method.

Here is an example of the use of this new partitioning method, a range-range partitioned table. In this case, we have a table that is partitioned on **SALES_DATE**, and subpartitioned on **SHIPPED_ON_DATE**. We might do this if we frequently look at sales from a specific date (or date range) that are shipped on a specific date (or date range):

```
Create table sales_information
(customer_number number, item_number number,
 quantity_sold number, date_sold date, date_shipped date)
partition by range (date_sold)
subpartition by range(date_shipped)
(partition sold_bef_01_07
  values less than(to_date('01-01-2007', 'mm-dd-yyyy') )
 (subpartition sold_bef_01_07_ship_bef_01_07
      values less than(to_date('01-01-2007', 'mm-dd-yyyy') ),
  subpartition sold_bef_01_07_ship_01_07
      values less than(to_date('02-01-2007', 'mm-dd-yyyy') ),
  subpartition sold_bef_01_07_ship_02_07
      values less than(to_date('03-01-2007', 'mm-dd-yyyy'))),
 partition sold_01_2007
  values less than(to_date('02-01-2007', 'mm-dd-yyyy') )
 (subpartition sold_01_07_ship_01_07
      values less than(to_date('02-01-2007', 'mm-dd-yyyy') ),
  subpartition sold_01_07_ship_02_07
      values less than(to_date('03-01-2007', 'mm-dd-yyyy') )) );
```

All the new types of composite partitioned tables support local and global indexing.

**Arup Says...**

Extended composite partitioning opens up new avenues to partition the tables more intelligently to reflect real-life situations. For instance, a hotel company might want to archive data and allocate disks based on reservation date and departure date. Instead of choosing one of the two as your partitioning scheme with regular range-based partitioning, you can use composite partitioning and use both columns as partition keys. This will ease the administration of management of the data in the partitions, allowing you to create an initial partition on the reservation date and then subpartition based on the departure date. This type of partitioning scheme might reflect the business situation more accurately.

## Reference Partitioning

Reference partitioning is a new partitioning method available in Oracle Database 11*g*. With reference partitioning you will have two tables that form a parent-child relationship, and you will logically equi-partition these tables. You reference-partition two tables by creating the parent table first. Then you create the child table, defining the foreign key constraint between the two tables and also including a partitioning clause that references the foreign key. This can also be done with the **alter table** command if both tables already exist. With reference partitioning, partition maintenance operations cascade down to the child table, easing administration of those objects. The result is that you cannot perform any partition maintenance operations on the child table.

Let's look at an example of reference partitioning. First, we create the partitioned parent table:

```
create table customer_orders
( customer_id  number, order_id number not null,
  order_date date not null, order_mode varchar2(8),
  order_status varchar2(1))
partition by range (order_date)
 ( partition p_before_jan_2007
   values less than (to_date('01-JAN-2007','dd-MON-yyyy'))
, partition p_2007_jan
   values less than (to_date('01-FEB-2007','dd-MON-yyyy')))
parallel;

alter table customer_orders
add constraint customer_orders_pk
primary key (order_id);
```

Now that we have created the parent table, we will create the table
CUSTOMER_ORDER_DETAILS, which is the child table in this relationship. Note
that in the **create table** statement, there is no need to list any partition details. The
partitions are aligned with the partitions of the CUSTOMER_ORDERS table we
created previously:

```
create table customer_order_items
( order_id number not null
, product_id number not null
, quantity number not null
, sales_amount number not null
, constraint customer_order_items_orders_fk
    foreign key (order_id) references customer_orders(order_id) )
partition by reference (customer_order_items_orders_fk)
parallel;
```

> **NOTE**
> *Reference partitioning is not supported with interval
> partitioning (discussed earlier in this section), index-
> organized tables, external tables, or a domain index
> storage table. Also the reference primary key or
> unique constraint cannot point to a virtual column
> (discussed later in this chapter).*

The data dictionary has changed a bit to support reference partitioning, as seen
in the following query output from USER_PART_TABLES, USER_TAB_PARTITIONS,
and USER_PART_TABLES:

```
-- Look at the partitioned tables.
select table_name, partitioning_type, ref_ptn_constraint_name
from user_part_tables
where table_name in ('CUSTOMER_ORDERS','CUSTOMER_ORDER_ITEMS');
TABLE_NAME                       PARTITION REF_PTN_CONSTRAINT_NAME
------------------------------   --------- ------------------------------
CUSTOMER_ORDERS                  RANGE
CUSTOMER_ORDER_ITEMS             REFERENCE CUSTOMER_ORDER_ITEMS_ORDERS_FK

-- Look at the partitions created.
select table_name, partition_name, high_value
from user_tab_partitions
where table_name in ('CUSTOMER_ORDERS','CUSTOMER_ORDER_ITEMS')
order by partition_position, table_name;
TABLE_NAME                       PARTITION_NAME            HIGH_VALUE
------------------------------   ------------------------- --------------------
CUSTOMER_ORDERS                  P_BEFORE_JAN_2007             TO_DATE(' 2007-01-01
00:00:00', 'SYYYY-MM-DD HH24:MI:SS', 'NLS_CALENDAR=GREGORIAN')
CUSTOMER_ORDER_ITEMS             P_BEFORE_JAN_2007
```

**Arup Says...**

The feature of reference partitioning is nothing less than spectacular. It allows you to create partitioned tables even when the partitioning key is not part of the table itself. In this example, note that the column ORDER_DATE is not part of the table CUSTOMER_ORDER_ITEMS, yet the table has been partitioned on that column. Isn't that amazing—partitioning on a nonexistent column?

In real life, this means a lot—it allows you to partition pretty much any table in some predetermined consistent format as long as there is a parent-child relationship. Prior to 11*g*, this was impossible. You either had to choose different partition keys or put the partition key in all tables, whether needed or not. Reference partitioning changed all that.

```
CUSTOMER_ORDERS                         P_2007_JAN                      TO_DATE(' 2007-02-01
00:00:00', 'SYYYY-MM-DD HH24:MI:SS', 'NLS_CALENDAR=GREGORIAN')
CUSTOMER_ORDER_ITEMS                    P_2007_JAN

-- Here we can see the references between the two tables.
select up.table_name, up.partitioning_type, uc.table_name ref_table
from user_part_tables up,
(select r.table_name, r.constraint_name
from user_constraints uc, user_constraints r
where uc.constraint_name=r.constraint_name and uc.owner=r.owner) uc
where up.ref_ptn_constraint_name = uc.constraint_name(+)
and up.table_name in ('CUSTOMER_ORDERS','CUSTOMER_ORDER_ITEMS');
TABLE_NAME                          PARTITION REF_TABLE
----------------------------------  --------- -----------------------------
CUSTOMER_ORDER_ITEMS                REFERENCE CUSTOMER_ORDER_ITEMS
CUSTOMER_ORDERS                     RANGE
```

# System Partitioning

Oracle Database 11*g* introduces system partitioning. System partitioning provides the ability to create a single table that has many physical partitions. With system partitioning you define a specific number of partitions, and you do not define a partition key. The resulting table partitions will have no defined partitioning method. As a result, when inserting data you must map the table rows to the assigned partition, typically through the use of the partition-extended syntax. One place that system partitioning is used is to support partitioning of domain indexes.

Creation of a system-partitioned table is straightforward. You just use the **create table** command along with the **partitioned by system** keyword as seen in this example:

```
CREATE TABLE TestTable (col1 integer, col2 integer)
PARTITION BY SYSTEM(
   PARTITION s1 TABLESPACE tbs_s1,  PARTITION s2 TABLESPACE tbs_s2,
   PARTITION s3 TABLESPACE tbs_s3,  PARTITION s4 TABLESPACE tbs_s4);
```

Delete and update operations on system-partitioned tables do not require any special syntax. However, when inserting into the TestTable, you must reference the partition that you want the data to be inserted into, as seen in this example. Note that if you remove the **partition** keyword, the statement will fail:

```
INSERT INTO TestTable PARTITION (s1) VALUES (4,5);
```

Most partition operations are supported with system-partitioned tables. They can be indexed with local indexes, local bitmap indexes, and global indexes. **Insert as select** operations are supported if they include a partition specification. Some operations are not supported including **create table as select** and an **insert as select** without a partition specification.

## System-Managed Domain Indexes

We now move to system-managed domain indexes. Oracle Database 11*g* now allows you to partition domain indexes. When partitioned, domain indexes are known as local domain indexes. Local domain indexes are created using the **create index** command as in this example where we add a comments column to CUSTOMER_ORDERS (which we created earlier in this chapter) and then we create a system-managed domain index on that column:

```
Alter table customer_orders add (comments varchar2(300) );

create index customer_orders_idx on
customer_orders (comments) indextype is ctxsys.context
local (partition tbs_s1, partition tbs_s2);
```

### Arup Says...

What possible value can system partitioning bring to the table? Plenty. What if a table just can't be partitioned in any way? But the table is so big that you do want to partition it, on maintenance and manageability grounds. So, you strike a deal with the developers that they will maintain the partitioning aspects of DML statements while you manage the partitions. System partitioning is the perfect solution for those cases.

Beware of one caveat, though. Suppose a developer issues this command:

```
update testable set col2 = 6 where col1 = 4;
```

This row exists in partition S1 and only that partition should be searched, but Oracle does not know that. It searches all partitions for this row, affecting performance. To remedy this issue, you should use this syntax:

```
update testable partition (s1) set col2 = 6 where col1 = 4;
```

The result is that we now have a domain index that is equi-partitioned with the base table that it is built on. This can improve performance of this index by allowing for partition pruning and other partition-related operations. This can also improve lookup times for certain types of queries (such as %value% types of queries).

**NOTE**
*The number of partitions you define on this index must equal the number of partitions in the base table of the index.*

# Virtual Columns

The ability to create virtual columns is a new feature in Oracle Database 11*g* that provides the ability to define a column that contains derived data, within the database. In this section we will introduce you to virtual columns, discuss how to create virtual columns, and discuss the use of virtual columns in partitioning.

## About Virtual Columns

Derived values for virtual columns are calculated by defining a set of expressions or functions that are associated with the virtual column when the table that the column is going to reside in is created. You can also use the **alter table** command to add a virtual column. The nice thing about virtual columns is that they do not consume any storage, as they are computed on the fly.

You can use virtual columns pretty much anywhere that you would use a normal column. You can query them, create indexes on them, and even collect statistics on them. There are a few restrictions including:

- You cannot write to a virtual column.

- There is no support for index-organized, external, object, cluster, or temporary tables.

- There is no support for Oracle-supplied datatypes, user-defined types, LOBs, or LONG RAWs.

Virtual columns can be used in queries, DML, and DDL statements. They can be indexed (the resulting index is essentially a function-based index), and you can collect statistics on them. Thus, they can be treated much as other columns. Let's look at how to create a virtual column in the next section.

# Creating Tables with Virtual Columns

To create a virtual column within a **create table** or **alter table** statement, you use the new **as** command, which is part of the virtual column definition clause. Figure 7-1 provides the basic syntax for the virtual column definition clause.

In the syntax of the **as** command, the parameters include:

- *Column* is the name of the virtual column.

- *Datatype* is optional, and can be used to define the datatype of the column.

- *Generated always* is optional, and is just used to clarify that the data is not stored on disk. Currently there is no need to include **generated always** in any virtual column definition.

- *As (column_expression)* defines the content of the virtual column. Column expressions for virtual columns are the same as those used in function-based indexes and are subject to the same restrictions. Some specific restrictions on column expressions include:

  - The expression cannot reference another virtual column, including using the same column expression used in another virtual column in the table.

  - All columns referenced in the expression for the virtual column must exist in the same table.

  - The virtual column expression can reference a user-defined function. That function must be deterministic, and the virtual column cannot be used as a partition key column.

  - The output of the column expression must be a scalar value.

- *Virtual* is optional.

Here is an example of the creation of a table with a virtual column. In this case, we are going to create an employee table that derives the current value of the

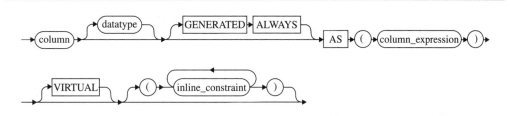

**FIGURE 7-1.** *The Virtual Column Definition clause syntax*

employees' retirement benefit, which is a formula based on the employee's years of service, the total salary, and a multiple:

```
Create table employee
( emp_id              number primary key,
  salary              number (8,2) not null,
  years_of_service    number not null,
  curr_retirement     as (salary*.0005 * years_of_service) );
```

Now that we have a virtual column, we will need to include the default keyword when we do inserts into the table, like this:

```
insert into employee values (1,100000,5,default);
```

We can then see the virtual column in action:

```
select * from employee;

    EMD_ID     SALARY YEARS_OF_SERVICE CURR_RETIREMENT
---------- ---------- ---------------- ---------------
         1     100000                5             250
```

You can see the virtual column setting by querying the DATA_DEFAULT column in the DBA_TAB_COLUMNS view as seen here:

```
select table_name, column_name, data_default from dba_tab_columns
where table_name='EMPLOYEE' and column_name='CURR_RETIREMENT';

TABLE_NAME      COLUMN_NAME          DATA_DEFAULT


--------------- -------------------- ------------------------------
EMPLOYEE        CURR_RETIREMENT      "SALARY"*.0005*"YEARS_OF_SERVICE"
```

You can also add a virtual column using the **alter table** command as seen in this example:

```
Alter table employee add
(curr_retirement   as (salary*.0005 * years_of_service) );
```

The fun does not stop there!! Perhaps we want to affix some form of message to a virtual column. In this example, we characterize the status of one's retirement benefit and its impact on our business with the use of a searched case expression:

```
Create table employee
( emp_id              number primary key,
  salary              number (8,2) not null,
  years_of_service    number not null,
  curr_retirement     as (salary*.0005 * years_of_service),
```

```
   retirement_impact varchar2(30) as (case
                       when (salary*.0005 * years_of_service) < 100
                       then 'MINIMAL'
                       when (salary*.0005 * years_of_service) < 500
                       then 'NORMAL'
                       else 'WARNING WILL ROBINSON! DANGER!'
                       end) );
insert into employee values (1,10000,1,default,default);
insert into employee values (2,100000,5,default,default);
insert into employee values (3,100000,10,default,default);
select emp_id, salary, years_of_service yos,
curr_retirement cr, retirement_impact ri from employee;

    EMP_ID     SALARY       YOS          CR RI
---------- ---------- ---------- ---------- ----------------------------
         1      10000          1          5 MINIMAL
         2     100000          5        250 NORMAL
         3     100000         10        500 WARNING WILL ROBINSON! DANGER!
```

## Partitioning Tables with Virtual Columns

You can use virtual columns as the partition key of the table. Say, for example, that we wanted to partition our employee table (for whatever reason) based on the current retirement amount. We would issue the following SQL statement:

```
Create table part_employee
( emp_id             number primary key,
  salary             number (8,2) not null,
  years_of_service   number not null,
  curr_retirement    as (salary*.0005 * years_of_service) )
partition by range (curr_retirement)
 ( partition dont_owe_much          values less than (100)
, partition owe_just_enough         values less than (500)
, partition oh_no_we_are_in_trouble values less than (maxvalue));
```

# Data Pump Single-Partition Imports

Oracle Data Pump now offers a partition mode that allows you to move specific partitions or subpartitions of a table instead of the whole table or a specific tablespace. In Oracle Database 10g, Data Pump Export allowed you to export one or more partitions or subpartitions of a table. Oracle Database 11g Data Pump Import now adds the **partition_options** parameter, which allows you to define how imported partitions should be handled.

Here is an example of using Data Pump export to export a specific partition of a table:

```
-- First, list the partition to be exported
select table_owner, table_name, partition_name
```

```
from dba_tab_partitions
where table_owner='ROBERT' and table_name='SALES_INFORMATION';

TABLE_OWNER TABLE_NAME          PARTITION_NAME
----------- ------------------- -------------------------
ROBERT      SALES_INFORMATION   SOLD_BEF_01_07
ROBERT      SALES_INFORMATION   SOLD_01_2007

-- Now, let's export the SALES_INFORMATION partitioned table
expdp robert/robert dumpfile=part_table.dmp directory=data_pump_dir
tables=(robert.sales_information.sold_bef_01_07) reuse_dumpfiles=y
```

**NOTE**
*In our example you can see the use of the*
**reuse_dumpfiles** *parameter. This is another new
feature of Oracle Database 11g that allows you to
overwrite an existing dump file!*

Using the new **partition_options** parameter, we can import this table as a partitioned table (the default), or we can import it as a single, nonpartitioned table. The options available when using the **partition_options** parameter are

- **None**   Creates the table as it exists in the dump file.

- **Departition**   Creates individual tables from each individual partition. Thus if you have a table with two partitions, you will end up with two separate tables after the import.

- **Merge**   Combines all partitions and subpartitions of the table into one single table.

Here is an example of importing the table as a nonpartitioned table:

```
impdp prod/prod dumpfile=part_table.dmp directory=data_pump_dir remap_
schema=Robert:prod partition_options=merge

-- Successful import...
select table_name from user_tables where table_name='SALES_INFORMATION';
TABLE_NAME
------------------------------
SALES_INFORMATION

-- And no partitions
select count(*) from user_tab_partitions
where table_name='SALES_INFORMATION';
  COUNT(*)
----------
        0
```

# Materialized Views and Query Rewrite

Oracle Database 11*g* introduces new and enhanced features associated with materialized views and query rewrite. In this section we will discuss the following:

- Materialized view logging control

- Online redefinition for tables with materialized view logs

- Query rewrite during refresh

- Partition Change Tracking (PCT) refresh for **union all** mviews

- New and enhanced materialized view catalog views

- Query rewrite enhancements

## Online Redefinition for Tables with Materialized View Logs

Oracle Database 11*g* now supports online redefinition of tables that have materialized view logs. You now just clone the materialized view log onto the interim table during the redefinition process as you do triggers, indexes, and so on. One requirement is that at the end of the redefinition process, you will need to perform a complete refresh of your materialized views.

## Query Rewrite During Refresh

Oracle Database 11*g* can now do query rewrite even if the materialized view is being refreshed. This feature requires the **query_rewrite_integrity** parameter be set to STALE_TOLERATED.

## Partition Change Tracking Refresh for Union All Mviews

Oracle Database 11*g* now supports PCT-based fast refresh for materialized views that include a **union all** operator.

## New and Enhanced Materialized View Catalog Views

New and enhanced catalog views are available in Oracle Database 11*g*. These changes provide information on

- Partition change tracking information for materialized views in the database

- Information on freshness or staleness of individual partitions

The new data dictionary views [DBA|ALL|USER]_MVIEW_DETAIL_PARTITION and [DBA_MVIEW_DETAIL_SUBPARTITION provide detailed information as to the staleness of individual partitions of a partitioned materialized view.

In addition to new catalog views, new columns have been added to the [DBA|ALL|USER]_MVIEWS view (NUM_PCT_TABLES, NUM_FRESH_PCT_REGIONS, and NUM_STALE_PCT_REGIONS) to indicate the total number of fresh and stale PCT regions and the number of PCT tables.

The [DBA|ALL|USER]_MVIEW_DETAIL_RELATIONS view has new columns to indicate whether the detail table is PCT-enabled and to also indicate the total number of fresh and stale PCT regions. Here is an example of the creation of a materialized view, on top of a partitioned table. We will then look at how the new PCT-related columns work. First we create the base table of the mview; then we create an mview log and then create the mview.

```
-- Create our demo table
CREATE table quarterly_sales (
     sales_month       number, sales_person_id  number
     ,date_of_sale     date,   cust_id          number
     ,quantity_sold    number, amount_sold      number)
   PARTITION BY LIST (sales_month) (
       PARTITION qtr_one    VALUES ( 1,  2,  3),
       PARTITION qtr_two    VALUES ( 4,  5,  6),
       PARTITION qtr_three  VALUES ( 7,  8,  9),
       PARTITION qtr_four   VALUES (10, 11, 12),
       PARTITION others     VALUES (DEFAULT));

-- Create the Mview log
CREATE MATERIALIZED VIEW LOG
   ON quarterly_sales WITH ROWID(sales_month)
   INCLUDING NEW VALUES;

-- Create the Mview
DROP MATERIALIZED VIEW mv_sales_sum;
CREATE MATERIALIZED VIEW mv_sales_sum
   BUILD IMMEDIATE
   REFRESH FAST ON DEMAND
   ENABLE QUERY REWRITE
AS
SELECT cust_id, sales_month, SUM(quantity_sold) as tot_qty_sold
   ,COUNT(quantity_sold) AS cnt_qty_sold
   ,SUM(amount_sold) as tot_amt_sold
   ,COUNT(amount_sold) AS cnt_amt_sold
  FROM quarterly_sales
 GROUP BY cust_id, sales_month;

-- Now, check the PCT info in user_mviews
select mview_name, num_pct_tables, num_fresh_pct_regions,
num_stale_pct_regions
```

```
from user_mviews
where mview_name='MV_SALES_SUM';

MVIEW_NAME      NUM_PCT_TABLES NUM_FRESH_PCT_REGIONS NUM_STALE_PCT_REGIONS
--------------- -------------- --------------------- ---------------------
MV_SALES_SUMM                1                     5                     0

-- What happens if we add a row..
insert into quarterly_sales values (1,22,sysdate,100,1,100.00);
commit;

-- Look at the catalog and we find that a partition is now stale:
select mview_name, NUM_FRESH_PCT_PARTITIONS, NUM_STALE_PCT_PARTITIONS
from user_mview_detail_relations
where mview_name='MV_SALES_SUM';
MVIEW_NAME      NUM_FRESH_PCT_PARTITIONS NUM_STALE_PCT_PARTITIONS
--------------- ------------------------ ------------------------
MV_SALES_SUM                           4                        1

select mview_name, num_pct_tables, num_fresh_pct_regions,
num_stale_pct_regions
from user_mviews
where mview_name='MV_SALES_SUM';

MVIEW_NAME      NUM_PCT_TABLES NUM_FRESH_PCT_REGIONS NUM_STALE_PCT_REGIONS
--------------- -------------- --------------------- ---------------------
MV_SALES_SUM                 1                     4                     1

-- which one is stale? As we expect, partition QTR_ONE..
-- as we can see from this query:
select mview_name, detail_partition_name, freshness
from user_mview_detail_partition
where mview_name='MV_SALES_SUM';

MVIEW_NAME      DETAIL_PARTITION_NAME          FRESH
--------------- ------------------------------ -----
MV_SALES_SUM    QTR_ONE                        STALE
MV_SALES_SUM    QTR_TWO                        FRESH
MV_SALES_SUM    QTR_THREE                      FRESH
MV_SALES_SUM    QTR_FOUR                       FRESH
MV_SALES_SUM    OTHERS                         FRESH
```

# Query Rewrite Enhancements

Oracle Database 10*g* offered limited support for query rewrite when inline views, or subqueries in the **from** clause were the same as inline queries in the materialized view. In these cases, the text in these queries had to match the materialized view query exactly or it could not be rewritten.

Oracle Database 11*g* improves on this with the notion of equivalency. When inline views of the query are "equivalent" with the inline views of the materialized views, then the query will be eligible for rewrite. The following constitutes equivalence in Oracle Database 11*g*:

■ The **select** list and **group by** lists are equivalent.

■ The **from** clause contains the same, or equivalent, objects.

■ The joins are equivalent, including all sections of the **where** clause.

■ The **having** clauses are equivalent.

This new functionality is demonstrated in the following example:

```
-- You can use the SH schema to test this...
-- Create the MVIEW
CREATE MATERIALIZED VIEW MV_SUM_SALES
ENABLE QUERY REWRITE AS
SELECT MY_MV.prod_id, MY_MV.cust_id,
sum(MY_MV.amount_sold) sum_amount_sold
FROM (SELECT sales.prod_id, sales.cust_id, sales.amount_sold
FROM sales, products
WHERE sales.prod_id = products.prod_id) MY_MV
GROUP BY MY_MV.prod_id, MY_MV.cust_id;

-- Now, query the table in a "equivalent" way..
SELECT SQ.prod_id, SQ.cust_id,
SUM(SQ.amount_sold) sum_amount_sold
FROM (SELECT sales.prod_id, sales.cust_id, sales.amount_sold
FROM sales, products
WHERE sales.prod_id = products.prod_id) SQ
GROUP BY SQ.prod_id, SQ.cust_id;
-- The execution plan tells the tale. Notice the rewrite.
```

| Id | Operation | Name | Rows |
|----|-----------|------|------|
| 0 | SELECT STATEMENT | | 1 |
| 1 | MAT_VIEW REWRITE ACCESS FULL | MV_SUM_SALES | 1 |

Bad news, I'm afraid, though. Inline view rewrite is not available for the following operations:

■ Set operators

■ Grouping set clauses

■ Nested subqueries

- Nested inline views

- Remote tables

You want more, you say? Okay, Oracle Database 11*g* now supports query rewrite on remote objects using materialized views that reference the remote object. So, if your SQL statement references a table like joe@my_db and an mview already is using joe@my_db, you might well find your query rewritten to use that mview. The mview has to be a local mview, and you must be running with **query_rewrite_integrity** parameter set to STALE_TOLERATED.

# The Pivot and Unpivot Clauses

Pivoting allows you to take a data structure (typically normalized) and essentially restructure that data into a different format in order to get the information you need, in a format that is easier to deal with. Pivoting may include summaries, averaging, and other types of aggregations. Oracle Database 11*g* has added new **pivot** and **unpivot** clauses to the **select** statement to make pivoting and unpivoting easier to accomplish. In this section we will address these two new clauses.

## The Pivot Clause

The **pivot** clause allows you to "flatten" a normalized table, if you will, providing the data in a more usable format for your application or reporting purposes. For example, say that we have a table or view that summarizes web hits to various web sites every day. What we want is an easy-to-produce cross-tab report that shows us the hits summarized for each quarter. Here is our table (note the use of a virtual column in this table to derive the quarter associated with the record. We will use this column in a little bit for our pivot operation):

```
create table web_hits
  ( website_name    varchar2(30),
    hit_date        date,
    hit_quarter     varchar2(5) as
        ('Q'||substr(ceil(to_number(to_char(hit_date,'mm')/3)),1,3) ),
    num_hits        number);
-- let's put some data in here...
truncate table web_hits;
begin
    dbms_random.initialize(1023);
    for tt in 1..365
    loop
        insert into web_hits
        values ('ROBERTSBLOG',sysdate-tt,
                default,tt*ceil(substr(abs(dbms_random.random),1,3) ));
        insert into web_hits values ('BILLSBLOG',sysdate-tt,
                default,tt*ceil(substr(abs(dbms_random.random),1,3) ));
```

```
            insert into web_hits values ('DAVIDSBLOG',sysdate-tt,
                    default,tt*ceil(substr(abs(dbms_random.random),1,3) ));
            insert into web_hits values ('JEDSBLOG', sysdate-tt,
                    default,tt*ceil(substr(abs(dbms_random.random),1,3) ));
            insert into web_hits values ('TERRYSBLOG',sysdate-tt,
                    default,tt*ceil(substr(abs(dbms_random.random),1,3) ));
            insert into web_hits values ('DANSBLOG',sysdate-tt,
                    default,tt*ceil(substr(abs(dbms_random.random),1,3) ));
        end loop;
end;
/
-- of course, create indexes and analyze the table as required
```

Now that we have our test data, we want to see it in the following format:

| Website_name | Q1 | Q2 | Q3 | Q4 |
|---|---|---|---|---|
| | # hits for quarter | # hits for quarter | # hits for quarter | # hits for quarter |

In Oracle Database 10*g* we could generate this report in this way:

```
select website_name,
    sum(case when hit_quarter='Q1' then num_hits else null end) Q1,
    sum(case when hit_quarter='Q2' then num_hits else null end) Q2,
    sum(case when hit_quarter='Q3' then num_hits else null end) Q3,
    sum(case when hit_quarter='Q4' then num_hits else null end) Q4
from ( select website_name, hit_quarter, num_hits
from web_hits) group by website_name;
```

Oracle Database 11*g* provides the new **pivot** clause, which provides a slightly more streamlined version of this operation. Here is the SQL query that we would use to generate the report:

```
-- Note that your output will differ from mine since we are using
-- random numbers.
select * FROM
    (select website_name, hit_quarter, num_hits from web_hits)
    pivot (sum(num_hits) for hit_quarter in ('Q1','Q2','Q3','Q4') )
    order by website_name;
```

and the result is:

| WEBSITE_NAME | 'Q1' | 'Q2' | 'Q3' | 'Q4' |
|---|---|---|---|---|
| BILLSBLOG | 4470125 | 2230694 | 7020588 | 7228769 |
| DANSBLOG | 4637120 | 2404018 | 8155904 | 7950024 |

| | | | | |
|---|---|---|---|---|
| DAVIDSBLOG | 4795485 | 2688444 | 7623701 | 7754571 |
| JEDSBLOG | 5607190 | 2194357 | 7495433 | 8045517 |
| ROBERTSBLOG | 5436279 | 1974066 | 6588326 | 6887461 |
| TERRYSBLOG | 5045030 | 2040091 | 7836385 | 7585883 |

**NOTE**
*Oracle documentation indicates that the pivot operation is optimized, which to me implies that the optimizer has some special code available that can improve its performance. In the testing I did (admittedly not exhaustive), I saw performance improvements in execution time of the **pivot** over the **case** method that were significant (in one test, consistently .85 seconds for **case** versus .34 seconds for **pivot**). Your results may vary, of course.*

*What was really interesting in these tests was that the cost of the two statements was equivalent except that the execution plan for the **case** method used a **hash group by** operation and the pivot plan used the new **sort group by pivot** operation.*

You can also pivot multiple columns if you like. For example, perhaps we would add a column to indicate whether the web hit is an intranet web hit or a normal web hit. Here is the SQL:

```
-- hit_type 1= regular and 2=intranet
alter table web_hits add(hit_type  number);
update web_hits set hit_type=1;
commit;
-- add intranet hits..
begin
    dbms_random.initialize(1023);
    for tt in 1..365*30
    loop
        insert into web_hits values ('ROBERTSBLOG', sysdate-tt,
            default,tt*ceil(substr(abs(dbms_random.random),1,2) ),2);
        insert into web_hits values ('BILLSBLOG',sysdate-tt,
            default,tt*ceil(substr(abs(dbms_random.random),1,2) ),2);
        insert into web_hits values ('DAVIDSBLOG',sysdate-tt,
            default,tt*ceil(substr(abs(dbms_random.random),1,2) ),2);
        insert into web_hits values ('JEDSBLOG',sysdate-tt,
            default,tt*ceil(substr(abs(dbms_random.random),1,2) ),2);
        insert into web_hits values ('TERRYSBLOG',sysdate-tt,
            default,tt*ceil(substr(abs(dbms_random.random),1,2) ),2);
```

```
        insert into web_hits values ('DANSBLOG',sysdate-tt,
             default,tt*ceil(substr(abs(dbms_random.random),1,2) ),2);
    end loop;
end;
/
```

So, now let's do a pivot report on both intranet hits and regular web hits for 2006 (we just show the first two quarters because the report is too long to show in this book otherwise):

```
select * FROM
    (select website_name, hit_type, hit_quarter, num_hits from web_hits)
    pivot (sum(num_hits) for (hit_type, hit_quarter)
    in ( (1,'Q1') as InternetQ01, (2,'Q1') as IntranetQ01,
         (1,'Q2') as InternetQ02, (2,'Q2') as IntranetQ02) )
    order by website_name;
```

| WEBSITE_NAME | INTERNETQ01 | INTRANETQ01 | INTERNETQ02 | INTRANETQ02 |
| --- | --- | --- | --- | --- |
| BILLSBLOG | 16714852 | 1649913 | 16072107 | 1586027 |
| DANSBLOG | 13067698 | 1287610 | 14765095 | 1458939 |
| DAVIDSBLOG | 16187401 | 1600155 | 13432231 | 1325907 |
| JEDSBLOG | 17048080 | 1682478 | 13603270 | 1342954 |
| ROBERTSBLOG | 15591637 | 1538418 | 14779765 | 1460401 |
| TERRYSBLOG | 17207025 | 1699643 | 13213661 | 1301877 |

## The Unpivot Clause

So, perhaps you have a view that is already "pivoted" and you want to flatten it out like a good little third-normal form (3NF) view. Oracle has introduced the **unpivot** clause for just such a case. Assume we have created a pivot table from our earlier queries as seen here:

```
Create table pivot_web_hits as
select * FROM
    (select website_name, hit_type, hit_quarter, num_hits from web_hits)
    pivot (sum(num_hits) for (hit_type, hit_quarter)
    in ( (1,'Q1') as InternetQ01, (2,'Q1') as IntranetQ01,
         (1,'Q2') as InternetQ02, (2,'Q2') as IntranetQ02) )
    order by website_name;
```

Now, we need to unpivot the data in that table, so we use the **unpivot** clause to do so:

```
Select website_name, substr(hit_quarter,9,3), num_hits
from pivot_web_hits
unpivot (num_hits for hit_quarter in (INTERNETQ01, INTERNETQ02) )
Order by website_name, substr(hit_quarter,9,3);
```

```
WEBSITE_NAME      SUB    NUM_HITS
---------------   ---    ----------
BILLSBLOG         Q01    16714852
BILLSBLOG         Q02    16072107
DANSBLOG          Q01    13067698
DANSBLOG          Q02    14765095
DAVIDSBLOG        Q01    16187401
DAVIDSBLOG        Q02    13432231
JEDSBLOG          Q01    17048080
JEDSBLOG          Q02    13603270
ROBERTSBLOG       Q01    15591637
ROBERTSBLOG       Q02    14779765
TERRYSBLOG        Q01    17207025
TERRYSBLOG        Q02    13213661
```

There are a few things to note in this example. First of all, note the slight data transformation with the **substr** command. I used that to remove the INTERNET part of the pivot table column name. Also notice that I explicitly list the column names in the **select** statement. This is because Oracle would try to return the values of the columns INTRANETQ01 and INTRANETQ02 in the query, so I had to filter those out. You can also unpivot multiple columns just as you can pivot multiple columns.

```
Select *
from pivot_web_hits
unpivot (num_hits for (hit_type, hit_quarter) in
  (INTERNETQ01 as ('INTERNET','Q1'),
   INTRANETQ01 as ('INTRANET','Q1'),
   INTERNETQ02 as ('INTERNET','Q2'),
   INTRANETQ02 as ('INTRANET','Q2') ) )
Order by website_name, hit_quarter;

WEBSITE_NAME      HIT_TYPE HI     NUM_HITS
---------------   -------- --     ----------
BILLSBLOG         INTERNET Q1     16714852
BILLSBLOG         INTRANET Q1      1649913
BILLSBLOG         INTERNET Q2     16072107
BILLSBLOG         INTRANET Q2      1586027
DANSBLOG          INTERNET Q1     13067698
DANSBLOG          INTRANET Q1      1287610
DANSBLOG          INTERNET Q2     14765095
DANSBLOG          INTRANET Q2      1458939
... extra output removed for brevity ...
```

# Table Compression

Oracle Database 10*g* offered the ability to compress data within a given table (or table partitions). However, this compression was subject to restrictions that limited the usefulness of the feature. In Oracle Database 11*g*, compression is enhanced and available when executing both regular and bulk-level DML. As a result, updating a row in a compressed table no longer decompresses the associated block. Compression is supported in the following cases:

■ Direct path SQL*Loader operations

■ **Create table as select** commands

■ Parallel inserts, or serial inserts with an append hint

■ Single-row or array insert and updates

Using compression on large tables that are frequently scanned can have a significant positive impact on performance. To compress a table or partition you use the **compress** keyword. Here we see a partitioned table that has only one of its partitions compressed:

```
CREATE TABLE compress_demo (
    tab_id     NUMBER(6),  tab_rec_time date, tab_store varchar2(300) )
PARTITION BY RANGE (tab_rec_time)
   (PARTITION long_ago
       VALUES LESS THAN (TO_DATE('01-JAN-2007', 'DD-MON-YYYY')) COMPRESS,
    PARTITION not_so_long_ago
       VALUES LESS THAN (TO_DATE('01-APR-2007', 'DD-MON-YYYY')),
    PARTITION close_but_not_yet
       VALUES LESS THAN (TO_DATE('01-JUN-2007', 'DD-MON-YYYY')),
    PARTITION now_or_future VALUES LESS THAN (MAXVALUE));
```

You can also use the **alter table move** command to compress existing tables (this would require an outage), or you could use the Oracle online redefinition abilities to reduce outage time to a minimum. Here is an example of using the **alter table** command to compress the contents of a table. Also all future contents will be compressed:

```
Alter table emp move compress;
```

**NOTE**
*Keep in mind that table compression comes with a price in CPU.*

We can determine whether a table or partition is compressed by looking at the compression column in the [DBA/ALL/USER]_TABLES or [DBA/ALL/USER]_TAB_ PARTITIONS views as seen here:

```
select table_name, partition_name, compression
from dba_tab_partitions
```

```
where table_name='COMPRESS_DEMO'
order by 1,2;

TABLE_NAME                          PARTITION_NAME                      COMPRESS
------------------------------      -------------------------------     --------
COMPRESS_DEMO                       CLOSE_BUT_NOT_YET                   DISABLED
COMPRESS_DEMO                       LONG_AGO                            ENABLED
COMPRESS_DEMO                       NOT_SO_LONG_AGO                     DISABLED
COMPRESS_DEMO                       NOW_OR_FUTURE                       DISABLED
```

So how big of a difference does compression make? I did a few experiments on a table that was about 900MB in size with **pctfree** set to 10. I then compressed the table and saw its size reduced to 9MB—yes, you read that right, from 900MB to 9MB compression. This was a table with a mix of numeric and character datatypes. In other testing I saw similar compression.

**NOTE**
*A side effect of compressing a table is that the **pctfree** value for that table is set to 0. Also note that when this book went to press, compression was a separately licensed feature of the Oracle Database. Although Oracle licensing changes over time, you will want to ensure that you are properly licensed before you start using this feature.*

**Arup Says...**
How valuable is the compression feature in 11*g*? Note that compression was available in 10*g* as well, but that was for bulk loads only. Compression in 11*g* allows tables subject to OLTP activity to be compressed as well. The advantage is not just saving space, which is probably trivial in this day and age where disks are really cheap. The real advantage is in saving IO. When the table is compressed, there are fewer blocks, fewer index blocks, and so on, which results in fewer block reads. This in turn reduces cache buffer chains and the need for buffers in the cache, improving the overall performance.

## End of Line

This has been a fun chapter to write, and I hope it was a fun one for you to read. The new features and enhancements in this chapter are very usable ones. The new partition options are outstanding, and some such as interval partitioning, long waited for. Table compression is a spectacular new offering and it's unfortunate that it's going to cost us more money to be able to use it. Oracle Database 11*g* is truly full of new innovation and functionality. I can almost hardly wait to see what's up with Version 11*g*R2!

# CHAPTER
# 8

# Application Development

everal new and improved features related to application development are present in Oracle Database 11*g*. These include SQL*Plus features, new online maintenance types of operations, new SQL features, and finally new PL/SQL-related features. So let's dive into these new features in some more detail.

# SQL*Plus

Oracle Database 11*g* has added new features to SQL*Plus including new **set** commands and Fast Application Notification (FAN) events. In this section we will discuss the new **set** commands first. We will then look at FAN events from RAC.

## New set Commands

In this first section we will discuss the SQL*Plus new **set** commands. First we will discuss the new **set esschar.** We will then cover the **set errorlogging,** command. So, let's get on with it!

### Set esschar

The new SQL*Plus command s**et escchar** is used to define characters that should be escaped in filenames. For example, the @ command is translated by SQL*Plus as the command to run a script. If the @ character is not escaped, then the use of the @ in a given filename could cause problems in SQL*Plus. Valid characters to escape are @, ?, %, and $. Use **set escchar off** to turn off the feature. Here is an example of the use of the **set escchar** command:

```
SQL>set escchar @
SQL>get "file@.sql"
```

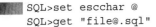
**NOTE**
*Some cases will not require the quotes around the filename.*

### Set errorlogging

SQL*Plus has added the **set errorlogging** command to provide additional methods of trapping errors. When enabled, **set errorlogging** will cause errors generated by SQL, PL/SQL, and SQL*Plus to be written to a logging table (SPERRORLOG by default) for you to review. Oracle will create the SPERRORLOG table if it is not present when you enable error logging. Here is an example of the use of the **set errorlogging** command:

```
-- enable error logging
SQL> set errorlogging on
-- bad query
```

```
SQL> select * from dud;
ORA-00942: table or view does not exist
-- Here is a desc of the sperrorlog that the error messages are written
-- to.
SQL> desc sperrorlog
 Name                                         Null?    Type
 -------------------------------------------- -------- -------------
 USERNAME                                               VARCHAR2(256)
 TIMESTAMP                                              TIMESTAMP(6)
 SCRIPT                                                 VARCHAR2(1024)
 IDENTIFIER                                             VARCHAR2(256)
 MESSAGE                                                CLOB
 STATEMENT                                              CLOB
-- Query the sperrorlog table.
SQL> select username, timestamp, statement, message from sperrorlog;


USERNAME    TIMESTAMP                         STATEMENT
----------  --------------------------------  ----------------------------
MESSAGE
-------------------------------------------
SYS         11-AUG-07 09.54.47.000000 PM      select * from dud
ORA-00942: table or view does not exist
```

## Fast Application Notification Events in an RAC Database

FAN events are events that Oracle RAC uses to notify applications about cluster state and workload service-level changes (such as an instance being started or stopped). SQL*Plus has a new **-F** argument that will allow it to receive these FAN events.

# Online Application Maintenance and Upgrade

Oracle Database 11*g* has added additional online application maintenance and upgrade features that will be helpful to the DBA. These new features include:

- New **ddl_lock_timeout** parameter

- New **lock table** parameter

- Fewer exclusive locks taken during online operations

- Invisible indexes

Let's look at each of these new features in a bit more detail.

## New lock table Parameter

The **lock table** SQL command has a new parameter that is much like the **ddl_lock_timeout** parameter. Using the new **wait** parameter, you can specify that the session should wait a specific amount of time to acquire the lock being requested. Unlike the **ddl_lock_timeout** parameter, there is no limit to how long you can wait to acquire the lock. You can also use the **nowait** parameter to indicate that the session should not wait at all. By default the **lock table** command will wait indefinitely to acquire the lock. Here are examples of the use of the **lock table** command using the **wait** and **nowait** parameters:

```
Lock table my_tab in exclusive mode wait 60;
Lock table my_tab in share mode nowait;
```

## Fewer Exclusive Locks Taken During Online Operations

Say good-bye completely to exclusive locks on the following operations:

- Create index online

- Create materialized view log

- Alter table enable constraint novalidate

## Invisible Indexes

Have you ever created and then dropped an index, just to find that doing so causes your database performance to take a nose dive? Perhaps in creating the index the optimizer starts using it out of the blue, and the results are ugly. Perhaps when you dropped that index, execution plans went wacko because they were dependent on it. Dropping an index can be difficult if a number of concurrent processes are using it. Rebuilding a dropped index can be time-consuming and nerve-wracking when the boss is sitting there eyeing you, and your phone is ringing off the hook.

Now you have a new friend in the index business, the invisible index. An *invisible index* is an index that the optimizer cannot see, and therefore will not consider when generating execution plans even if the index is specifically mentioned in a hint. You can make a new index invisible when you create it. You can then test it with representative SQL statements, including the new index in the hint of the SQL statement, and determine the impact of the SQL statements. Likewise, if you are planning on dropping an index, you can make it invisible. This will invalidate all shared SQL statements that have execution plans using that index, and the optimizer will stop considering that index for use.

You can make an index invisible when you create it with the **create index** command by using the **invisible** keyword as seen in this example:

```
Create index ix_test on test(id) invisible;
```

You can also make an existing index visible or invisible using the **invisible** or **visible** keywords with the **alter index** command as seen in these examples:

```
Alter index ix_test visible;
alter index ix_test invisible;
```

You can override the **invisible** attribute of all indexes by setting the **optimizer_use_invisible_indexes** parameter at the system or session level. Setting this parameter to TRUE will cause the optimizer to consider index usage regardless of the **invisible** setting. You can use the [DBA/ALL/USER]_INDEXES view to determine if an index is visible or invisible as seen in this example:

```
Select index_name, visibility from dba_indexes
where index_name='IX_TEST';
INDEX_NAME                       VISIBILIT
-------------------------------- ---------
IX_TEST                          INVISIBLE
```

Here is an example of the use of an invisible index:

```
-- first the index is visible
SQL> alter index ix_test visible;
Index altered.
SQL> select * from test where id=1;
        ID
----------
         1
---------------------------------------------------------------------------
| Id  | Operation        | Name    | Rows  | Bytes | Cost (%CPU)| Time     |
---------------------------------------------------------------------------
|   0 | SELECT STATEMENT |         |     1 |    13 |     1   (0)| 00:00:01 |
|*  1 |  INDEX RANGE SCAN| IX_TEST |     1 |    13 |     1   (0)| 00:00:01 |
---------------------------------------------------------------------------
-- Now, make it invisible
SQL> alter index ix_test invisible;
Index altered.
SQL> select * from test where id=1;
        ID
----------
         1
---------------------------------------------------------------------------
| Id  | Operation         | Name  | Rows  | Bytes | Cost (%CPU)| Time     |
---------------------------------------------------------------------------
|   0 | SELECT STATEMENT  |       |     1 |    13 |    24   (5)| 00:00:01 |
|*  1 |  TABLE ACCESS FULL| TEST  |     1 |    13 |    24   (5)| 00:00:01 |
---------------------------------------------------------------------------
```

**NOTE**
*If you rebuild an invisible index, the resulting operation will make the index visible.*

# SQL

Several new SQL-related features have been introduced in Oracle Database 11*g*. These include:

- Read-only tables

- The SQL Query Result Cache

- The Client Side Result Cache

- Regular expression enhancements

- Named and mixed notation

Let's look at each of these new features in a bit more detail next.

## Read-Only Tables

The **alter table** command can now be used to make a table read-only. This allows the DBA to make a table read-only across the database, including the owner of the table. The following examples demonstrate the use of the **alter table** command along with the **read only** keywords to make a table read-only, and then the use of the **read write** keywords to make the table read-write:

```
Alter table my_table read only;
SQL> delete from my_table;
delete from my_table
             *
ERROR at line 1:
ORA-12081: update operation not allowed on table "SCOTT"."MY_TABLE"
alter table my_table read write;
```

A new column in the [DBA/ALL/USER]_TABLES view, READ_ONLY, has been added to help you determine if a table is read-write or read-only. Valid values for the READ_ONLY column are YES and NO.

## SQL Query Result Cache

The SQL Query Result Cache is useful in cases where you have large amounts of data that is fairly static, and you query that data on a frequent basis. With SQL Query Result Cache the results of a query are stored in the SGA (the shared pool in an area called the result cache), and then can be used in subsequent queries, or even query fragments. In this section we discuss the SQL Query Result Cache. First we will discuss the parameters used to configure the SQL Query Result Cache. Then we will discuss how the SQL Query uses Result Cache.

**Arup Says...**
This feature can be somewhat simulated in pre-11*g* versions using triggers that raise an exception whenever a DML statement is issued against the table. This was effective but somewhat performance-inhibiting due to context switching. Another way was to define a Virtual Private Database (VPD) policy that always failed. Although that eliminated context switching (especially when the policy is defined static), it also didn't produce any meaningful feedback for the user. This new feature in 11*g* solves both the problems with this simple implementation.

## SQL Query Result Cache Parameters

The parameter **result_cache_max_size** can be set to indicate the maximum size of the SQL Query Result Cache. This parameter is dynamically allocated by Oracle at database startup if you do not set it. Setting this parameter to 0 will disable the feature. Note that the PL/SQL Function Result Cache (discussed later in this chapter) also shares this memory area.

**NOTE**
*Remember that the SQL Query Result Cache is part of the shared pool. This is an upgrade consideration since this is a new area of memory in Oracle Database 11g and will thus reduce the amount of total memory available to other areas of the shared pool.*

The defaults that Oracle will use when configuring the result cache differ based on which database parameters are set. Oracle will never allocate more than 75 percent of shared pool memory to the result cache. The following table lists the parameters that can be set, and which default percentage Oracle will use for allocating shared pool memory to the result cache.

Note that the result cache will not be very efficient if the data changes frequently, as Oracle will invalidate a cached result when transactions modify the data, or any of the metadata of the associated objects used in the cached results. Oracle uses a least-recently-used algorithm to age out result cache results.

| Parameter | Default Percentage of Shared Pool to Result Cache |
| --- | --- |
| memory_target | 0.25% |
| sga_target | 0.50% |
| Shared_pool_size | 1% |

You can globally control result caching by setting the **result_cache_mode** parameter. Valid values are

- **MANUAL** Oracle will not use SQL Query Result Cache by default. You must use the **result_cache** hint in order to use SQL Query Result Cache.

- **FORCE** If possible, all results will use SQL Query Result Cache. The **no_result_cache** hint can be used to bypass the result cache.

Another parameter, **result_cache_max_result**, controls the maximum percentage of the total result cache memory that any one result can consume. The default for this value is 5 (5 percent) and can be from 1 to 100. Something else to note is that in Oracle Database 11*g* Release 1 the result cache is not included in the view V$SHARED_POOL_ADVICE.

When **result_cache_mode** is set to **manual**, you need to use the **result_cache** hint in your SQL statements to indicate to Oracle that you want to store the results of the query in the result cache. If the **result_cache_mode** is set to **force** then all query results will be cached in the result cache. In this case, if you issue a SQL statement and you want it to bypass the result cache, you can use the **no_result_cache** hint.

### Using the Result Cache

You can tell if you are using the result cache by looking at the execution plan of your SQL statement. Here is an example of a SQL statement that uses the **result_cache** hint, along with its associated execution plan (the output is cleaned up for the benefit of the size of this page):

```
select /*+ result_cache */ sum(sal) sum from emp;
      SUM
----------
    29025
```

| Id | Operation | Name | Rows | Bytes | Cost |
|----|-----------|------|------|-------|------|
| 0 | SELECT STATEMENT | | 1 | 4 | 3 |
| 1 | **RESULT CACHE** | **67v5fz5wzz2ad7ruhbmr8wqanu** | | | |
| 2 | SORT AGGREGATE | | 1 | 4 | |
| 3 | TABLE ACCESS FULL | EMP | 14 | 56 | 3 |

Note the result cache line in the execution plan. It indicates that the SQL Query Result Cache is being used. Oracle provides a view, V$RESULT_CACHE_OBJECTS, that you can use to review the status of the result cache item. The parameter **cache_id** relates to the value in the NAME column of the execution plan. Thus I can execute this query:

```
Select name, status, row_count,creation_timestamp
from v$result_cache_objects
where cache_id='67v5fz5wzz2ad7ruhbmr8wqanu';
```

| NAME | STATUS | ROW_COUNT | CREATION_ |
|------|--------|-----------|-----------|
| select /*+ result_cache */ sum(sal) sum from emp | Published | 1 | 07-AUG-07 |

So, looking at the execution plan, the result cache operation will always appear. How do you tell if you are actually using the result cache? The biggest hint will be in reduced consistent GETs. For example in the first run of the example **select** statement in this section, I had four consistent reads as it read the EMP table and populated the cache. After the first run, my consistent reads were reduced to 0.

### Arup Says...

Those who are familiar with materialized views (MV) can surely draw a parallel between the result cache and materialized views. While they may appear similar, they are very different and are suitable for separate scenarios. An MV creates a stored object on the database, akin to tables. You can convert a regular table into an MV, create indexes, create MVs on other MVs, and so on. Result caches are stored in memory, not in the database; they are sort of MVs created on the fly. Query rewrite must be enabled to let a query use the MV instead of running the query against a table; no such thing is needed for result cache, as long as the session or system parameter says so. But the most important difference is the way the data is considered to be stale. In MVs, if the data is stale, the optimizer still gets it, provided the parameter **stale_tolerated** is set. In result cache, when the underlying data changes, the cache is recomputed, so you get the best of both worlds.

Remember those pesky queries that took forever to run against dictionary objects such as X$BH or DBA_FREE_SPACE, especially in a very large database? In some cases such as our 64TB data warehouse, it's virtually impossible to run the queries against the view DBA_FREE_SPACE, as it sucks up the resources and probably never comes back at all so we have to kill it. So, we resorted to creating a table from the view and run the query against it. One tempting question that might pop up is: will result cache make these types of queries faster? It is a perfect condition for result cache, since the dictionary view is fairly static. Sadly, the answer is no. Result cache can't be applied to dictionary tables and views.

One other caveat in using result cache is that you must use a *deterministic* function. A deterministic function always returns the same value when the same data is passed to it. One example of a deterministic function is SUM(), which always returns the same value every time two specific values are passed into it, regardless of the time of the day. On the other hand, consider SYSDATE, whose return value changes every time it is called, making it nondeterministic. If you use such a function in the query, result cache will not be used.

## Managing the Result Cache

Oracle provides a PL/SQL package, **dbms_result_cache**, that provides information on the result cache. For example, you can generate a report on the result cache memory utilization with **dbms_result_cache.memory_report**. You can flush the result cache with **dbms_result_cache.flush**. Also, Oracle provides new views to help manage the result cache. These include:

- **V$RESULT_CACHE_STATISTICS**   Provides information and statistics on cache settings and memory usage

- **V$RESULT_CACHE_MEMORY**   Provides a list of all memory blocks and related statistics

- **V$RESULT_CACHE_OBJECTS**   Provides a list of all cached results (objects and dependencies)

- **V$RESULT_CACHE_DEPENDENCY**   Provides a dependency list for items in the result cache

You can generate a report on the result cache using the Oracle PL/SQL procedure **dbms_result_cache.memory_report** as seen in this example:

```
SQL> set serveroutput on
SQL> dbms_result_cache.memory_report
 SQL> exec dbms_result_cache.memory_report
R e s u l t   C a c h e   M e m o r y   R e p o r t
[Parameters]
Block Size          = 1K bytes
Maximum Cache Size  = 864K bytes (864 blocks)
Maximum Result Size = 43K bytes (43 blocks)
[Memory]
Total Memory = 103528 bytes [0.077% of the Shared Pool]
... Fixed Memory = 5132 bytes [0.004% of the Shared Pool]
... Dynamic Memory = 98396 bytes [0.073% of the Shared Pool]
....... Overhead = 65628 bytes
....... Cache Memory = 32K bytes (32 blocks)
........... Unused Memory = 30 blocks
........... Used Memory = 2 blocks
.............. Dependencies = 1 blocks (1 count)
.............. Results = 1 blocks
................. SQL     = 1 blocks (1 count)
PL/SQL procedure successfully completed.
```

You can flush the result cache with the PL/SQL procedure **dbms_result_cache.flush**.

### Result Cache Restrictions

There are some restrictions to be aware of with regards to the result cache. These include:

- Result cache does not support queries against data dictionary objects

- Result cache does not support queries against temporary tables

- Sequence pseudo columns (**currval** and **nextval**) are not supported.

- Queries that use the following SQL functions: **current_date**, **current_ timestamp**, **local_timestamp**, **userenv/sys_context**, **sys_guid**, **sysdate** and **sys_timestamp**.

- Non-deterministic PL/SQL functions.

# Client Side Result Cache

Related to the SQL Query Result Cache is the Client Side Result Cache. The Client Side Result Cache is use to improve query results on client-side applications. Client Side Result Cache differs from SQL Query Result Caching in that the query result set can be cached on both the server and the client side. The client side of the result cache is enabled by setting two parameters:

- **CLIENT_RESULT_CACHE_SIZE**   This is the maximum size of the client result cache in bytes. This is a per-process limit, thus it is cumulative on a per-process basis.

- **CLIENT_RESULT_CACHE_LAG**   This is the maximum time in milliseconds between client round trips to the server to determine if any database changes related to the query have occurred.

# Regular Expression Enhancements

Oracle Database 11*g* has added two new features to regular expressions. The first is the ability to access the *n*th subexpression from **regexp_substr** and **regexp_instr**. The second is the ability to return the number of times that a pattern match is found based on an input string when using the **regexp_count** function. Let's look at each of these in a bit more detail.

### Access to the *N*th Subexpression from regexp_substr and regexp_instr

A new parameter, **subexpr**, has been added to **regexp_instr** and **regexp_substr** that allows you to find the *n*th occurrence of a subexpression of an input string. Here is an example: Let's assume that we have a string of characters that represents a set of flight pairs and we want to find the second subexpression of that pair. Our string might look like 1okcslclas2lasslcokc3okcslclas4lasslcokc, which might read "flight 1 goes from OKC to SLC to LAS, flight 2 goes from LAS to SLC to OKC," and so on. If I want to find the position of the SLC string in the second OKCSLCLAS flight string, I might run this **select** statement:

```
SELECT  REGEXP_INSTR('1OKCSLCLAS2LASSLCOKC3OKCSLCLAS4LASSLCOKC',
'(OKC)(SLC)(LAS)', -- The regular expression patterns
2, -- Where to start searching
1, -- Which occurrence
0, -- This is the return option
'i', -- This is the match option (case insensitive)
2) -- This is the sub-expression (SLC) on which to search
"Position" FROM dual;

   Position
 ----------
         5
```

### The REGEXP_COUNT Function

The REGEXP_COUNT function returns the number of times that a given pattern appears in a string. Here is an example:

```
SELECT  REGEXP_COUNT('1OKCSLCLAS2LASSLCOKC3OKCSLCLAS4LASSLCOKC',
'OKCSLCLAS', -- The regular expression pattern
 2, -- Where (position) to start searching
'i') -- case insensitive search
"Count" FROM dual;
      Count
 ----------
         2
```

# Named and Mixed Notation from SQL

Oracle Database 11*g* now supports named and mixed notation for PL/SQL calls within a SQL statement. For example:

```
Create or replace function my_func
                  (p_one in number default 1, p_two in number default 5)
return number
is
    v_num  number;
begin
    v_num:=p_one+(p_two*3.14159);
    return v_num;
end;
/
select my_func(p_two=>20) from dual;
```

**NOTE**
*The **call** statement also accepts named and mixed notation.*

# PL/SQL

Oracle continues to improve on PL/SQL in Oracle Database 11*g* with a number of new features and enhancements. These include:

- The ability to create triggers as enabled or disabled
- The **create trigger follows** clause
- Compound triggers
- Inlining
- The SIMPLE_INTEGER datatype
- PL/SQL function result cache
- Dynamic SQL
- Dynamic SQL and REF cursors
- PLW06009 warning
- PL/SQL sequence enhancements
- PL/SQL **continue** statement

We will look at these new and enhanced features in the next several sections.

## Create Triggers as Enabled or Disabled

Oracle Database 11*g* allows you to create a trigger either as enabled (the default) or disabled using the new **enabled** or **disable** clause. If you want to create a trigger as disabled, you would use the **disable** clause as seen in this example:

```
Create or replace trigger trigger_two
before insert on test
disable
begin
    null;
end;
/
```

## Create Trigger Follows Clause

The **follows** clause in the **create trigger** command lets you define the order in which a set of triggers will follow when executing. For example, suppose you had two triggers that were both **before insert** triggers. One was called TRIGGER_ONE and the other was called TRIGGER_TWO. If you wanted TRIGGER_TWO to always follow TRIGGER_ONE in execution, you would write TRIGGER_TWO using the **follows** clause as in this example:

```
Create or replace trigger trigger_two
before insert on test
follows trigger_one
begin
    null;
end;
/
```

### Arup Says...

The FOLLOWS functionality is also known as ordered trigger execution facility, which ensures the order in which the triggers are executed if there are multiple triggers of the same type. Now, this begs a question: How big a deal is it to have triggers executed in a specified order?

It's a big deal in some cases. For instance, a trigger populates some variable or value, which is then used by all other triggers of the same type. In this case, the first trigger must be executed first; otherwise the variable will not be set at all, or set incorrectly. Prior to Oracle 11*g*, you had only one option: put all the code in one trigger to guarantee the execution order. However, that also took away a big functionality—the ability to modularize the code into coherent, manageable pieces. In many cases it actually makes sense to put multiple triggers of the same type to do many types of work. For instance, consider a table that has a BEFORE INSERT ROW trigger to put some calculated value into one of the columns. Later, another functionality was needed—to encrypt the value. Before 11*g* you had only one choice—putting the encryption code in the same trigger. However, in doing so, you introduced a risk by modifying an existing code. The better approach is to put the encryption code on a separate before-insert-row trigger and leave the original trigger alone. This also allows you to selectively disable/enable the triggers. Before 11*g*, you couldn't do that since the order of firing was not guaranteed; in 11*g*, you can easily set the clause that guarantees that the encryption code trigger will fire only after the value-setting trigger. You get the best of both worlds.

# Compound Triggers

If you have ever dealt with mutating trigger problems, then you will be interested in compound triggers. In this section we will review compound triggers, and then look at an example of one in use.

## Compound Trigger Overview

A compound trigger is a PL/SQL trigger (no C or Java, nor can it call C or Java procedures) that allows you to define actions that should occur at one of four trigger points. These points are

- Before the firing statement

- Before each row that the firing statement impacts

- After each row that the firing statement impacts

- After the firing statement

When one of these states is reached, a common set of PL/SQL code will fire, but that code is independent of the state of the trigger that fired it (kind of the way the package you modeled to handle mutating table errors was a separate object prior to Oracle Database 11*g*). Once the PL/SQL code executes, the state is destroyed, regardless of the success of the PL/SQL code that was executed. Note that a compound trigger can only be fired in the event of a DML statement.

The compound trigger has two main sections. The first is the initial section where variables and subprograms are declared. This is essentially like a normal trigger, and code written in this part of the trigger will execute before any of the code defined in the optional sections.

The optional section is where the code is created for the four trigger points in the preceding list. The triggering points must appear in the order listed in the preceding bulleted list.

Compound triggers can be associated with both tables and views. Also note that if the compound trigger executes and then a rollback occurs, the local variables associated with the compound trigger will be reset. Also if you have more than one trigger on a table, you cannot be assured of the firing order of the compound trigger.

## Compound Trigger Example

In this example we will assume that there is a table called SECRET_STUFF. It's a pretty simple table that looks like this:

```
create table secret_stuff(id number primary key,
                    description varchar2(30),
                    last_upd_user_id number );
```

Whenever something is changed in the SECRET_STUFF table, we want an audit record created in WHO_TOUCHED_SECRET_STUFF, which looks like this:

```
create table who_touched_secret_stuff(id number,
                                       touch_date date,
                                       user_id number );
alter table who_touched_secret_stuff add constraint pk_wtss
primary key (id, touch_date);
```

In the olden days it took a mess of code to do this auditing. We would have to create our trigger, and we would also create a package that would collect the information that needed to go into the WHO_TOUCHED_SECRET_STUFF table and then write it out to that table when yet another trigger fired. With a compound trigger, we just have one set of code to encapsulate all the trigger logic. Let's look at an example and then we will look at some of the details of that example:

```
CREATE OR REPLACE TRIGGER ctr_audit_secret_stuff
FOR INSERT OR UPDATE ON secret_stuff
COMPOUND TRIGGER
--Initial section begins
--Declarations
threshhold CONSTANT SIMPLE_INTEGER := 10;
TYPE secret_stuff_t IS TABLE OF who_touched_secret_stuff%rowtype
INDEX BY PLS_INTEGER;
v_secret_stuff secret_stuff_t;
idx SIMPLE_INTEGER:=0;
-- subprogram
PROCEDURE Flush_Secret_Array IS
n CONSTANT SIMPLE_INTEGER := v_secret_stuff.Count();
BEGIN
FORALL j IN 1..n
INSERT INTO who_touched_secret_stuff VALUES v_secret_stuff (j);
v_secret_stuff.Delete();
idx := 0;
END Flush_secret_Array;
-- Initial section ends
-- Optional section
BEFORE STATEMENT IS
BEGIN
v_secret_stuff.Delete();
idx := 0;
END BEFORE STATEMENT;
AFTER EACH ROW IS
BEGIN
idx := idx + 1;
v_secret_stuff(idx).ID:= :New.ID;
v_secret_stuff(idx).touch_Date := SYSDATE();
```

```
v_secret_stuff(idx).user_id := :New.last_upd_user_id;
IF idx >= Threshhold THEN
Flush_Secret_Array();
END IF;
END AFTER EACH ROW;
AFTER STATEMENT IS
BEGIN
Flush_Secret_Array();
END AFTER STATEMENT;
END ctr_audit_secret_stuff;
/
```

There are several things to note in this code. First we configured the ability to do bulk loading of records into the WHO_TOUCHED_SECRET_STUFF audit table. In this case, if you insert a number of records in one **insert** statement, every 10 statements will result in a bulk load into the audit table. Note the **forall** call in the **flush_secret_array** procedure that does the bulk loads.

**NOTE**
*The other two trigger points we didn't use were the **before statement** and **before each row** trigger points.*

We created a collection called V_SECRET_STUFF that holds the data that we need to load into the audit table. In this code, we use two of the four trigger points, **after each row** and **after statement**. In the **after each row** section, as a row is inserted into the table, we populate V_SECRET_STUFF with the data from that row and increment the index. Note that in this section, if the array index reaches the value of **threshold**, the array is flushed and the data is written. Each time an **insert** statement completes, the **after statement** section runs, which flushes the array, thus ensuring all changes are recorded in the audit table.

Here is a demonstration of the resulting trigger in action:

```
SQL> insert into secret_stuff values (1,'test',1);
1 row created.
SQL> select * from who_touched_secret_stuff;
        ID TOUCH_DAT     USER_ID
---------- --------- ----------
         1 07-AUG-07           1
SQL> rollback;
Rollback complete.
SQL> select * from who_touched_secret_stuff;
no rows selected
SQL> select * from secret_stuff;
no rows selected
```

**Arup Says...**

Compound triggers embody the concept of a tight little package of code that must be self-contained in the sense that it should be initialized when called and destroyed at the end. The example of mutating table error, as Robert mentions, is a classic example where you have to employ **before** and **after** statements and row triggers, along with a complex array of packaged variables, to pass tons of data back and forth between the triggers. Compound triggers changed all that. A compound trigger is a single piece of code. To pass data back and forth between multiple parts of the code, you don't need to have packaged variables, but simple PL/SQL variables, which are not only easier to use, but offer a broad choice of datatypes and collections as well. Compound triggers also place all the logic for a particular functionality inside one piece of code, which makes it easier to maintain.

```
SQL> insert into secret_stuff values (2,'testagain',3);
1 row created.
SQL> commit;
Commit complete.
SQL> select * from secret_stuff;
        ID DESCRIPTION                        LAST_UPD_USER_ID
---------- ------------------------------- ----------------
         2 testagain                                       3
SQL> select * from who_touched_secret_stuff;
        ID TOUCH_DAT    USER_ID
---------- --------- ----------
         2 07-AUG-07          3
```

Compound triggers on views follow the same basic design except they have three trigger points, the **before statement**, **instead of each row,** and the **after each row**.

## Inlining

In the previous section, did you notice that we had a piece of code (**flush_secret_array**) that was called from within the body of the code in a couple of places? There are cases where it will be more efficient for Oracle to actually move that piece of code into the different sections, in place of the actual call to the code. This is an optimization that the Oracle PL/SQL optimizer can do, called *inlining*. You can also identify code that you think should be inlined by using the **pragma inline** call in your PL/SQL code, which would look something like this pseudocode:

```
Create or replace procedure add_pragma is …
    function proc_run(a pls_integer) is
        <function code>
    end;
```

**Arup Says…**

Inlining is an example of how conventional wisdom could be detrimental in some cases. Best practices in many languages preach a common theme—divide and conquer; in other words, break the code into smaller pieces (modules) and call the modules. They make maintenance of the code so much simpler. However, unfortunately, they impacted performance in PL/SQL programs. In Oracle Database 11g, inlining now allows you to write maintainable code while letting Oracle transform the code into better-performing code.

```
begin
    pragma inline(proc_run, 'YES');
    a:=proc_run(1);
end;
```

To get Oracle to consider inlining when not using a PRAGMA, we need to set the **plsql_optimize_level** to 3. For example, if we wanted to have Oracle consider inlining for the compound trigger , we would issue the following call:

```
ALTER SESSION SET PLSQL_Warnings = 'enable:all';
ALTER SESSION SET PLSQL_Optimize_Level = 3;
ALTER SESSION SET PLSQL_Code_Type = native;
```

When we compiled the trigger we would find that we get two warnings indicating our calls to **flush_secret_array** were inlined:

```
SQL> show err
Errors for TRIGGER CTR_AUDIT_SECRET_STUFF:
LINE/COL ERROR
-------- -------------------------------------------------------------------
32/1     PLW-06005: inlining of call of procedure 'FLUSH_SECRET_ARRAY' was
         done
37/1     PLW-06005: inlining of call of procedure 'FLUSH_SECRET_ARRAY' was
         done
```

## SIMPLE_INTEGER Datatype

The **simple_integer** datatype is a subtype of the **pls_integer** datatype. The **simple_integer** datatype has the same numeric range as **pls_integer** (-2147483648 to +2147483648) but lacks overflow checking (entering the largest number+1 will wrap to the smallest number, and the reverse). Additionally this datatype will not allow NULL values. These two differences serve to make the internal operation of **simple_integer** faster than that of **pls_integer** when using native PL/SQL compilation. There is also some reported performance improvement with non-native PL/SQL.

**NOTE**
*Since the **simple_integer** datatype is declared as a **not null** datatype, you must assign it a value when defining it.*

# PL/SQL Function Result Cache

The PL/SQL Function Result Cache is much like the SQL Query Result Cache. It allows PL/SQL function results to be cached in the SGA, reducing memory requirements overall, improving performance and scalability. A PL/SQL function can take advantage of the PL/SQL Function Result Cache by adding the **result_cache** clause to the function definition. When enabled, Oracle will check the result cache to see if a previous call to the function exists (using the same parameters) and if so it will return the cached result instead of executing the function.

Restrictions on PL/SQL Function Result Cache include:

- The function cannot be defined in a module using invoker's rights.

- The function cannot be used in an anonymous block.

- The function cannot have any OUT or IN OUT parameters.

- The function cannot have IN parameters that are BLOB, CLOB, NCLOB, REF CURSOR, collections, objects, or records.

- The function cannot return a **blob**, **clob**, **nclob**, **ref cursor**, objects, or records. It can return a collection as long as the collection does not contain one of these types.

An example of using the **result_cache** clause is seen in this sample PL/SQL function. Note that we have also included the optional **relies_on** clause to indicate that the EMP table is a dependency of the cached result:

```
Create or replace function get_name (id number)
return varchar2
result_cache relies_on(emp)
is
     v_return varchar2(30);
begin
    select ename into v_return from emp where empno=id;
    Return v_return;
end;
/
```

The PL/SQL Function Result Cache is controlled by the same parameters as the SQL Result Cache, which is discussed earlier in this chapter.

## Dynamic SQL

Oracle has enhanced both the **dbms_sql** package and native dynamic SQL (**execute immediate**) functionality in several ways including:

- Native dynamic SQL statements can now exceed 32kb.

- **dbms_sql.parse** is now overloaded for **clobs**.

- **dbms_sql** now supports abstract datatypes such as collections, **refs**, and **opaque** types.

- **dbms_sql** allows bulk binds using user-defined collection types.

## Dynamic SQL and REF Cursors

A REF CURSOR can now be converted into a **dbms_sql** cursor. The reverse is also true. This is supported with the new procedures in **dbms_sql** called **dbms_sql.to_ refcursor** and **dbms_sql.to_cursor_number**. Here is an example of using **dbms_sql .to_refcursor** to take a **dbms_sql** cursor and convert it into a **ref cursor**:

```
CREATE OR REPLACE PROCEDURE find_emp_by_mgr (mgr_id NUMBER)
IS
TYPE name_list IS TABLE OF VARCHAR2(30) INDEX BY BINARY_INTEGER;
TYPE cur_type IS REF CURSOR;
src_cur cur_type;
c_hndl NUMBER;
emp_nos name_list;
ename_list name_list;
ret INTEGER;
sql_stmt CLOB;
BEGIN
c_hndl := DBMS_SQL.OPEN_CURSOR;
sql_stmt := 'SELECT empno, ename FROM emp
WHERE mgr = :b1';
DBMS_SQL.PARSE(c_hndl, sql_stmt, DBMS_SQL.NATIVE);
DBMS_SQL.BIND_VARIABLE(c_hndl, 'b1', mgr_id);
ret := DBMS_SQL.EXECUTE(c_hndl);
-- switch from dbms_sql to native dynamic SQL
src_cur := DBMS_SQL.TO_REFCURSOR(c_hndl);
-- fetch with native dynamic SQL
FETCH src_cur BULK COLLECT INTO emp_nos, ename_list;
IF emp_nos.COUNT > 0 THEN
DBMS_OUTPUT.PUT_LINE ('   Empno Name');
DBMS_OUTPUT.PUT_LINE ('-------- ------------');
FOR i IN 1 .. emp_nos.COUNT LOOP
DBMS_OUTPUT.PUT_LINE(emp_nos(i) || ' ' || ename_list(i));
```

```
END LOOP;
END IF;
CLOSE src_cur;
END find_emp_by_mgr;
/
```

And the result:

```
SQL> exec find_emp_by_mgr(7902);
Empno Name
-------- ------------
7369 SMITH
```

# PLW 06009 Warning

If you use PL/SQL warnings much, you will notice a new one in Oracle Database 11g. The PLW-06009 warning is now provided to indicate if there is a **when others** exception handler that does not pass the exception up to the calling routine. For example, if I have a procedure such as the following, it will raise this new error because there is nothing done in the **when others** exception:

```
ALTER SESSION SET PLSQL_Warnings = 'enable:all';
Create or replace procedure my_proc
is
v_val     varchar2(30);
begin
    select ename into v_val from emp where rownum < 2;
exception
when others then NULL;
End;
/
SP2-0804: Procedure created with compilation warnings
SQL> show err
Errors for PROCEDURE MY_PROC:
LINE/COL ERROR
-------- -----------------------------------------------------------------
----
7/6      PLW-06009: procedure "MY_PROC" OTHERS handler does not end in
         RAISE or RAISE_APPLICATION_ERROR
```

# PL/SQL Sequence Enhancement

Oracle Database 11g has improved sequence use in PL/SQL. You can now directly assign the next and current value of a sequence as an assignment as in this sample PL/SQL code:

```
Declare
     Seq_id  number;
     seq_two number;
```

> **Arup Says...**
> If I were to compile a list of felonious offenses in PL/SQL programming practices,
> the practice of writing **when others then null** would rank high, very high.
> Unfortunately, it's also a very commonly used sloppy programming practice that
> is a breeding ground for bugs later. It's high time Oracle put some type of quality
> check into the PL/SQL compilation process; and now it has done so—in the
> form of the warning.
>
> However, the check for **when others then null** does not happen automatically.
> To make the compiler check for it, you have to compile with the special compiler
> directive **plsql_warnings** as shown in this example:
>
> ```
> alter procedure p compile plsql_warnings = 'enable:all';
> ```
>
> If you omit the clause **plsql_warnings**, the compiler will not check for this
> construct.

```
Begin
     Seq_id:=the_sequence.nextval;
     seq_two:=the_sequence.currval;
     dbms_output.put_line(seq_id);
     dbms_output.put_line(seq_two);
End;
/
```

# PL/SQL Continue Statement

Many programming languages have a **continue** statement that can be used inside a
looping structure to cause the next iteration of the loop to occur, rather than process
the remainder of the current loop iteration. In complex looping structures this can
save some processing time. Oracle Database 11*g* now provides the **continue**
statement for this very purpose. Here is a simple example:

```
Set serveroutput on
Declare
     v_counter    number:=0;
begin
     for count in 1..10
     LOOP
         v_counter:=v_counter + 1;
         dbms_output.put_line('v_Counter = '||v_counter);
         continue when v_counter > 5;
         v_counter:=v_counter+1;
     END LOOP;
end;
/
```

```
v_Counter = 1
v_Counter = 3
v_Counter = 5
v_Counter = 7
v_Counter = 8
v_Counter = 9
v_Counter = 10
v_Counter = 11
v_Counter = 12
v_Counter = 13
```

You can also continue to outer loops by creating a label before the outermost loop and then issuing a **continue** statement as in this example:

```
Set serveroutput on
Declare
     v_counter    number:=0;
begin
     <<BeforeLoop>>
     for outer_loop in 1..10
     LOOP
          for count in 1..10
          LOOP
               v_counter:=v_counter + 1;
               dbms_output.put_line('v_Counter = '||v_counter);
               continue BeforeLoop when v_counter > 5;
               v_counter:=v_counter+1;
          END LOOP;
     END LOOP;
end;
/
```

# End of Line

Once again we have seen in this chapter that Oracle Database 11*g* has a number of new features. In this chapter we looked at new features revolving around SQL*Plus, Online Application Maintenance, SQL and PL/SQL. As always, the new features that Oracle introduces make our lives much easier, and make the database product much more powerful. Arup has done a great job of further highlighting these new features!

# CHAPTER
## 9

## Performance Tuning

erformance tuning in Oracle has always been an important part of the DBA's life. We have already discussed certain features such as Database Replay and the SQL Performance Analyzer (both in Chapter 5). This chapter covers more on Oracle Database 11*g* performance-related features. We look at improvements in monitoring Oracle Database–related processes, several statistics-related changes, SQL Plan Management, and several other new performance-tuning–related features in Oracle Database 11*g*. Now strap in, throttle up, and let's go ballistic!

# Enhanced Oracle Process Monitoring

Sometimes an Oracle process (like SMON) will cause database performance-related issues. You can now identify the events that are causing the database problems by looking at new columns in the V$SYSTEM_EVENT view. The new columns are

- **TOTAL_WAITS_FG**   This is the total number of waits that a foreground/background session waited for the event.

- **TOTAL_TIMEOUTS_FG**   This is the total number of timeouts for an event that a foreground/background session waited.

- **TIME_WAITED_FG**   This is the amount of time that a foreground/background session waited for the event in centaseconds.

- **AVERAGE_WAIT_FG**   This is the average wait time that a foreground/background process waited for the event in centaseconds.

- **TIME_WAITED_MICRO_FG**   This is the total time in microseconds that a foreground session spent waiting on an event.

For example, I could run the following query to find all cumulative waits of more than one second that occurred on foreground/background processes:

```
select event, total_waits_fg twg, total_timeouts_fg ttf,
time_waited_fg twf, average_wait_fg awf,
time_waited_micro_fg twmf
from v$system_event
where time_waited_micro_fg > 1000000
and wait_class !='Idle';
```

| EVENT | TWG | TTF | TWF | AWF | TWMF |
|---|---|---|---|---|---|
| db file sequential read | 10,449 | 0 | 2,347 | 0 | 23,474,002 |
| db file scattered read | 894 | 0 | 384 | 0 | 3,843,803 |

```
library cache load lock      11        0        136      12  1,362,976
resmgr:cpu quantum           66        0        770      12  7,703,445
reliable message              4        2        251      63  2,511,143
control file heartbeat        1        1        400     400  3,999,654
```

So, in this case it seems that the background processes are having issues with the disk. Since it's a cumulative time of 23 seconds, I probably would not worry too much about the disks if the database has been up for any length of time. The V$SYSTEM_WAIT_CLASS view has many of the same new columns as V$SYSTEM_EVENT.

Further, the AWR-related view DBA_HIST_SYSTEM_EVENT provides these new columns:

- **TOTAL_WAITS_FG**   This is the total number of waits for an event, from a foreground session.

- **TOTAL_TIMEOUTS_FG**   This is the total number of timeouts for an event, from a foreground session.

- **TIME_WAITED_MICRO_FG**   This is the total time in microseconds that a foreground session spent waiting on an event.

So, we could look in the DBA_HIST_SYSTEM_EVENT view to see if our snapshots are picking up a trend and see if background processes are waiting for the db file sequential file read event as seen in this query:

```
select a.begin_interval_time,
substr(a.end_interval_time-a.begin_interval_time,11,9) snap_time_hms,
-- Note we use the lag function here to get the difference in the waits
-- between the two snapshots. A negative number indicates an instance
restart.
b.total_waits_fg
- lag(b.total_waits_fg,1) over (order by a.begin_interval_time) twg,
b.total_timeouts_fg
- lag(b.total_timeouts_fg,1) over (order by a.begin_interval_time) ttf,
b.time_waited_micro_fg
- lag(b.time_waited_micro_fg,1) over (order by a.begin_interval_time) twmf
from dba_hist_snapshot a, dba_hist_system_event b
where a.snap_id=b.snap_id
and a.dbid=b.dbid and a.instance_number=b.instance_number
and b.event_id=2652584166 -- db file sequential read event id
and a.begin_interval_time > sysdate - 4
order by a.begin_interval_time;


BEGIN_INTERVAL_TIME          SNAP_TIME      TWG      TTF          TWMF
-------------------------    ---------    -------  -------  ----------------
09-AUG-07 10.59.41.000 AM    01:00:34
09-AUG-07 12.00.15.262 PM    01:00:06        699        0        2,496,748
09-AUG-07 01.00.21.649 PM    01:00:07        121        0          380,375
```

```
09-AUG-07 02.42.57.000 PM  00:17:09  -9,393        0      -136,038,275
09-AUG-07 03.00.06.749 PM  01:00:06     306        0          691,525
09-AUG-07 04.00.12.952 PM  01:00:06      19        0           30,100
09-AUG-07 05.00.19.068 PM  01:00:06     140        0          298,194
09-AUG-07 06.00.25.883 PM  01:00:07      42        0           91,049
09-AUG-07 07.00.33.078 PM  01:00:07      14        0           46,215
09-AUG-07 08.00.40.416 PM  01:00:07       1        0            1,044
09-AUG-07 09.00.47.609 PM  01:00:08   9,764        0       49,575,851
09-AUG-07 10.00.56.003 PM  00:59:08  11,831        0       24,009,039
```

# Statistics

These days our Oracle databases live and breathe statistics. Statistics can have such a profound impact on execution plans, and we need to be aware of all the new features associated with statistics. In this section we will cover new features including:

- Pending and published statistics

- Recovering previous statistics

- Extended statistics

## Pending and Published Statistics

Oracle Database 11*g* gives you the option of publishing statistics after they are collected (this is the default behavior), or you can have newly collected statistics saved in a pending state. In this section we will look at how to determine whether statistics are published when collected or pending. We will then look at how to control whether collected statistics are published or pending in the database. We will then look at data dictionary views associated with statistics.

### Determine Whether Statistics Are Automatically Published

To determine whether the database will publish statistics when they are generated or they will be held in pending status, you use the **dbms_stats.get_prefs** function. It will return TRUE if the statistics will be published or FALSE if they will not be published. By default the setting for an Oracle Database is TRUE (thus, statistics are published when generated). Here is an example:

```
Select dbms_stats.get_prefs('PUBLISH') from dual;

DBMS_STATS.GET_PREFS('PUBLISH')
--------------------------------
TRUE
```

Oracle also provides a parameter, **optimizer_use_pending_statistics**, that will cause the optimizer to always use pending statistics, if available, rather than published ones. If pending statistics are not available, then Oracle will use the published statistics.

## Modify the Publish Setting

You can change the PUBLISH setting (indicating whether statistics should be published or not when collected) at either the schema or table level. To set an entire schema so that collected statistics should not be published, you would use the **dbms_stats.set_schema_prefs** procedure as seen in this example:

```
Exec dbms_stats.set_schema_prefs('SCOTT', 'PUBLISH', 'false');
```

To modify a table so that it will use not use newly collected statistics until they are published, we can use the **dbms_stats.set_table_prefs** procedure. In this example, we are setting the PUBLISH preference for the EMPLOYEE table to FALSE. As a result, newly collected statistics will be staged, and will not be used until they are published:

```
Exec dbms_stats.set_table_prefs('SCOTT','EMPLOYEE', 'PUBLISH', 'false');
```

## Pending Statistics and the Data Dictionary

Having collected statistics that are pending, you will want to review them to make sure they make sense. Pending table statistics are kept in the USER_TAB_PENDING_STATS data dictionary view. Pending column statistics in the USER_COL_PENDING_STATS data dictionary view and pending index statistics are kept in the USER_IND_PENDING_STATS data dictionary views.

If you determine that you do not wish to publish the pending statistics, you can remove them through the **dbms_stats.delete_pending_stats** procedure. The following example shows how to delete statistics for the entire database, a given schema, and a specific object in a given schema:

```
-- Delete all pending statistics
Exec dbms_stats.delete_pending_stats(null, null);
-- Delete pending statistics for SCOTT
Exec dbms_stats.delete_pending_stats('SCOTT', null);
-- Delete pending statistics for SCOTT.EMPLOYEE
Exec dbms_stats.delete_pending_stats('SCOTT', 'EMPLOYEE');
```

## Publishing Statistics

To publish pending statistics you use the **dbms_stats.publish_pending_stats** procedure. You can publish all pending database statistics as seen in this example:

```
Exec dbms_stats.publish_pending_stats(null,null);
```

You can also choose to publish statistics for a specific schema, as in this example where we are going to publish all pending statistics for the SCOTT schema:

```
Exec dbms_stats.publish_pending_stats('SCOTT',null);
```

We can also publish statistics for a specific object, as seen in this example where we are publishing pending statistics for SCOTT.EMPLOYEE:

```
Exec dbms_stats.publish_pending_stats('SCOTT', 'EMPLOYEE');
```

# Recovering Previous Statistics

It happens. In fact, it happened where I work not all that long ago. You generate statistics on an object only to find that, for whatever reason, you have only made things worse. Maybe the way you generated the statistics was wrong; maybe the problem was related to the time when you generated the statistics (perhaps the table was empty at the time); or maybe you are just having one of those days when nothing goes right.

Oracle sympathizes with your plight. In earlier days, if you were lucky, you had exported your statistics before you regenerated them, so you could import those statistics back into the data dictionary if things went badly. Now Oracle Database 11*g* allows you to restore previous versions of statistics (I'm surprised they don't call this flashback statistics, but what do I know?).

In the following sections we will discuss how to restore statistics, how to maintain the repository of historical statistics, and where to find your old statistics.

### Restoring Old Statistics

Oracle provides several procedures in the **dbms_stats** PL/SQL package that can be used to restore statistics based on a specific timestamp (see the section titled Data Dictionary and Historical Statistics Views later in this section for data dictionary views that will provide timestamps for you to use when restoring statistics). These procedures include:

- **Dbms_stats.restore_dictionary_stats**   Restore data dictionary stats

- **Dbms_stats.restore_fixed_objects_stats**   Restore fixed object stats

- **Dbms_stats.restore_schema_stats**   Restore schema stats

- **Dbms_stats.restore_system_stats**   Restore system stats

- **Dbms_stats.restore_table_stats**   Restore table stats

Let's look at an example. First, let's find out when we last gathered statistics:

```
select * from dba_optstat_operations;
OPERATION       TARGET          START_TIME
--------------------------------- ------------------------------------
END_TIME
------------------------------------
```

```
gather_database_stats(auto)    19-AUG-07 06.00.08.477333 AM -06:00

19-AUG-07 06.02.28.607562 AM -06:00
```

Let's restore the SCOTT schema statistics back to that point in time:

```
Exec dbms_stats.restore_schema_stats('SCOTT',     -
'19-AUG-07 06.00.08.477333 AM -06:00');
```

### Maintaining the Historical Statistics Repository

Oracle will manage the historical statistics repository, purging old statistics on a regular basis, by default every 31 days (meaning that the furthest back you can restore optimizer stats would be within the last 31 days). You can adjust this retention by using the procedure **dbms_stats.alter_stats_history_retention**.

You can manually purge statistics with the **dbms_stats.purge_stats** procedure. There are two other functions that might come in handy:

- **dbms_stats.get_stats_history_retention**   Returns the current retention value

- **dbms_stats.get_stats_history_availability**   Returns the oldest timestamp that can be used to restore statistics

### Data Dictionary and Historical Statistics Views

Oracle Database 11*g* provides different data dictionary views that you can use to view historical statistics. These include:

- **DBA_OPTSTAT_OPERATIONS**   Contains a history of statistics-related operations performed at the schema and database level

- **[DBA/ALL/USER]_TAB_STATS_HISTORY**   Contains a history of table statistics modifications

## Extended Statistics

Oracle Database 11*g* provides the ability to gather additional statistics. These are collectively known as extended statistics. Extended statistics include the following:

- Multicolumn statistics

- Expression statistics

Let's look at each of these new statistic types in more detail next.

### Arup Says...

As long as I remember, this has been a great debate in many forums—the mailing lists, personal discussion forums, and now blogging—whether collection of statistics on a regular basis is useful or not. Some argue that the periodic collection of statistics enables the Cost-Based Optimizer (CBO) to gather more accurate distribution of data to make a sensible decision about execution path, while others argue that the repeated collection forces hard parses and might create a suboptimal plan. Well, there is merit to both arguments. In the prior versions, it has been always been my practice to export the statistics to a table before collecting new stats. But there was this element of fear—what if the new stats wreak havoc on my humming database? And the operations involved in exporting the stats and importing them are not trivial.

Two eagerly awaited features ease that burden. One is what Robert has described here—the decoupling of collection and publicizing of stats and exposing them at will. This will allow you to collect stats when the system is least used, for example, at night, but put off the parsing until a more opportune time. Perhaps morning is not a good time to experiment with a new execution path. No problem; collect the stats at night and publish them in the afternoon. Did something go wrong? Just reinstate the older version. If you have time, you can also reinstate the old version and replay the SQL code through SQL Performance Analyzer to get a sense of how these stats are useful (or the contrary).

The second feature is SQL Plan Management, discussed later in this chapter. SPM allows you to be protected from the potentially harmful execution paths due to the newly collected stats.

## Multicolumn Statistics

Prior to Oracle Database 11*g* Oracle had no way of understanding the relationship of data within multiple columns of a **where** clause. Oracle Database 11*g* adds multicolumn statistics to the mix to try to solve this problem. How do multicolumn statistics work? Let's look at an example. Suppose that in Oracle Database 10*g* we had the following query:

```
Select count(*)
from employee
Where deptno=30;
  COUNT(*)
----------
      6144
```

Now let's add a predicate to the **where** clause to make it more selective:

```
Select count(*)
from employee
```

```
Where deptno=30
and job='SALESMAN';
  COUNT(*)
----------
      4096
```

```
-- Execution Plan
-----------------------------------------------------------------
| Id  | Operation          | Name         | Rows | Bytes| Cost(%CPU)|
-----------------------------------------------------------------
|   0 | SELECT STATEMENT   |              |    1 |   11 |    5  (0)  |
|   1 |  SORT AGGREGATE    |              |    1 |   11 |           |
|*  2 |   INDEX RANGE SCAN | IX_EMPLOYEE  |  892 | 9812 |    5  (0)  |
-----------------------------------------------------------------
```

But what about this case, where we query for a job that does not exist?

```
Select count(*)
from employee
Where deptno=30
and job='JANITOR';
COUNT(*)
----------
        0
```

```
-- Execution Plan
-----------------------------------------------------------------
| Id  | Operation          | Name         | Rows | Bytes| Cost(%CPU)|
-----------------------------------------------------------------
|   0 | SELECT STATEMENT   |              |    1 |   11 |    5  (0)  |
|   1 |  SORT AGGREGATE    |              |    1 |   11 |           |
|*  2 |   INDEX RANGE SCAN | IX_EMPLOYEE  |  892 | 9812 |    5  (0)  |
-----------------------------------------------------------------
```

Note that the execution plan has not changed at all. Oracle has no way of knowing that the JOB column is querying a value that is not present. How can we provide Oracle with better information so that it can know these columns are grouped together, and so that it might generate an execution plan that more accurately reflects the reality of the query? We can use multicolumn statistics.

**Generate Multicolumn Statistics**   We generate multicolumn statistics by first creating the column group, and then collecting statistics. We create the column group with the **dbms_stats.create_extended_stats** call, as seen in this example where we define the EMPLOYEE column group consisting of the DEPTNO and JOB columns:

```
Declare
    cg_name varchar2(30);
```

```
begin
     cg_name := dbms_stats.create_extended_stats(null,
               'EMPLOYEE','(DEPTNO, JOB)' );
end;
/
```

Now that we have defined the column group, let's collect the statistics for the table. In this case, we will use the **method_opt** parameter of the **dbms_stats.gather_table_ stats** procedure to indicate that we want to collect statistics on the DEPTNO/JOB column group:

```
begin
    dbms_stats.gather_table_stats(null,'EMPLOYEE',
      method_opt=>'for all columns size skewonly for columns (DEPTNO,JOB)');
end;
/
```

Alternatively you can use the **method_opt** option **for all columns size auto** to gather statistics for all defined column groups. Now that we have collected the extended multicolumn statistics, let's look at the execution plan for our query:

```
---------------------------------------------------------------
| Id | Operation         | Name        | Rows | Bytes| Cost(%CPU) |
---------------------------------------------------------------
|  0 | SELECT STATEMENT  |             |    1 |   11 |   2    (0) |
|  1 |  SORT AGGREGATE   |             |    1 |   11 |            |
|* 2 |   INDEX RANGE SCAN| IX_EMPLOYEE |  548 | 6028 |   2    (0) |
---------------------------------------------------------------
```

Note that the number of rows reported by the optimizer has decreased significantly in the index range scan. Since the index is built on DEPTNO and JOB, it's still going to have to scan down the DEPTNO rows, but now Oracle is aware that there are likely to be few JOB entries because of the histogram built on the column pairing. Thus, the number of rows returned that the plan reports is reduced.

**NOTE**
*As with many new features, during testing, this seemed to work in a somewhat hit-and-miss way. The technical reviewer could never duplicate the results I had. What is the moral of the story? Carefully test all new features and make sure that they are working, as you would expect.*

**Drop Multicolumn Statistics**   If you find you need to drop a column group that you have previously defined, the **dbms_stats.drop_extended_stats** procedure

can be used. Here is an example where I drop the column group for DEPTNO and
JOB that was created earlier:

```
Exec dbms_stats.drop_extended_stats('SCOTT', 'EMPLOYEE', '(DEPTNO,JOB)');
```

**Multicolumn Statistics Dictionary Views**   You can use the [DBA/ALL/USER]_
STAT_EXTENSIONS data dictionary view to retrieve information on column groups
that have been created. Note the meaningful name (which we have no control over)
assigned to the extension in the EXTENSION_NAME column in this example (that's
dripping sarcasm, just in case you were wondering):

```
Select extension_name, extension
from user_stat_extensions
where table_name='EMPLOYEE';
EXTENSION_NAME                    EXTENSION
------------------------------    ------------------------------
SYS_STU$7LJEWQEV#_NNT_P4FXAU5K ("DEPTNO","JOB")
```

## Expression Statistics

Prior to Oracle Database 11*g*, if you included a function as a predicate in a **select**
statement, Oracle had no way of determining the selectivity of that function. In this
section we will look at why expression statistics are important and how to generate
expression statistics. We will then look at how to drop expression statistics and
review data dictionary views associated with expression statistics.

**What's the Big Deal Anyway?**   Assume that you had a table called EMPLOYEE
with a column called HOME_STATE that indicated the state that the employee lived
in. Here is a partial list of the distribution of the number of employees in each state:

```
Select home_state, count(*)
from employee
group by home_state;

HO   COUNT(*)
--   ----------
ND           1
TX       15359
```

Note that in the state of TX (Texas) we have a large number of employees. In the
state of ND (North Dakota) we have one lonely (and probably very cold) employee.
Now assume that we have the following SQL statements:

```
Select count(*)
from employee
Where lower(home_state)='tx' and empno < 500;
```

```
Select count(*)
from employee
Where lower(home_state)='nd' and empno < 500;
```

In the first statement, we would expect that a full table scan would likely be the best way of getting at our data, and in the second we would assume that index access (using a function-based index, of course) would be best.

In Oracle Database 10*g* and 11*g* by default we find the following execution plans for both of these statements:

```
-------------------------------------------------------------------------------
| Id  | Operation                      | Name        | Rows  | Bytes |
-------------------------------------------------------------------------------
|   0 | SELECT STATEMENT               |             |     1 |     8 |
|   1 |  SORT AGGREGATE                |             |     1 |     8 |
|*  2 |   TABLE ACCESS BY INDEX ROWID| EMPLOYEE    |     5 |    40 |
|*  3 |    INDEX RANGE SCAN            | PK_EMPLOYEE |   499 |       |
-------------------------------------------------------------------------------
```

Note that these plans don't even use our function-based index. Clearly the optimizer in Oracle Database 10*g* is not up to determining the best way to access data when a function is in use. Let's see what happens in Oracle Database 11*g*.

**Enter Expression Statistics**   Oracle Database 11*g* offers expression statistics to solve this problem. First, we have to analyze the table, gathering specific expression statistics on our object. We use the **method_opt** parameter to build these expression statistics, as seen in this example:

```
Begin
    dbms_stats.gather_table_stats(null, 'EMPLOYEE',
        method_opt=>
        'for all columns size skewonly for columns (lower(home_state))');
end;
/
```

Now, when we run our queries, look how the execution plan changes:

```
Select count(*)
from employee
Where lower(home_state)='tx' and empno < 500;
-------------------------------------------------------------------------------
| Id  | Operation           | Name        | Rows  | Bytes |
-------------------------------------------------------------------------------
|   0 | SELECT STATEMENT    |             |     1 |    15 |
|   1 |  SORT AGGREGATE     |             |     1 |    15 |
|*  2 |   TABLE ACCESS FULL | EMPLOYEE    |   500 |  7500 |
-------------------------------------------------------------------------------
```

```
Select count(*)
from employee
Where lower(home_state)='nd' and empno < 500;
```

```
------------------------------------------------------------------
| Id  | Operation                     | Name        | Rows | Bytes |
------------------------------------------------------------------
|   0 | SELECT STATEMENT              |             |    1 |    19 |
|   1 |   SORT AGGREGATE              |             |    1 |    19 |
| * 2 |     TABLE ACCESS BY INDEX ROWID| EMPLOYEE   |    1 |    19 |
| * 3 |       INDEX RANGE SCAN        | FX_EMPLOYEE |    1 |       |
------------------------------------------------------------------
```

Looking at the later execution plan, clearly Oracle now knows that there are a lot of 'tx' rows, and is using a full table scan there. On the other hand, it also knows that 'nd' is a rare bird and is modifying the execution plan as a result of that. Also note that the number of rows in the execution plan is being displayed properly.

**NOTE**
*Of course, several factors can influence the execution plan you get for any query. Here's an example in which two perfectly good new features rather battle themselves. When I first executed the query after analyzing the EMPLOYEE table with the **lower()** function, I was still getting the index range scan. I discovered that the main reason was that I had a SQL baseline plan that was being picked up and used (we will talk about SQL baselines later in this chapter), which defeated my efforts. Only after disabling SQL baselines for the session (by setting the new parameter **optimizer_use_sql_ plan_baselines** to FALSE) did I get the plan I was expecting! Fortunately, this problem only cost me two laptops that I hurled from my office in total frustration. It could have been much worse.*

**Drop Expression Statistics**   You use the **dbms_stats.drop_extended_stats** procedure to drop extended expression statistics. Note that you will not be able to drop an extended expression statistic if a function-based index is dependent on that statistic. Here is an example of the removal of an extended expression statistic:

```
exec dbms_stats.drop_extended_stats(null,'EMPLOYEE','(LOWER("HOME_STATE"))');
```

**NOTE**
*If you get an ORA-20000 error when you run this command, this means that you have a function-based index that depends on this extended statistic. You will have to drop that index in order to drop the statistic. The error text itself is not very helpful in this case.*

**Expression Statistics Dictionary Views**    You can use the [DBA/ALL/USER]_STAT_
EXTENSIONS data dictionary view to retrieve information on expression statistics
that have been created in the database, as seen in this example:

```
Select extension_name, extension
from user_stat_extensions
where table_name='EMPLOYEE';

EXTENSION_NAME                    EXTENSION
-------------------------------   ------------------------------
SYS_STU$7LJEWQEV#_NNT_P4FXAU5K    ("DEPTNO","JOB")
SYS_NC00012$                      (LOWER("HOME_STATE"))
```

# PL/SQL Native Compilation

Oracle Database 11*g* has improved PL/SQL native compilation. First, you no longer
need a C compiler to use this feature. Also, while DLLs are still generated, they are
stored in the database and will load the DLL directly from the catalog. In some cases
Oracle says that you may see performance improvements over Oracle Database 10*g*
by as much as an order of magnitude. Here is an example of creating Oracle
Database 11*g* PL/SQL that is natively compiled:

```
Alter session set plsql_code_type=native;
Create or replace procedure hello_world as
begin
     Dbms_output.put_line('Hello World, I''m a native!');
End;
/
-- We can check the status by looking at dba_plsql_object_settings
select plsql_code_type from all_plsql_object_settings
where name='HELLO_WORLD';
PLSQL_CODE_TYPE
---------------
NATIVE
```

If you have a lot of PL/SQL in your database, you may want to recompile all of
the PL/SQL in the database using native compilation. Oracle provides a process that
you can use to do this. The steps in this process are

1.  Set the **plsql_code_type** parameter to NATIVE (**alter system set plsql_code_
    type=NATIVE).**

2.  Shutdown the database (**shutdown immediate).**

3.  Startup the database in **upgrade** mode (**startup upgrade).**

**Arup Says...**

This is perhaps one of the most useful features in this release. Native compilation is not new; it was available in 9*i* R2. So, what is the big fuss? The major difference between the previous version and this one is the need to have a C compiler. The 11*g* version does not need a C compiler to be installed and defined in the initialization parameter. Most shops loathe or downright prohibit installing a C compiler on a production database for a variety of reasons, security being the topmost, usually. So, even though native compilation was available, it was hardly used. This version makes that feature truly accessible.

4. Execute the script dbmsupgnv.sql in $ORACLE_HOME/rdbms/admin. This will invalidate all of the PL/SQL programs units in the data dictionary, so utlrp.sql will recompile them. You can choose to exclude package specifications when you run this script. Personally I'd just recompile everything.

5. **Shutdown** the database and restart in restricted mode (**startup restrict**).

6. Execute the utlrp.sql script in $ORACLE_HOME/rdbms/admin.

7. Disable restricted session after utlrp.sql completes (**alter system disable restricted session**).

# SQL Plan Management

SQL Plan Management is used to help improve the performance of SQL statements, especially those that are executed frequently. In this chapter we will introduce you to SQL Plan Management. First we will look at an overview of SQL Plan Management. Next we will look at plan capture, including automated plan capture and manual plan capture.

## SQL Plan Management Overview

As SQL statements are executed, Oracle will record the SQL execution plans and maintain a record of which are the most efficient. These plans are known as SQL plan baselines, and these baselines are later used to ensure that system performance will not be negatively impacted by changes that might occur in the system. For example, if a given SQL statement runs subsecond with a given plan, and some change in the system causes that plan to change such that it is no longer subsecond, Oracle will try to revert to the baseline plan to preserve the performance of that SQL statement.

When Oracle captures a plan and determines that it is acceptable, then that plan will be marked by the optimizer as accepted for use. Subsequent execution plans will be analyzed by Oracle Database, and if it is verified that the plan will not cause negative performance, then that plan will be added to the SQL plan baseline. Plans that are captured will "evolve" over time, as Automatic SQL Tuning tries to evolve the plans, improving performance. Plans that you wish to remain unchanged can be marked as fixed within the SQL Plan baseline, which will cause them to remain unchanged.

# Plan Capture

Oracle Database provides two ways of capturing plans. The first is through the use of the automatic plan capture facility. The second method is to manually load the execution plans. In this section we will discuss both of these methods.

## Automatic Plan Capture

Oracle provides a method of automatically capturing SQL execution plans. When automatic plan capture is enabled, Oracle will create and maintain the SQL execution plan history. Various information with regard to the plan is stored including the SQL statement, the execution plan, bind variable information, and other relevant information. Automatic plan capture is not enabled in Oracle Database by default. The parameter **optimizer_capture_sql_plan_baselines** must be set to **true** (**alter system set optimizer_capture_sql_plan_baselines=TRUE**) in order to enable this feature (**false** is the default). This parameter is dynamic and can also be set at the session level with the **alter session** command.

## Manual Plan Loading

You can manually load SQL plans from several sources. These include:

- SQL Tuning Sets

- AWR snapshots

- The cursor cache

Let's look at each of these methods of loading SQL plans in more detail next.

**Loading a Plan Using a SQL Tuning Set**   Loading plans from a SQL Tuning Set (discussed later in this chapter) is quite easy. You use the **dbms_spm.load_plans_from_ sqlset** function to load the SQL Tuning Set into SQL plan baselines (if the account is not a DBA account, you will need the **administer SQL management object** privilege along with the **execute** privilege on the **dbms_spm** package). The plans loaded are not verified for performance and will be marked as accepted plans when loaded. In this example we load SQL plans from the SQL Set Robert into SQL plan baselines:

```
Declare
My_plan_id     pls_integer;
```

```
begin
   my_plan_id:=dbms_spm.load_plans_from_sqlset(
               sqlset_name=>'Robert');
end;
/
```

**NOTE**
*The **dbms_spm.load_plans_from_sqlset** function
provides options to filter plans from the SQL set using
the **basic_filter** parameter. Other options include
the ability to indicate if the plans are fixed, which
indicates that they cannot evolve over time. By
default plans are not fixed, and thus can evolve over
time through the Automatic SQL Tuning process.*

**Loading a Plan Using an AWR Snapshot**   You can load SQL plans from AWR
snapshots into SQL plan baselines. First you will need to convert the AWR snapshot
into a SQL Tuning Set (we discuss how to do this later in this chapter). Once the
tuning set is loaded, you can then create the SQL plan baselines as described in the
previous section.

**Loading a Plan Using the Cursor Cache**   The **dbms_spm.load_plans_from_cursor_
cache** function provides the ability to create a SQL plan baseline from plans stored
in the cursor cache. You will need to query the SQL cache first to determine the
SQL_ID of the statement that you are interested in. You can then load that SQL
statement as a SQL plan baseline, referencing that SQL_ID.

Here is some PL/SQL that will find a specific SQL statement in the cursor cache
and load it in a SQL plan baseline:

```
Declare
   My_sql_plan    pls_integer;
   v_sql          varchar2(1000);
begin
   for dd in (select sql_id from v$sqlarea where
              sql_text like 'select * from scott.emp')
   loop
      if length(dd.sql_id) > 0
      then
          my_sql_plan:=dbms_spm.load_plans_from_cursor_cache
                       (sql_id=>dd.sql_id);
      end if;
   end loop;
end;
/
```

## Use of SQL Plan Baselines

SQL plan baselines are used to avoid SQL plan degradation. When you issue a SQL statement, Oracle will cost that statement using the CBO. Oracle will then compare the cost of that statement against the SQL plan baseline, looking for a match. If it finds a match, then the plan is considered acceptable.

If a match is not found, Oracle will compare the plan against the cost of each accepted plan (plans are accepted using a process called *evolving*, which we will discuss in the next section) that is present in the SQL plan baseline (of course, only plans related to the SQL statement are considered). If a plan with a lower cost is found in the SQL plan baseline, then that plan will be used instead of the one generated by the CBO. If a plan with a lower cost is not found, then the newly generated plan will be stored in the SQL plan baseline and it will not be used until it has been accepted. In this case, the lowest-cost plan, with an accepted status, will be used from the SQL plan baseline. If there is no acceptable plan in the SQL plan baseline, then the generated plan will be used.

You may decide, after testing, that you don't want to use SQL plan baselines. If this is the case, simply set the parameter **optimizer_use_sql_plan_baselines** to **false**. This parameter can be set at either the session or database level. Note that the use of SQL plan baselines can sometimes be confusing when you are trying to tune SQL statements (see a perfect example of this earlier in this chapter).

## Querying SQL Plan Baselines

You can query SQL plan baseline information via the DBA_SQL_PLAN_BASELINES view (there is no ALL or USER view available) as seen in this example:

```
Select sql_handle, plan_name, accepted, version
from dba_sql_plan_baselines
where creator='SCOTT'
and dbms_lob.substr(sql_text, 34,1)='select * from emp where empno=7369';

SQL_HANDLE                       PLAN_NAME                        ACC
-------------------------------- -------------------------------- ---
VERSION
-----------------------------------------------------------------
SYS_SQL_353e8c17a551f70c         SYS_SQL_PLAN_a551f70c695cc014    YES
11.1.0.6.0
```

In this case, there is just one baseline plan for this query. There is just one plan for now, and it is accepted (and thus, it will always be used as long as it is the lowest-cost plan that is accepted).

Now that you have identified the SQL plan baseline for a given SQL statement, you can look at the execution plan of that statement. The **dbms_xplan** PL/SQL package now adds the **display_sql_plan_baseline** call, which will show you the current execution plan for a given SQL_HANDLE (which we found via the call to the DBA_SQL_PLAN_BASELINES view in the preceding code). Here is an example of using **dbms_xplan.display_sql_plan_baseline** to get the execution plan:

```
Select * from table (dbms_xplan.display_sql_plan_baseline    -
      (sql_handle=>'SYS_SQL_353e8c17a551f70c',format=>'basic'));


PLAN_TABLE_OUTPUT
------------------------------------------------------------------------
SQL handle: SYS_SQL_353e8c17a551f70c
SQL text: select * from emp where empno=7369
------------------------------------------------------------------------
Plan name: SYS_SQL_PLAN_a551f70c695cc014
Enabled: YES     Fixed: NO      Accepted: YES      Origin: AUTO-CAPTURE
------------------------------------------------------------------------
Plan hash value: 2949544139
----------------------------------------------
| Id  | Operation                 | Name    |
----------------------------------------------
|   0 | SELECT STATEMENT          |         |
|   1 |  TABLE ACCESS BY INDEX ROWID| EMP   |
|   2 |   INDEX UNIQUE SCAN       | PK_EMP  |
----------------------------------------------
```

A few things to note from the preceding code. First, note that the plan is enabled, which means that Oracle will use that plan. Note that the plan is not fixed. Enabled and fixed plans will be used in preference to enabled and not fixed. Manually loaded plans are automatically fixed. Oracle will mark plans as fixed when they are evolved (see the next section). If a plan is fixed, the optimizer will not add new plans to that fixed SQL plan baseline. Also, if the plan is fixed, no new plan will be evolved either. When a SQL statement is tuned with the SQL Tuning Advisor or Automatic SQL Tuning, new plans can be added to the fixed SQL plan baseline. You can alter the **fixed** attribute via the **dbms_spm.alter_sql_plan_baseline** function.

**NOTE**
*From testing, it appears that if there is a change in the dependent objects in the query (for example, an index is dropped), the stored plans are dynamically regenerated, and accepted, at the time the object is dropped or added. This behavior does not appear to be documented anywhere in the current Oracle Database 11g documentation. For example, if I drop the PK_EMP index, the baseline plan is changed dynamically, removing the index unique scan and replacing it with a full table scan.*

## Evolving SQL Plan Baselines

You probably noticed that when SQL plan baselines are in use, a new CBO plan will not get used right off the bat (unless it's the only CBO plan, or other plans have been invalidated). This is good, because it avoids plan regression. It's not so good because if the plan is a better one, it's not going to get used since it must first be accepted. So, how do we accept, or evolve, SQL plans? There are three ways a plan can be evolved:

- When the plan is manually loaded to the SQL plan baseline
- When a SQL plan baseline plan is manually evolved
- Via Automatic SQL Tuning

We discussed manual plan loading into the SQL plan baseline already in this chapter (see the section titled "Manual Plan Loading"). When plans are manually loaded, they will be set as accepted in the SQL plan baseline, and thus those plans are available for use.

**NOTE**
*A plan is considered evolved when an unaccepted plan is changed into an accepted plan.*

If a plan is already in the SQL plan baseline, then we can use the PL/SQL function **dbms_spm.evolve_sql_plan_baseline** to verify the performance of the plan, and then accept it if the performance is acceptable. Here is an example of evolving a baseline plan using the **dbms_spm.evolve_sql_plan_baseline** function:

```
Set serveroutput on
set long 100000
Declare
     Output_report    clob;
begin
     output_report:=dbms_spm.evolve_sql_plan_baseline(
                     sql_handle=>'SYS_SQL_353e8c17a551f70c');
     dbms_output.put_line(output_report);
end;
/
```

Note that options exist when evolving the SQL Plan Baseline to not verify the plan (and thus it will be accepted without determining the performance aspects of the new plan). You can also choose to not change the status of the plan to ACCEPTED if you prefer.

The result of the execution of the **dbms_spm.evolve_sql_plan_baseline** will be a report on the plans, comparison statistics on the different plans considered for evolving, and whether the plans were evolved or not.

**NOTE**
*When you use autotrace, you can tell if a baseline is being used. You will see the following note in the autotrace output:*

```
- SQL plan baseline "SYS_SQL_PLAN_
a3185cea611ea913" used for this statement
```

# Managing SQL Plan Baselines

As you might expect, cases will arise where you need to manage SQL plan baselines. In this section we will discuss the use of the **dbms_spm.alter_sql_plan_baseline** function and the **dbms_spm.configure** procedure. We will then look at the **dbms_spm .drop_sql_plan_baseline** procedure, which you can use to drop SQL plan baselines.

### Using dbms_spm.alter_sql_plan_baseline

You may wish to change the attribute of baseline plans from time to time. This can be done with the **dbms_spm.alter_sql_plan_baseline** procedure. With this procedure you can

- Enable or disable a baseline plan for use

- Fix the SQL plan so that it does not evolve over time

- Enable or disable purging of plans

For example, let's look at this baseline plan for a SQL statement:

```
Select sql_handle, plan_name, accepted, fixed
from dba_sql_plan_baselines
where creator='SCOTT'
and dbms_lob.substr(sql_text, 34,1)='select * from emp where empno=7369';
SQL_HANDLE                      PLAN_NAME                      ACC FIX
------------------------------- ------------------------------ --- ---
SYS_SQL_353e8c17a551f70c        SYS_SQL_PLAN_a551f70c695cc014  YES NO
```

Here we have a plan that is not fixed (the FIX column is set to NO). Let's mark the first plan as fixed:

```
Declare
     v_number pls_integer;
```

```
Begin
    v_number:=dbms_spm.alter_sql_plan_baseline(
    sql_handle=>'SYS_SQL_353e8c17a551f70c',
    plan_name=>'SYS_SQL_PLAN_a551f70c695cc014',
    attribute_name=>'FIXED',
    attribute_value=>'YES');
end;
/
```

Now, let's see the results. Note that the **fixed** attribute (FIX) is now set to YES:

```
Select sql_handle, plan_name, accepted, fixed
from dba_sql_plan_baselines
where creator='SCOTT'
and dbms_lob.substr(sql_text, 34,1)='select * from emp where empno=7369';
SQL_HANDLE                       PLAN_NAME                         ACC FIX
------------------------------   ------------------------------    --- ---
SYS_SQL_353e8c17a551f70c         SYS_SQL_PLAN_a551f70c695cc014     YES YES
```

Now this plan is fixed and will be used in lieu of plans that are not fixed, or new optimizer plans.

> **NOTE**
> *You may have wondered about hints. Hints will override SQL Plans, since they end up with a different hash value. As a result, they will have their own baseline plan.*

## Using dbms_spm.configure

SQL baseline information is stored in a structure that Oracle calls the SQL Management Base (SMB). The SMB is located in the SYSAUX tablespace. Oracle provides the **dbms_spm.configure** procedure to manage the SMB. Using this procedure you can configure the amount of space that can be consumed by SQL plan baselines and how long plans will be retained for. By default the default amount of space that can be used by SQL Plan Management is no more than 10 percent of the size of the SYSAUX tablespace. You can adjust this up to a value of 50 percent of the SYSAUX tablespace size. Baseline plans that are unused will be retained for one year and one week, and then will be automatically purged. You can opt to retain unused plans for 523 weeks. In the following example we have modified the space budget to 20 percent of the SYSAUX tablespace and configured unused plans to be removed after 30 weeks:

```
Exec dbms_spm.configure('space_budget_percent',20);
Exec dbms_spm.configure ('plan_retention_weeks',30);
```

You can query the DBA_SQL_MANAGEMENT_CONFIG data dictionary view to determine the current configuration of the SMB.

### Using dbms_spm.drop_sql_plan_baseline

You can drop SQL plan baselines with the **dbms_spm.drop_sql_plan_baseline**
function. You simply pass it the SQL_HANDLE and the PLAN_NAME and it will
remove the plan (either of these has defaults, so you can remove all plans with the
same SQL_HANDLE or the same PLAN_NAME). The function will return the
number of plans that were removed. Here is an example of the use of **dbms_spm
.drop_sql_plan_baseline**:

```
Declare
    v_plans_dropped pls_integer;
Begin
    v_plans_dropped:=dbms_spm.drop_sql_plan_baseline(
        sql_handle=>'SYS_SQL_353e8c17a551f70c',
        plan_name=>'SYS_SQL_PLAN_a551f70c695cc014');
end;
/
```

### Arup Says...

After reading this section you must be wondering how this is different from other
plan stabilization techniques like stored outlines and SQL Profiles, which also
provide a fixed plan for a specific SQL statement. Good question, and there is an
equally good answer. Stored outlines are fixed for the SQL statement for life;
they are not affected by changes in data distribution and other variables such as
**optimizer_index_cost_adj**. This will work in most cases, but in some cases you
actually lose. Consider the example of selecting from a 1-million-row customer
table where country_code = 'US', which is probably the biggest chunk of the
table, and an index should not be used. However, when the **country_code** is set
to, say, Luxemburg, there are only a few records and the index should be used.
A stored outline is fixed with full table scans, and that will be the case in all
cases, which hurts the Luxemburg queries.

SQL Plan Management differs by developing a new plan, but making it
available only if the new plan is superior to the old one. So, the plan is fixed for
the SQL statement, but that plan changes if a need arises. Consider it sort of a
constantly evolving stored outline.

SQL Profiles are also fixed, but unlike outlines, they are dependent on the
data distribution among the tables and how the query affects it. Once set, they
also attach themselves to the SQL statement. What if the data distribution pattern
changes? For instance, suddenly you may find that 99 percent of your customers
are from Luxemburg while fewer than 1 percent are from the U.S. A profile that
was generated earlier will not know this change in pattern unless you drop
the profile and run SQL Tuning Optimizer once again. SQL Plan Management
takes care of that by constantly evaluating the statements that may benefit from a
plan change.

# Automatic SQL Tuning

Oracle Database 10*g* introduced the SQL Tuning Advisor to help you tune SQL statements for better performance. The main problem with using the SQL Tuning Advisor was that it required a manual process. Additionally there was some disconnect between the SQL Tuning Advisor and ADDM that would sometimes require more manual work to analyze SQL identified by ADDM. Associated with SQL Plan Management is Automatic SQL Tuning. Let's look at Automatic SQL Tuning in more detail. First I will provide an overview of Automatic SQL Tuning. Then we will discuss configuration and management of Automatic SQL Tuning.

## Overview of Automatic SQL Tuning

Oracle Database 11*g* improves on the SQL Tuning Advisor by automating the identification of problem SQL. Now, SQL statements are identified automatically, the SQL Tuning Advisor is executed automatically during the scheduled maintenance window on those SQL statements and SQL Baseline Profiles are created. To identify SQL statements the AWR is used. Top queries from the previous week are reviewed for tuning. There are four basic query "buckets" that are selected:

- Top queries for the past week

- Top queries for any day in the past week

- Top queries for any hour

- Top queries by average single execution

The queries collected are combined into a single result, and are then weighted.

> **NOTE**
> *The Automatic SQL Tuning Tasks will not detect all of your problem SQL statements. SQL that is rarely executed (such as ad-hoc SQL), parallel queries, recursive SQL, and DML/DDL are examples of SQL that will not be analyzed. Also if your system has a lot of SQL that repeats with literals instead of bind variables, the Automatic SQL Tuning may not detect these SQL statements. Also note that Automatic SQL Tuning will ignore long-running queries if they have been initially profiled, but the performance is not improved after profiling. In cases where Automatic SQL Tuning does not tune a specific SQL statement, you can still manually tune these statements with the SQL Tuning Advisor.*

Supporting Automatic SQL Tuning is the optimizer. The optimizer now runs in two different modes. First is the mode you are most acquainted with, the normal mode. This is the mode that the optimizer runs in when you execute a SQL statement, and the optimizer generates a plan for that statement.

The optimizer now runs in another mode called tuning mode. In tuning mode, the optimizer will look at SQL statements that run in the system historically, and analyze them to determine if tuning recommendations can be generated for those SQL statements. The result of this tuning exercise will be a profile. This tuning is done during the system maintenance window as an automated task and will run by default for only one hour (minimizing overall system impact).

When running in tuning mode, Automatic SQL Tuning performance these four basic steps:

1.  Identify SQL candidates for tuning from the AWR.

2.  Tune each SQL statement by calling the SQL Tuning Advisor and generate a resulting profile.

3.  Test the SQL profiles generated by executing the SQL statement. Determine if the profile generated in step 2 is accepted.

4.  Implement the SQL profiles if they meet the accepted implementation criteria.

Note in step 2 that the Automatic SQL Tuning process calls the optimizer to tune the SQL. The optimizer in tuning mode will perform four different kinds of tuning analysis on selected SQL statements:

■ **Statistical Analysis**   This is used to determine the freshness of statistics on the underlying objects used by the query. The resulting information from this check may be specific recommendations for gathering statistics and/or collection of "auxiliary information" on the objects being analyzed. This auxiliary information will get stored in the relevant profile generated for the SQL statement by the optimizer.

■ **SQL Profiling**   During SQL profiling, the optimizer will use all available information on the object associated with the SQL statement to generate a SQL profile. This information includes the normal statistics gathered for the object, but also additional statistics and analytical calculations that are possible during a more intense profiling of a SQL statement.

■ **Access Path Analysis**   The automatic tuning analyzer will analyze the SQL statement and make recommendations if additional indexing would be helpful. The SQL Access Advisor will review the index recommendation and determine it's overall impact on the system.

■ **SQL Structure Analysis** This analysis reviews the structure of SQL statements and determines if changes to the structure of the SQL statement could improve its performance.

Once a profile is generated, it is tested by Oracle Database 11*g* to ensure that it improves performance and is then implemented automatically. Oracle Database 11*g* requires a minimum of a 3x performance improvement before it will automatically implement the profile; therefore, the improvement must be significant before it will be implemented. The DBA_SQL_PROFILES column STATUS will be set to AUTO-TUNE if the Automatic SQL Tuning process created them.

As mentioned earlier, the Automated Tuning Advisor tasks will also provide recommendations with regard to new indexes, and other tuning changes that might help your SQL statement perform better. These recommendations are not implemented automatically but can be reviewed and implemented through OEM or using the various views available with the Advisor framework.

Oracle provides for reporting of these automated activities. You can check on which SQL Profiles have been generated and validate or remove any generated SQL profile. All this automation is facilitated with the AutoTask framework discussed in Chapter 2 and thus this process runs nightly.

There are cases where a given SQL statement might be tuned to optimum performance, but over time conditions change with the underlying data, such that the SQL statement is no longer efficient when using the created SQL profile. The SQL Tuning Advisor will detect these regressively performing statements and retune them for better performance. This way, your SQL statements continue to perform optimally over time.

## Automatic SQL Tuning with OEM

Oracle Database 11*g* provides the ability to easily interface with Automatic SQL Tuning via OEM. To begin click on the Advisor Central link on the OEM home page. From the Advisor Central home page you will see a list of the different advisors that have run (by default the last runs of the individual advisors are displayed). To manage the Automatic SQL Tuning Advisor or review its results, click on the radio button by the SQL Tuning Advisor and click on the View Result button (Figure 9-1). OEM will provide the Automatic SQL Tuning Result Summary page (Figure 9-2).

Note in the Task Status region of the Automatic SQL Tuning Result Summary Page, you can enable or disable Automatic SQL Tuning by clicking on the configure button which takes you to the Automated Maintenance Tasks Configuration page (Figure 9-3). From the configure page you can turn off Automatic SQL Tuning or choose which day you wish Automatic SQL Tuning to be run.

Note that you could opt to look at a previous run from this page if you wanted. You can look at all runs for a specific advisor. You can also look at the last runs over a specific period of time (the last 24 hours, seven days, or all of the runs).

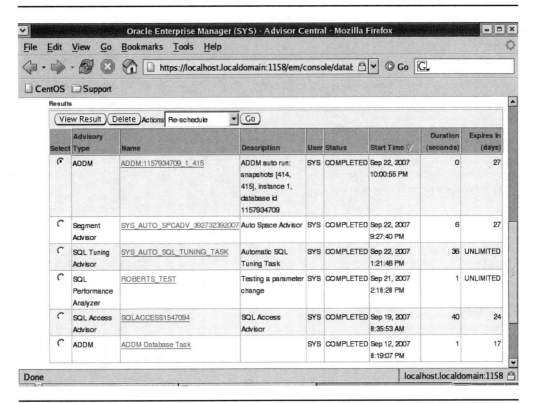

**FIGURE 9-1.** *OEM SQL Tuning Advisor results page from Advisor Central*

Other filter criteria include the task name and the status of the task. Notice another configure button on the Automated Maintenance Tasks Configuration Page. This provides the ability to further manage Automatic SQL Tuning. You can configure things like the maximum time spend on a specific SQL during SQL tuning and so on. This Automatic SQL Tuning Settings page can be seen in Figure 9-4.

Returning to the Automatic SQL Tuning Result Summary page (back to Figure 9-1), still on the Task Status Region you will see that Oracle lists the number of Highly Recommend SQL Profiles that it has created. You can choose to implement all of the highly recommended SQL Profiles by clicking on the Implement All button.

If you are perhaps a bit less than willing to just trust Oracle, you can view the SQL Profiles that are recommended. You do this from the Task Activity Summary region in the Automatic SQL Tuning Result Summary Page (again, Figure 9-1). You can view a specific report (such as the last one executed), a time period (such as the last week) or view a report for all runs of the Automatic SQL Tuning Advisor. You can click on the Time Period you wish and then click on the View Report button to

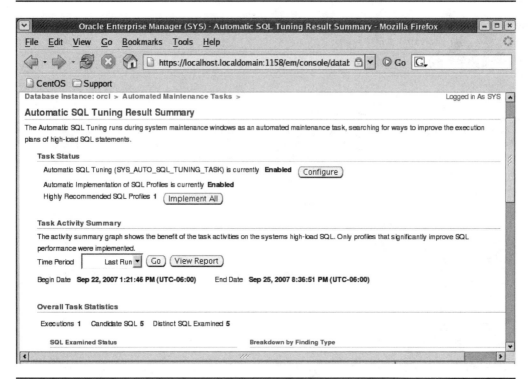

**FIGURE 9-2.** *OEM Automatic SQL Tuning Result Summary page*

bring up the Automatic SQL Tuning Result Details page seen in Figure 9-5. From this page you can view specific recommendations for a given SQL statement and implement specific SQL profiles generated by Automatic SQL Tuning.

Looking more at the Automatic SQL Tuning Result Details page (Figure 9-5) note that the Automatic Tuning Advisor provides us with a wealth of recommendations beyond just adding SQL Profiles. It will let us know if statistics are stale (in which case the statistics box would be selected), if we need to add indexes, if there are recommendations to rewrite the SQL, and other recommendations.

**NOTE**
*It is perhaps a bit disheartening that the Oracle-related schemas (like SYS) come up with so many SQL Tuning Advisor recommendations.*

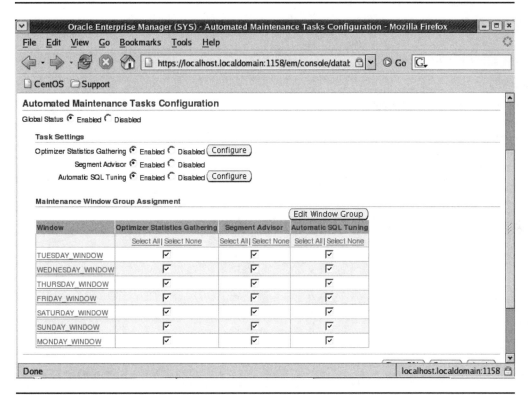

**FIGURE 9-3.** *OEM Automated Maintenance Tasks Configuration page*

## Manage Automatic SQL Tuning Manually

I'll be honest: When someone tells me they are automating something, my first thought as a DBA is, how do I control this thing? This thought is followed shortly by the question, how do I turn this thing off if I need to? You might also wonder how you monitor what it's doing. Oracle Database 11g makes it easy to manually manage and report on Automatic SQL Tuning. In this section we will discuss enabling and disabling Automated SQL Tuning.

### Enable and Disable Automatic SQL Tuning

You can manually turn Automatic SQL Tuning on or off as you wish using the **dbms_auto_task_admin.disable** or **dbms_auto_task_admin.enable** procedures from the SQL prompt, as seen here:

```
-- Disable
BEGIN
dbms_auto_task_admin.disable(client_name => 'sql tuning advisor',
```

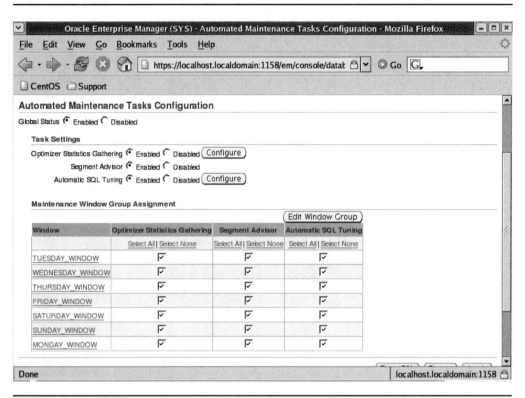

**FIGURE 9-4.** *OEM Automated Maintenance Tasks Configuration page*

```
operation => NULL, window_name => NULL);
END;
/
-- Enable
BEGIN
dbms_auto_task_admin.enable(client_name => 'sql tuning advisor',
operation => NULL, window_name => NULL);
END;
/
```

Automatic profile implementation can also be disabled via the supplied PL/SQL procedure **dbms_sqltune.set_tuning_task_parameter** as seen in this example (we will discuss other parameters that can be set through a call to **dbms_sqltune.set_tuning_task_parameter** later in this section:

```
--Disable
BEGIN
dbms_sqltune.set_tuning_task_parameter('SYS_AUTO_SQL_TUNING_TASK',
```

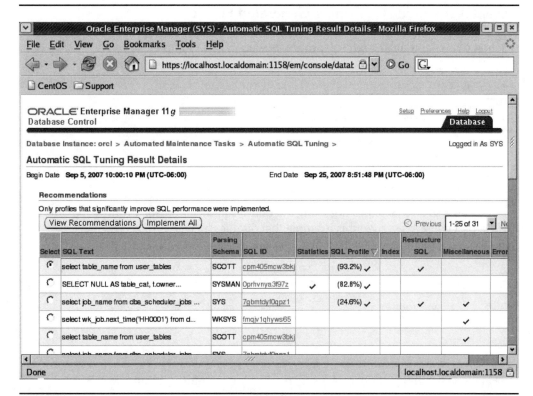

**FIGURE 9-5.** *OEM Automatic SQL Tuning Result Details page*

```
'ACCEPT_SQL_PROFILES', 'FALSE');
END;
/
-- Enable
BEGIN
dbms_sqltune.set_tuning_task_parameter('SYS_AUTO_SQL_TUNING_TASK',
'ACCEPT_SQL_PROFILES', 'TRUE');
END;
/
```

**NOTE**
*If **statistics_level** is set to basic or you turn off AWR snapshots or you modify AWR snapshot retention to <7 days, this will also disable Automatic SQL Tuning.*

## Accept Automatic SQL Tuning Generated Profiles

You can manually accept a recommended SQL profile using the supplied PL/SQL function **dbms_sqltune.accept_sql_profile** as seen in this example:

```
DECLARE
  my_sqlprofile_name VARCHAR2(30);
BEGIN
  my_sqlprofile_name := DBMS_SQLTUNE.ACCEPT_SQL_PROFILE (
     task_name    => 'ROBERTS_TASK',
     name         => 'PROFILE_001',
     force_match  => TRUE);
END;
/
```

You can also alter SQL profiles using the **dbms_sqltune.alter_sql_profile** supplied PL/SQL procedure, as seen in this example that disables a given profile (you can find profile information in the DBA_SQL_PROFILES view):

```
BEGIN
   DBMS_SQLTUNE.ALTER_SQL_PROFILE(
      name             => 'PROFILE_001',
      attribute_name   => 'STATUS',
      value            => 'DISABLED');
END;
/
```

Finally you can drop SQL profiles manually with the **dbms_sqltune.drop_sql_profile** supplied PL/SQL procedure, as seen here:

```
BEGIN
   DBMS_SQLTUNE.DROP_SQL_PROFILE(name => 'PROFILE_001');
END;
/
```

The **dbms_sqltune** PL/SQL procedure provides a number of other procedures and functions that allow you to manually customize the work you want to do with the SQL Tuning Sets. Check out the *Oracle Database Performance Tuning Guide* for more in-depth examples.

## Configure Automatic SQL Tuning

Several parameters can be configured that control the way that Automatic SQL Tuning works. You can use the PL/SQL procedure **dbms_sqltune.set_tuning_task_parameter** procedure to set the different parameters associated with Automatic SQL Tuning. The procedure takes the following parameters:

- **Task_name**  For auto tuning tasks this is always SYS_AUTO_SQL_TUNING_TASK

- **Parameter**  Defines the parameter you want to set. Parameters include the following:

  - **Accept_sql_profile**  When set to **true** (the default) will allow the SQL Tuning Advisor to accept a given SQL profile automatically (that meets the performance requirements). A value of **false** will disallow any profile being set automatically.

  - **Max_sql_profiles_per_exec**  Defines the limit of SQL profiles that are accepted for each Automatic SQL Tuning run.

  - **Max_auto_sql_profiles**  Defines the maximum number of SQL profiles that can be accepted in total.

  - **Execution_days_to_expire**  Defines the number of days to save task history in the advisor framework schema. By default task history expires after 30 days.

- **Value**  The value that you wish to set this particular parameter too.

Here is an example of setting the **accept_sql_profile** attribute:

```
BEGIN
   DBMS_SQLTUNE.SET_TUNING_TASK_PARAMETER(
      task_name => 'SYS_AUTO_SQL_TUNING_TASK',
      parameter => 'ACCEPT_SQL_PROFILES', value => 'TRUE');
END;
/
```

## Automatic SQL Tuning Manual Reporting

If you are an old command line type like I am, then you want to do some good old-fashioned manual reporting on things. Oracle Database 11*g* provides the Automatic SQL Tuning Report which provides information on executions of the SQL Tuning Advisor. You generate the report using the PL/SQL function **dbms_sqltune.report_auto_tuning_task**, which returns the report in the form of a **clob**. Here is an example of the generation of a report for tasks from today back in time to two days ago:

```
variable my_rept CLOB;
BEGIN
   :my_rept :=DBMS_SQLTUNE.REPORT_AUTO_TUNING_TASK(
      begin_exec => sysdate - 2,
      end_exec => sysdate,
      type => 'TEXT',
      level => 'TYPICAL',
      section => 'ALL',
      object_id => NULL,
      result_limit => NULL);
END;
/
print :my_rept
```

# Manual Creation and Use of SQL Tuning Sets

As we mentioned earlier, the advisors in Oracle Database 10g use SQL Tuning Sets instead of SQL workloads. SQL Tuning Sets can be created via OEM, of course, but you may also want to create them manually. There are a number of ways to do this, but we thought we would give you a quick highlight of one method. If you need to investigate this further, the *Oracle Database Performance Tuning Guide* is very helpful. The basic steps for the creation of a SQL tuning set are

1. Create the task that the SQL Tuning Set will be associated with (such as a SQL Access Advisor task).

2. Create the SQL Tuning Set.

3. Load the SQL Tuning Set.

4. Link the SQL Tuning Set to the task created in Step 1.

5. Set any task parameters.

6. Execute the task.

7. View the results.

Let's look at these steps in some more detail.

## Create the Task

This step is pretty much the same as in Oracle Database 10g. In this example we are creating a SQL Access Advisor task.

```
-- Create the SQL Access Advisor Task
VARIABLE task_id NUMBER;
VARIABLE task_name VARCHAR2(255);
EXECUTE :task_name := 'ROBERTS_TASK';
-- This next command will fail if this is running for the first time.
EXECUTE DBMS_ADVISOR.DELETE_TASK (:task_name);
EXECUTE DBMS_ADVISOR.CREATE_TASK ('SQL Access Advisor', :task_id, :task_name);
```

## Create the SQL Tuning Set

Next, we need to create the SQL Tuning Set. This is like creating a container, and for right now it will contain nothing. In the next section we will load up the SQL Tuning Set. In this example we will create a SQL Tuning Set called **sqltuningset_001**.

We use the new Oracle supplied procedure **dbms_sqltune.create_sqlset** to create the SQL Tuning Set:

```
-- Drop the SQLSET if it exists. Will generate an error if it
-- does not exist.
BEGIN
  DBMS_SQLTUNE.DELETE_SQLSET(sqlset_name => 'SQLTUNINGSET_001',
     sqlset_owner=>'ROBERT');
END;
/
-- Create the SQL tuning set
BEGIN
  DBMS_SQLTUNE.CREATE_SQLSET(sqlset_name => 'SQLTUNINGSET_001');
END;
/
```

We can see the newly created SQL Tuning set using the DBA_SQLSET view:

```
select name, owner from dba_sqlset
where name='SQLTUNINGSET_001';
NAME                             OWNER
------------------------------   --------
SQLTUNINGSET_001                 ROBERT
```

## Load the SQL Tuning Set

After creating the SQL Tuning Set, we need to load it with some content. There are a number of different ways to do this including loading from baselines, the AWR, another SQL Tuning Set, or the cursor cache. In our example we are going to load it from a SQL baseline (see Chapter 2 for more on SQL baselines) called **system_baseline**. Note that we are using a table function called **dbms_sqltune.select_workload_repository**. This allows us to query the AWR and query only the information in the AWR that we are interested in. In this case, we are going to query for the baseline called **system_baseline**. We are going to query only the top 20 statements sorted by elapsed time:

```
-- PL/SQL to load the SQL Tuning Set from an AWR baseline
DECLARE
 baseline_cursor DBMS_SQLTUNE.SQLSET_CURSOR;
BEGIN
 OPEN baseline_cursor FOR
    SELECT VALUE(p)
    FROM TABLE (DBMS_SQLTUNE.SELECT_WORKLOAD_REPOSITORY(
        'system_baseline', NULL, NULL, 'elapsed_time',  NULL,
        NULL, NULL, 20)) p;
    DBMS_SQLTUNE.LOAD_SQLSET(
```

```
            sqlset_name      => 'SQLTUNINGSET_001',
            populate_cursor => baseline_cursor);
END;
/
```

You can see the SQL statements loaded in the SQL Tuning Set once it's loaded, by using the following query:

```
SELECT SQL_TEXT FROM TABLE(DBMS_SQLTUNE.SELECT_SQLSET('SQLTUNINGSET_001') );
```

Note that this uses another table function to easily provide you with the data you are interested in. You could also refer to the DBA_SQLSET, DBA_SQLSET_STATEMENTS, and DBA_SQLSET_BINDS views for this and additional information on the SQL tuning set you have just created.

## Link the SQL Tuning Set and the Task

We now have a SQL Access Advisor task and a SQL Tuning Set ready to go. We just need to link the two together and then execute the task. We use the **dbms_advisor .add_sts_ref** supplied PL/SQL procedure to do just that as seen here:

```
-- Link to tuning set to the task
EXECUTE DBMS_ADVISOR.ADD_STS_REF('ROBERTS_TASK', null, 'SQLTUNINGSET_001');
```

## Set Any Task Parameters

Any task you run may have certain parameters that can be set to define, for the task, what kind of information you are looking for. For example, we would like our task to only report any valid information of a specific table, ROBERT.MY_TAB. We make a call to the PL/SQL supplied procedure **dbms_advisor.set_task_parameter** to set just a condition:

```
-- set task parameters
BEGIN
   DBMS_ADVISOR.SET_TASK_PARAMETER ( 'ROBERTS_TASK',
        'VALID_TABLE_LIST', 'ROBERT.MY_TAB');
END;
/
```

## Execute the Task

Finally, after all the setup work is complete, we can execute the task using the PL/SQL provided procedure **dbms_advisor.execute_task** as seen in this example:

```
-- Execute the task
EXECUTE DBMS_ADVISOR.EXECUTE_TASK('ROBERTS_TASK');
```

## Review the Results

Once the task has been executed, you probably would like to see some results. Again, OEM provides an easy graphical interface into the results as we have demonstrated in earlier sections of this chapter. If you want to manually view the results you can view the recommendations that have been generated by the task through a call to the [DBA|USER]_ADVISOR_RECOMMENDATIONS view as seen in this example:

```
VARIABLE workload_name VARCHAR2(255);
VARIABLE task_name VARCHAR2(255);
EXECUTE :task_name := 'ROBERTS_TASK';
SELECT REC_ID, RANK, BENEFIT
FROM DBA_ADVISOR_RECOMMENDATIONS WHERE TASK_NAME = :task_name;
```

Oracle provides other views that you can use as required. These views include:

- **DBA_ADVISOR_EXECUTIONS**   Provides information on specific advisor task executions.

- **DBA_ADVISOR_FINDINGS**   Provides findings related to a specific advisor task execution.

- **DBA_ADVISOR_RECOMMENDATIONS**   Provides recommendations related to a specific advisor task execution.

- **DBA_ADVISOR_RATIONALE**   Provides the rationale for specific findings of a given advisor task execution.

- **DBA_ADVISOR_TASKS**   Provides a parent record for each advisor task. Can be executed many times (seen in DBA_ADVISOR_EXECUTIONS).

### Arup Says...

One of the best usages of the SQL Tuning Advisor I found was to combine it with the SQL Performance Analyzer. Get the recommendations from the STA and then run these in the SPA to get a side-by-side comparison of the before and after change scenarios. Not only will you see the recommendations, but you will be able to run them on your actual system for a genuine impact analysis. For an even better comparison, use Database Replay to capture a significant workload and then run it in the replay with the recommended changes in place, to measure the impact. This allows you to assess the impact not only on specific SQL statements, but on a whole range of other SQL statements as well.

# Intelligent Cursor Sharing (Bind-Aware Peeking)

In the past, cursor sharing has struggled when bind variables were used. This is because different bind variable values could have different selectivity, and thus might well require different execution plans. Oracle Database 11*g* introduces intelligent cursor sharing (also known as bind-aware peeking), which is an extension of cursor sharing and bind variable peeking. In this section we will look at what bind-aware peeking is, and look at data dictionary views associated with bind-aware peeking.

**NOTE**
*Don't confuse cursor sharing with intelligent cursor sharing. Intelligent cursor sharing is independent of cursor sharing and is not impacted by the setting of the **cursor_sharing** parameter.*

## About Bind-Aware Peeking

Bind-aware peeking provides Oracle with the ability to determine the selectivity of any **where** clause condition that uses bind variables. Unlike cursor sharing in the past, bind-aware peeking is a more intelligent approach to cursor sharing in that it allows for multiple execution plans for a single SQL statement using bind variables. Intelligent cursor sharing cannot be disabled.

A cursor that uses bind variables will start its life with a hard parse, as would be expected. Bind variable peeking will be used and a histogram is used to compute the selectivity of the predicate. A selectivity cube will be generated (this can be seen in V$SQL_CS_SELECTIVITY).

When a subsequent execution occurs, the statement will be soft-parsed and the matching cursor and execution plan found. After the execution, the execution statistics of the run will be compared to the previous execution statistics for that cursor. Oracle will monitor the pattern of the statistics as SQL runs progress, and if Oracle finds that the cursor will benefit from being bind-aware (because of the pattern of usage of that cursor and the overall selectivity of the executions of that cursor overt time), it will mark the cursor as bind-aware.

On the following query executions, the query will still be soft-parsed. However, Oracle will review the selectivity of the predicate since it is now marked for cursor matching. The selectivity of the predicate will be determined, and the appropriate stored execution plan (or a new execution plan if required) will be generated. Note that one result of intelligent cursor sharing, then, is that a given SQL statement could end up with more than one execution plan depending on the history of past executions and the use of the bind variables.

## Bind-Aware Peeking Views

There are four views that can be used to monitor bind-aware peeking. Three of these views are new. The new views are

■ The V$SQL_CS_STATISTICS view provides execution statistics on shared cursors, including information on whether the cursor has been peeked, how many executions there were for the cursor and so on. This view can be used to determine performance, comparing cursor performance with different bind sets.

■ The V$SQL_CS_SELECTIVITY view materializes the selectivity cubes created by Oracle for each predicate in the SQL statement.

■ The V$SQL_CS_HISTOGRAM view displays the distribution of the execution count across a three-bucket execution history histogram.

Additionally the V$SQL view has two new columns added:

■ **IS_BIND_SENSITIVE**   This column indicates if the cursor is bind-sensitive. If set to YES, then the column is bind-sensitive. If a cursor is marked bind-sensitive, then this indicates that the optimizer peeked at the bind variable values and has determined that changes to the bind variable may lead to a need to a different plan.

■ **IS_BIND_AWARE**   This column indicates if a given cursor is bind-aware. If set to YES, this cursor will use bind-aware cursor sharing.

**NOTE**
*In the early documentation the V$SQL_CS* views
were not documented in the Oracle Reference Guide.*

## Starting a System with Bind-Aware Peeking

Recall that SQL plan baselines will only use the first plan generated. Subsequent plans, even those resulting from bind-aware peeking, will be stored but not used until it has been validated, defeating the benefit of bind-aware peeking. One way around this is to set the parameter **optimizer_capture_sql_plan_baselines** to **false** after starting the database, allowing the plans to all be loaded into the cache. You can then set this parameter to **true** after some up time and manually load the cursor cache into the SQL plan baseline.

# Temporary Tablespace Features

Two new features are available in Oracle Database 11*g* related to temporary tablespaces. The first is the **alter tablespace shrink space** and **alter tablespace shrink tempfile** commands. Second is a new view, DBA_TEMP_FREE_SPACE. Let's look at each of these in some more detail next.

## Temporary Tablespace Shrink

Certain database operations may require unusually large amounts of temporary tablespace usage, which leads to large tempfiles. If these operations are rare, or one-time operations, then it would nice to be able to shrink those tempfiles down to some smaller size. Oracle Database 11*g* provides two options to reduce the size of a temporary tablespace. The **alter tablespace shrink space** command will cause Oracle to reduce the overall size of the temporary tablespace to its originally defined size. The **alter tablespace shrink tempfile** command allows you to shrink a given tempfile to its originally defined size. Both commands come with a **keep** option, which allows you to indicate that you want the temporary tablespace or data file to be a minimum of the **keep** size.

For example, these commands will resize the TEMP tablespace to its original size:

```
Alter tablespace temp shrink space;
alter tablespace temp shrink tempfile '/oracle01/oradata/orcl/temp01.dbf';
```

Here is an example of using the **keep** parameter to manage how much space is left in the tablespace or the tempfile. Note that using the **keep** parameter will not cause the size of the temporary tablespace or tempfiles to grow if they are already smaller than the **keep** size:

```
Alter tablespace temp shrink space keep 100m;
alter tablespace temp shrink
tempfile '/oracle01/oradata/orcl/temp01.dbf' keep 100m;
```

**NOTE**
*So, why not just use the **alter database tempfile resize** command? The main difference is that the **shrink space** command will not try to deallocate extents that are allocated and in use. The **resize** command will try to deallocate all the space, and will return an error if the space is in use and cannot be deallocated.*

## The DBA_TEMP_FREE_SPACE View

A new view, DBA_TEMP_FREE_SPACE, has been added to Oracle Database 11*g* to make it easier to manage temporary tablespaces. This view provides a single place to determine the total size of a temporary tablespace, how much space is allocated, and how much is free. Here is an example of a query against DBA_TEMP_FREE_SPACE:

```
select * from dba_temp_free_space;
TABLESPACE_NAME     TABLESPACE_SIZE     ALLOCATED_SPACE     FREE_SPACE
---------------     ---------------     ---------------     ----------
TEMP                     18,939,904           4,259,840     14,680,064
```

# Real-Time SQL Monitoring

Oracle Database 11*g* adds additional monitoring for currently executing SQL statements with the introduction of Real-Time SQL Monitoring. In this section we will discuss Real-Time SQL Monitoring, views associated with this feature, and how to generate a report using the features of Real-Time SQL Monitoring. Finally we will look at how to control Real-Time SQL Monitoring.

## Real-Time SQL Monitoring Overview

Real-Time SQL Monitoring allows you to see accumulating execution statistics for a given SQL statement, updated every second, as that SQL statement is executing. Real-Time SQL Monitoring is started by default when the SQL statement runs in parallel or if the SQL statement has consumed at least 5 seconds of CPU or IO time during a single execution.

## Real-Time SQL Monitoring Views

New views, V$SQL_MONITOR and V$SQL_PLAN_MONITOR, are available to provide the new runtime-related execution statistics. You can use these views in conjunction with other available Oracle views (such as V$SESSION_LONGOPS) to get a more complete picture of the SQL being executed.

The V$SQL_MONITOR view provides the main set of statistics for the execution of a given SQL statement. It is much like the V$SQL view, except that the associated statistics apply to only the single execution of the execution being monitored. As a result, if an identical SQL statement is executing in two different sessions, each execution will have a separate entry in V$SQL_MONITOR.

You can differentiate the different executions by looking at the KEY column in V$SQL_MONITOR. (Uniqueness is also determined by a combination of the SQL_ID, the SQL_EXEC_START, and the SQL_EXEC_ID columns). Here is an example of a query against V$SQL_MONITOR for a long-running execution:

```
select b.key, b.sql_exec_start,
b.sql_exec_id,
b.buffer_gets BG, b.disk_reads DR, b.elapsed_time ET, b.cpu_time CPU,
```

```
a.sql_text
from v$sql a, v$sql_monitor b
where a.sql_id=b.sql_id;
          KEY SQL_EXEC_ SQL_EXEC_ID         BG       DR          ET         CPU
------------- --------- ----------- --------- ------ ---------- ----------
SQL_TEXT
-----------------
 158913789964 21-AUG-07    16777216  10172616    8392  104543994    79934848
delete from child
```

The V$SQL_PLAN_MONITOR view provides additional information related to the cursor being executed. There is a row for each operation in the execution plan of the SQL statement. Here is an example:

```
select b.key, c.plan_line_id, c.plan_operation, c.output_rows
from v$sql a, v$sql_monitor b, v$sql_plan_monitor c
where a.sql_id=b.sql_id
and b.key=c.key
order by c.plan_line_id;
```

```
          KEY PLAN_LINE_ID PLAN_OPERATION   OUTPUT_ROWS
------------- ------------ ---------------- -----------
 158913789964            0 DELETE STATEMENT           0
 158913789964            1 DELETE                     0
 158913789964            2 TABLE ACCESS         2520000
```

## Real-Time SQL Monitoring Report

If you want to save some typing, you can use the **dbms_sqltune.report_sql_monitor** function to produce the SQL monitor report. Here is an example:

```
declare
    v_output    clob;
begin
    v_output:=dbms_sqltune.report_sql_monitor();
dbms_output.put_line(v_output);
end;
/
```

Several different parameters are available that allow you to adjust the report output to suit your needs.

## Control Real-Time SQL Monitoring

For real-time monitoring to operate, the **statistics_level** parameter must be set to **all** or **typical**. Additionally you must have enabled the OEM management packs as discussed in the next section.

Hints are available to enable or disable SQL Monitoring. The MONITOR hint will force SQL Monitoring for a query, and the NO_MONITOR hint can be used to disable monitoring for a given SQL Statement.

# Control the Use of OEM Management Packs

Unfortunately, not everyone has coughed up the money to use the Oracle Diagnostic and Tuning Pack features. We are all good citizens, of course, and would not want to accidentally start using features that we are not licensed for. To help you avoid this moral dilemma, Oracle added the **control_management_pack_access** parameter. This parameter provides the following settings:

- **NONE**   Access to the Diagnostic and Tuning packs is not available.

- **DIAGNOSTIC**   Only the Diagnostic Pack will be available.

- **DIAGNOSTIC+TUNING**   The default setting, which enables both the Diagnostic Pack and the Tuning Pack.

# End of Line

We have provided coverage of a number of the new and enhanced performance related features in Oracle Database 11g.

Performance is always something that a DBA seems to be busy dealing with and features such as pending statistics, the ability to recover previous versions of object statistics, and extended statistics can all make the DBA's job easier. These features can also help to stabilize a database environment, which is also a plus!

SQL Plan management is something to watch out for. While a powerful feature in and of itself, it can also cause you some problems if you are not thinking about the potential impacts of this feature on your tuning efforts. Stable plans, in and of themselves are a great idea. Coupled with Automatic SQL Tuning though, SQL Plan management is a powerful feature. In the end, I think the DBA is going to have to embrace these new features and just work with them. My guess is Oracle will keep building on them and in the end, using them will be a far better thing than not using them.

But then again, I've been wrong before.

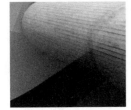

# CHAPTER
## 10

## Other New Features
## and Enhancements

n this chapter, we present a variety of other features that need to be included in this book. In some cases, these new features could comprise their own book (such as the XML-related feature set), and in other cases the feature set is fairly small (for example, RAC-related features). In this chapter we will review:

■ Real Application Clusters

■ XML

■ Java

■ New Oracle supplied packages and procedures

# Real Application Clusters

Oracle Database 11*g* offers new RAC-related features. These features include:

■ Oracle call-level interface (OCI) runtime connection load balancing

■ Using XA transactions with RAC

■ RAC Configuration Assistants

■ Network Configuration Assistant (NetCA)

■ Database rolling upgrade

■ Parallel execution honors service placement

■ Direct NFS

We will cover these new features in more detail in the next several sections.

## OCI Runtime Connection Load Balancing

Several options have been available for managing workload in RAC clusters since version 10.2. Starting with Oracle Database 11*g*, there are two options for load balancing for OCI clients: connect-time load balancing and runtime load balancing. These options were available with Java Database Connectivity (JDBC) or ODP.NET connection pools in version 10.2, and now similar features have been extended to OCI session pools as well.

Connect-time load balancing works by distributing new incoming sessions to the best node for a given service when that connection is made. This is facilitated by the listeners servicing the cluster instances since they periodically receive load-balancing advisories from the individual instances to help the listeners determine the "best" node for a new session at any given time. So, connections to instances aren't spread randomly across all instances, but take into account some of the existing workload factors as well.

Runtime load balancing is performed after sessions are connected to instances in the cluster and requires pooling to be used. The session pool opens connections to all instances in the cluster. Ideally, these sessions are equally distributed to all instances. The pool receives load-balancing advisories (just as the listeners do) and uses that information to determine which connections in the pool can provide the best service at any given time. So, when a client requests a connection from the pool (via the **OCISessGet()** call), the pool returns a session on the instance that is best able to handle additional workload at that time.

Runtime load balancing for OCI session pools is enabled by default in 11*g* when connecting to Oracle Database servers version 10.2 and higher. To disable this behavior, you must set the mode parameter to **oci_spc_no_rlb** when calling the **OCISessionPoolCreate()** function to create the pool.

## Using XA Transactions with RAC

Oracle Database 11*g* introduces a new background process, GTXn, to support distributed XA transactions. The new parameter **global_txn_processes** controls how many processes are started and is set to 1 by default. In systems where XA transactions account for a small amount of the workload, the default setting should be sufficient. In previous versions of RAC, XA transactions needed to adhere to special considerations to avoid locking and resource issues due to the lack of shared resources for all branches of a distributed transaction. By allowing an XA transaction to span instances, the scalability and availability of RAC environments can be harnessed.

Note that if you set **global_txn_processes** to 0, XA transactions will not be allowed in an RAC cluster (an ORA-55712 error will be raised when you attempt to start one). You can, however, change the parameter value via **alter system**, and instances do not need to have the same number of processes.

Transaction identifiers (XIDs) are used to globally connect parts of a distributed transaction. Before Oracle Database 11*g*, Oracle was not able to determine if duplicate XIDs were created on different instances. Starting with 11*g*, Oracle will determine if the XID is a duplicate and raises an error, preventing the new transaction from starting. This means that applications may need to handle this exception (ORA-00150: duplicate transaction ID) and appropriately attempt a new XID.

## RAC Configuration Assistants

Configuration assistants for RAC environments received several improvements in 11*g*. Among the improvements were new and improved features for

- Database Upgrade Assistant (DBUA)
- Network Configuration Assistant (NetCA)

Next, we'll review the new features for each of these assistants.

### Database Upgrade Assistant (DBUA)

In previous versions of Oracle Database, patching an RAC cluster to a new version of the Oracle Database software required many manual steps that were prone to error. Starting with versions 10.1.0.6 and 10.2.0.3, the DBUA may be used to patch an RAC cluster, significantly easing the upgrade process.

You may know that the DBUA does prerequisite checks before you can upgrade the database. This is to ensure a successful upgrade. Prerequisite checks in DBUA have been improved in Oracle Database 11g, further ensuring a successful upgrade. New pre-upgrade checks include reviewing initialization parameters to determine if new ones are required or obsolete ones are present. Other checks include statistics gathering, available free space, and other warning conditions.

## Network Configuration Assistant (NetCA)

The Network Configuration Assistant (NetCA) has added the following features:

- Converts single-instance listeners to cluster listeners

- Removes the CRS resources for listeners during deinstallation

Each of these features is discussed in the next sections.

### NetCA Converts Single-Instance Listeners to Cluster Listeners

During the Oracle Universal Installer's (OUI) installation process, it invokes the NetCA to configure the listeners in the cluster. If the NetCA encounters listeners that are not cluster listeners, it will convert them to cluster listeners.

### NetCA Deinstall Removes Listener CRS Resources

During deinstallation, the NetCA removes cluster listeners configured in the ORACLE_HOME being deinstalled. If the definition for those listeners in the listener .ora file does not contain static endpoints, NetCA will additionally remove the CRS resources for those listeners.

## Database Rolling Upgrade

Of particular interest to RAC administrators is the introduction of rolling upgrades that do not require creation of standby databases. Starting with 11g, all future upgrades will support rolling upgrades to later releases. This includes major releases, patchsets, and many individual patches as well. We expect we will see the true measure of this new feature after the first patch is released.

**Arup Says...**

If DBAs ever felt that they were being held hostage, it was at least during application of patches. You need to bring the database down for patching, but doing so invalidates your commitment of the high-uptime SLA. I had a manager once who actually put in my performance appraisal a condition that the database can't come down for any reason for more than four times a year— planned or unplanned. Well, the four quarterly security patches alone would have blown that limit. So, what did I do? I just didn't apply any security patches for three quarters and then applied the fourth one! Needless to say, that was detrimental to the business in the long run, but was necessary to support the high outage requirements for patching.

Keeping this in mind, Oracle's introduction of online patching is a very welcome sign. There are two types of patches: software and database objects. Bear in mind, though, that some, not all, patches will be online. The way it works is that the online software patches, when applied, modify the code running in memory directly so that the database instance is altered without a recycle. This may sound like rocket science, but in reality this is something like changing a code path dynamically or force-loading a library. Since these alterations may affect the code and data segments of a process stack, it will not be possible for all the patches to be online, but some will be.

The other type of patch—database object patch—where a supplied package or procedure is updated by a patch follows a slightly different path. You saw earlier in the book that certain types of package changes do not invalidate the package, especially if you add functions to the end, not at the top. Oracle has made a commitment that all the patches will be developed keeping that property in mind. So, we should see a lot fewer invalidations due to object patching.

But the biggest question is how many of the patches will be online. Only time will tell that. As of writing this book, there were no patches for Oracle Database 11*g*—online or otherwise.

## Parallel Execution Honors Service Placement

Parallel query is an option commonly used in RAC environments to spawn additional query slaves, which each execute a portion of the query's workload. In an RAC environment, these query slaves can be placed on different instances to utilize all the resources available in the cluster. In versions of RAC before Oracle Database 11*g*, Oracle could assign query slaves to run on any available instance in the cluster, regardless of whether that instance offered the service to which the client had connected. Starting with Oracle Database 11*g*, the default behavior is to only place query slaves on nodes that run the service to which the client has connected. This feature helps make the workload more manageable by ensuring that only sessions related to the running services are assigned to each instance. You may override this behavior by using the **parallel_instance_group** initialization parameter.

## Direct NFS

Direct NFS is an implementation of NFS built directly into the RDBMS kernel via the Oracle Disk Manager (ODM). Direct NFS allows the database to communicate directly with NFS storage, bypassing the operating system's NFS client. Note that this feature isn't specific to RAC and may be used with single-instance databases as well.

By performing the NFS calls directly from the database code, the operating system can focus on performing network calls more efficiently and avoid allocating memory to the NFS client processes and NFS file system client cache. The Oracle buffer cache provides all caching, performs all I/O to the NFS file system directly, and just relies on the operating system to make the network calls to the NFS server or appliance.

Additionally, this also provides a uniform NFS client implementation across all platforms supported by the database including all flavors of UNIX, Windows, Linux, and others. That means that not only will NFS clients be available on platforms that normally don't provide one (like Windows), but also that all platforms should have performance characteristics that are more similar given the same CPU and network specifications.

To configure Direct NFS, you must first put the proper Oracle Disk Manager library in place. On most platforms, that will involve replacing the $ORACLE_HOME/lib/libodm11.so file with a copy of the $ORACLE_HOME/lib/libnfsodm11.so file (or a symbolic link if the platform supports them). Then, you need to properly mount the NFS share on the operating system according to Oracle's instructions specific to your operating system.

Once the NFS share is mounted, the next step for most platforms will be to create a data file on the new mount point. Oracle will check the $ORACLE_HOME/dbs/oranfstab, /etc/oranfstab, and /etc/mtab files in that order to find a matching mount point. If it does, then Direct NFS will attempt to perform IO directly to the new mount point using the Direct NFS calls. If that fails, it will fall back to using the operating system kernel's NFS client. To determine if the client is using Direct NFS or not, consult the V$DNFS_SERVERS and V$DNFS_FILES views. The following output from V$DNFS_FILES shows a data file that is being accessed by Direct NFS:

```
SQL> select * from v$dnfs_files;
FILENAME                FILESIZE       PNUM      SVR_ID
-------------------- ---------- ---------- ----------
/mnt/all1/dan101.dbf  104865792         15           1
```

# XMLDB New Features

Oracle Database 11*g* introduces a myriad of new features within the XMLDB arena. The new features address many of the complaints developers and database administrators have had. These enhancements include:

■  Binary XML storage

■  Partitioning support for XMP

■  XQuery enhancements

■  Database native Web Services

■  XML DB Repository enhancements

■  XML Developer's Kit

We will discuss these features in the next several sections.

## Binary XML Storage

Oracle Database 11*g* introduces a new storage model for schema-less XML storage in 11*g*. This binary storage model compresses the XML data with several benefits including improved performance, resulting in faster parsing, lower transfer times on the network, and less CPU consumption. The binary model also supports returning more than one leaf node when doing one pass over an XML document.

While this storage model is called schema-less, that does not mean that XML schemas are not supported. In fact, multiple documents can be stored in the same table or even the same column and still be validated against their different schemas. Schema validation is also faster with binary XML due to its token-based storage model.

Binary XML is great when you need to store XML documents for which you do not want to create an XML schema or have to change the metadata of your XML schema a lot. Multiple fragment-level and leaf-level operations on these large documents are much faster because they can be pulled out of the document with a single scan.

### Compression and Tokens

Binary XML compresses XML documents by creating tokens for the XML tags within a document. For example, the tag <name> could be replaced with a token ſ. Every time <name> is encountered it would be replaced with ſ. This would reduce the storage needed for <name> from 6 down to 1. A 6-to-1 compression ratio isn't too bad, but it only applies to the tags and not on the text itself.

If an XML schema is registered in the database as a binary XML schema and a document is stored referencing that schema, then the database encoder uses the stored schema to generate the token definitions for the XML document. Schema-less binary XML does not have tokens already generated for it and so must include the token to tag mapping within the encoded data. This compressed format is faster because the same format is used in memory and when transferring data over the network as is stored on disk. Compression also reduces the overhead of full schema validation.

### Binary XMLType Columns and Tables

In Oracle Database 11*g* XMLType columns and tables can be specified to use binary XML storage when you use the **store as binary xml** parameter when defining an XMLType column or table as binary during its creation. You can also reference an XML schema when creating a binary XMLType by using the **xmlschema** option of the **create table** command. Oracle also provides an additional parameter, **allow anyschema**, which provides the ability to store documents related to different XML schemas in the same table or column. Each of the documents can use different encodings because of their different schemas. This is good for flexibility but bad for copy-based schema evolution. Here is an example of the creation of a binary XML table:

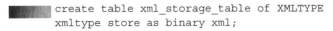
```
create table xml_storage_table of XMLTYPE
xmltype store as binary xml;
```

And here is an example of the use of the **allow anyschema** parameter:

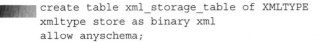
```
create table xml_storage_table of XMLTYPE
xmltype store as binary xml
allow anyschema;
```

**NOTE**
*Using copy-based schema evolution can result in documents that do not conform to the schema you are upgrading. The direct result of nonconformity is that documents are not decodable after the evolution is complete.*

### Virtual Columns

We discussed virtual columns earlier in Chapter 7 and here we will add to that discussion a bit. Virtual columns can be used with XML LOB-based columns or tables. The result is the ability to add referential integrity and other constraints to LOB-based XML documents. You cannot define constraints while creating virtual columns using the **virtual columns** option of the **create table** statement. You can, however, add them after the table or column has been created. These columns will not show up in a **describe** statement if the column is created on an XMLType table. They will show up, however, if the columns were created on an XMLType column within a non-XMLType table. Here is an example of the creation of a virtual column for an XML LOB column:

```
Create table example_xml of XMLType XMLType
store as binary xml
virtual columns (name as (extractValue(object_value, '/person/fullname')));
```

## Leaf-Level and Fragment-Level Extraction

Continuing our binary storage discussion, we find that binary storage provides the ability of Oracle Database 11*g* to return multiple leaf nodes and fragments in one read through an XML document. Updates to the XML LOB-based storage have also improved with binary XML due to its ability to update the XML document starting at the point when the document was changed instead of writing the entire document back out. Secure-file LOBs using binary XML go one step further and only update the data that has been changed.

## Validation

When you insert a new XML document into a schema-based binary XMLType column or table, the database performs a full validation of the document against the schema for you. If you are using other types of XML storage, validation either doesn't occur or is a partial validation. Partial validation is not an Oracle Database 11*g* new feature, but it is important to understand the change from partial to full validations when working with binary XML.

Also associated with binary XML in Oracle Database 11*g* is a new parser that does not require a DOM (Document Object Model) tree. The validation that occurs for documents stored in binary XML also does not need to use a DOM. This provides a considerable performance improvement, which is probably why Oracle now does a full validation on schema-based binary XML XMLType storage columns and tables on inserts, and it's also what allows them to do validation on fragments that change instead of the full document after the document has been stored.

## Support for Language Translation

Binary XML storage, like other types of XML storage, comes with language translation support. This allows you to store strings that need to be translated into different languages within your XML document. The XML schema must identify these strings by specifying the attribute **xdb:translate** within each element you want translated. Tags within the XML document that you want translated must then specify the attribute **xml:lang** or **xml:srclang**.

### XMLIndex Index Type

In Oracle Database 10*g* indexing options for the CLOB-based storage model of XML documents was limited. Function-based indexes were available, but they were limited in the overall functionality they provided. **Ctxsys.ctxxpath**, part of Oracle Text, attempted to help us out but was also limited. Oracle Database 11*g* has added XMLIndex types, which address many of the limitations associated with indexing the LOB-based XML storage model. As a result of the introduction of XMLIndex types, CTXXPATH indexes are now deprecated.

XMLIndex indexes are supported for both binary and CLOB-based XML storage models, and can be used on schema-based and schema-less columns or tables. They provide the power to search an XML document without having to specify specific elements to index. You can, instead, specify a specific path or index the entire document in one index. You can also use an XMLIndex index in the **select** and **from** clauses of a statement. This provides a means of working with pieces of a document instead of the whole document.

This new index type can also be used to search collections of nodes within a document. A collection is a set of nested nodes, as we see in the following example where we have a list of nested nodes. Function-based indexes cannot index all of these nodes, but the new XMLIndex index can:

```
<COLLECTION>
<PERSON>
<NAME>Fred Smith</NAME>
<TITLE>DOCTOR</TITLE>
</PERSON>
<PERSON>
<NAME>Jon McCall</NAME>
<TITLE>NURSE</TITLE>
</PERSON>
</COLLECTION>
```

Here is an example of the creation of an XMLIndex. In this case the index will be synchronized every three days:

```
create index xml_example_index on xml_storage_table(OBJECT_VALUE)
indextype is XDB.XMLINDEX
parameters ('async (sync every "freq=daily; interval = 3")');
```

**NOTE**
*The **every** clause requires the **create job** privilege.
This is because a job must be scheduled to
synchronize the index.*

You can also create an index that will be manually synchronized:

```
CREATE INDEX xml_example_index on xml_storage_table(OBJECT_VALUE)
indextype is XDB.XMLINDEX
PARAMETERS ('ASYNC(SYNC MANUAL)');
```

After the index is created it can be updated by running the following command.

```
BEGIN
DBMS_XMLINDEX.SYNC-INDEX('myuser', 'XML_EXAMPLE_INDEX');
END;
/
```

Parallel operations are also supported for XMLIndex index types. This means you can create the indexes faster and rebuild them faster than function-based indexes. Updates to the indexes are also faster because only pieces of the indexes are updated instead of the entire index each time data is changed or deleted within the XML document.

**NOTE**
*Not all XPATH expressions are indexed by XMLIndex types. They are user-defined XPATH functions, XPATH axes (other than child, descendant, and attribute), and statements using the union operator.*

An XMLIndex is created using a path table. The path table contains identifying information for each node it indexes. You can see the structure of this table via a **describe** statement. You can specify the name of the table at index creation time by adding **parameters ('path table table_name')** to your **create index** command. You can even create indexes on the path table. But you cannot access the path table any other way. You don't even need to gather statistics on the path table as Oracle does this for you when processing the table the XMLIndex was created on.

There are two update options with XMLIndex index types. They are synchronous and asynchronous updates. If you choose synchronous updates (the default), the index is updated as rows are inserted, updated, or deleted from an XML document. Asynchronous updates are done when a commit is issued, a DDL is created on the table or the index, a user is scheduled, or when you choose to kick off an update manually.

## In-place XML Schema Evolution

In Oracle Database 10*g* we had to evolve our XML schemas the hard way—uphill, in the snow, during a blizzard. We copied data out, deleted it, upgraded the schema, and then copied it back in. The cries of the oppressed and downtrodden XML schema version upgraders have not gone unheard. Oracle has seen fit to grant us the ability to evolve schemas without all of the copies. There are conditions, of course, but in-place XML schema evolution is a great step in the right direction.

There are a few restrictions to consider when planning on an in-place schema evolution. The basic rule is that you have to maintain backward compatibility. You cannot change the schema so much that existing documents would fail validation. These rules are quite involved, so please refer to the Oracle documentation for specifics on what is allowed, what is not, and when you can do it.

Binary XML sometimes will allow changes not normally allowed on non-binary schemas and disallow changes normally allowed. Please refer to Oracle's documentation on the conditions surrounding upgrading XML schemas with and without binary XML.

The first thing we have to do to evolve an XML schema in-place is to create an XMLDiff file. Using the **xmldiff** function as seen in this example will cause the XMLDiff file to be created:

```
var mydiff clob;
select xmldiff(xmltype(bfilename('XMLDIR2', 'example.xsd'),
NLS_CHARSET_ID('AL32UTF8')), xmltype(bfilename('XMLDIR2', 'example_v2.xsd'),
NLS_CHARSET_ID('AL32UTF8'))).getClobVal into :mydiff from dual;
```

Once the diff is created, we use it and the **dbms_xmlschema.inPlaceEvolve** procedure to evolve the schema:

```
begin dbms_xmlschema.inPlaceEvolve('http://localhost:8080/opt/oracle/
example.xsd',
xmltype(:mydiff));
end;
/
```

## Partitioning Support for XMP

Oracle Database adds the ability to partition XMLType columns and tables. This can have significant impacts when you have large sets of data and want to use partition pruning or set up an archival strategy based on partitions. The only drawback to partitioning an XMLType column or table is that XMLIndex index types cannot be created on partitioned XMLType tables or columns.

## XQuery Enhancements

XQuery within Oracle Database 11*g* supports the WC3 XQuery 1.0 standard and the JSR 225 XQJ standard. Oracle has also improved XQuery performance when using XQuery on XML data stored in the schema model. Compound document support has been added as well as two new SQL operators, **XMLExists** and **XMLCast**.

## XMLExists

**XMLExists** is similar to the **exists** SQL operator. It checks to see if an XQuery expression returns an empty result. The result of an XQuery expression evaluates to node sequences instead of node sets, unlike XPATH expressions. Previous to Oracle Database 11*g* you may have used **existsNode** with XPATH expressions. **XMLExists** is a better solution than using **existsNode** because it accepts XQuery expressions instead of only the XPATH expressions. Another difference is that **XMLExists** also returns TRUE or FALSE instead of 0 or 1 as we find with **existsNode**. One other important difference between **XMLExists** and **existsNode** is that **existsNode** can only be used in the **where** clause of a SQL statement. XMLExists can be used within the **select** clause of a query but it must be inside a **case** statement.

## XMLCast

**XMLCast** is much like the **cast** statement, casting the value of an expression to a specific datatype. This is, of course, a one-way cast from XML to one of the supported SQL datatypes. You cannot convert those types to XML or convert XML to XML using **XMLCast**.

## Xlink Support

Oracle Database 11*g* provides the ability to use the Xlink language to define referential integrity in XML documents. Xlink has the ability not only to relate one document to another but also to specify how, or give definition to, why the relationship exists. For example, if you wanted to specify a link between the author of a book and every location where the author has been in the world, you could do so with an Xlink that not only specified the location but also identified what the location meant to the author. One location might just be a vacation spot while another might be a place where the author lived. Maybe a specific location was where the author came up with the inspiration to one of the books they wrote. All of these identifications within the relationship between author and location can be specified with the Xlink language.

## Compound Document Support

Oracle Database 11*g* supports compound documents via the **xi:xinclude** element. Oracle can deliver **xi:xinclude** elements as they are entered, or it can expand the element to contain the document the **Xinclude** is referencing. By default Oracle does not expand **xi:xinclude** elements. Expansion of **xi:include** elements can be done by calling the **XDBURIType** constructor. This constructor takes two arguments. The first is the path to operate on, and the second tells the constructor to either expand all **xi:xinclude** elements by specifying a "1," suppress errors by specifying a "2," or both by specifying a "3".

**NOTE**
*Although Oracle supports the **xi:xinclude** element, it does not support the **xpointer** attribute.*

## Database Native Web Services

Oracle Database 11*g* has improved its web services by allowing PL/SQL stored objects to be accessed as Web Services. This does not require additional coding on a developer's part and also allows dynamic XQuery and SQL statements to be issued via the web interface instead of using a SQL Client.

To enable Oracle's native SOAP interface, the xmlconfig.xml file that resides in the XMLDB repository must be updated. You can access this file using FTP, HTTP, WebDav, Enterprise Manager, development APIs, or the DBMS_XDB packet using the **cfg_get**, **cfg_refresh**, and **cfg_update** objects.

The following example shows how to add a Web Services servlet using the **dbms_xdb** interface:

```
Begin
     DBMS_XDB.addServlet(NAME => 'orawsv',
     LANGUAGE => 'C', DISPNAME => 'SQL Web Service',
     DESCRIPT => 'Added to use with SQL queries',
     SCHEMA => 'XDB');
end;
/
begin
     DBMS_XDB.addServletSecRole(SERVNAME => 'orawsv',
     ROLENAME => 'XDB_WEBSERVICES', ROLELINK => 'XDB_WEBSERVICES');
end;
/
begin
     DBMS_XDB.addServletMapping(PATTERN => '/orawsv/*', NAME => 'orawsv');
end;
/
```

You can verify that the servlet has been added by issuing an XQuery against the XML repository. The new entry should be in servlet-name = 'orawsv' at the location: /xdbconfig/sysconfig/protocolconfig/httpconfig/webappconfig/wervletconfig/servlet-list/servlet in the dbconfig.xml file.

Users are granted rights to use the enabled Web Services by granting the **xdb_webservices_over_http** and/or **xdb_webservices_with_public** roles to a user. The **xdb_webservices_over_http** role grants web access to all objects, via the web, that the user has access to within the database except for objects that are PUBLIC. Web access to PUBLIC objects requires the user to have the **xdb_webservices_with_public** role.

Submitting SQL queries after that is as simple as constructing an XML document that conforms to Oracle's XML schema for database queries. The document is sent to

the database using an HTTP POST request on the web address http://<host>:<port>/
orawsv (where <host> and <port> are the host and port of the HTTPD server running
on your database).

Here's an example of an XML query request:

```
<?xml version="1.0" ?>
<envL:Envelope xmlns:env="http://www.w3.org/2002/06/soap-envelope">
<env:body>
<query xmlns="http://xmlns.oracle.com/orawsv">
<query_text type="SQL">
SELECT * from DBA_TABLES
</query_text>
</query>
</env:body>
</env:Envelope>
```

## XML DB Repository Enhancements

Oracle has provided several new enhancements to the XML DB Repository in 11*g*.
One of the larger enhancements is the addition of repository events. Events can be
generated on repository resource operations. To handle events an event listener is
created. The listener is composed of event handlers that process individual events.
The event listener is a package (PL/SQL), class (Java), or object type, while the event
handlers are methods or procedures or methods of the event listener. Events can be
enabled or disabled either within a session or at the system level. To enable or
disable events in the session dynamically, issue the command **alter session set xml_
db_events = disable** or **alter session set xml_db_events = enable**. Events can also be
set at the system level with the **alter system** command, as seen in these examples:

```
alter system set xml_db_events = disable;
alter system set xml_db_events = enable;
```

Event listeners are defined within an XML document that follows the XDBResConfig
.xsd schema definition. This schema definition can be found in Oracle's XML DB
repository in the path /sys/schemas/PUBLIC/xmlns.oracle.com/xdb/XDBResConfig.xsd.
Once the event listener's XML resource configuration document has been created, it is
then created in the repository using the **DBMS_XDB.createResource** function. Once
the resource has been created, it is added to Oracle's resource configuration through
the **dbms_resconfig.appendResConfig** procedure.

Procedures that are called by events are passed an event object called
**XDBRepositoryEvent** defined in the **dbms_xevent** package. Procedures can use this
event object to gather information about the event and the resource the event is for.
The **dbms_xevent** package is used to access information about the event and can
also be used to extract the resource object from the event. Once the resource object
is extracted from the event, the **dbms_xdbresource** package can be used to access
information about the extracted resource.

## XML Developers Kit

Oracle Database 11*g* provides full support of binary XML in both C and Java. First, Java now supports encoding, decoding, and vocabulary management. Encoding and decoding are accomplished via the **BinXMLStream** interface. The decoder can return SAX events or an **InfosetReader** type to access decoded XML. Vocabulary management within Java is done through the **BinXMLMetadataProvider** interface.

When using binary XML in C or Java, the code must be metadata-aware. In order for this to happen, several additional steps need to be taken to access binary XML data. After creating a connection handle a program must also create a metadata repository. Calling the **OCIBinXMLCreateReposCTXFromCPool** function for a connection pool or the **OCIBinXMLCreateReposCtxFromConn** function for a dedicated connection creates the repository. Once the repository is created it must be associated with the data connection being used for binary XML. This is done by calling the **OCIBinXmlSetRepos CtxForConn** function. This is a very simple overview of what has to happen in C programs using binary XML. Oracle's documentation has complete examples and calls on using C and Java with binary XML.

## Java

Oracle Database 11*g* offers a number of new Java features including:

- Oracle Java Virtual Machine (JVM)–related Features

- Utility improvements

- JDBC enhancements

Let's look at each of these features in the next section.

## Oracle JVM-Related Features

Several JVM-related components have new features and enhancements in Oracle Database 11*g*. In this section we will discuss the following:

- Oracle JVM upgraded to JDK 1.5

- Oracle JIT compiler

- Oracle JVM improved user interface

### Oracle JVM Upgraded to JDK 1.5

The JVM that runs inside the database has been upgraded to JDK version 1.5. This enhancement provides support for the new features introduced in JDK 1.5. These new features provide better usability and portability for applications that previously were difficult to run in the Oracle JVM.

## Oracle JIT Compiler

A just-in-time (JIT) compiler was added to the Oracle JVM in Oracle Database 11*g*. The JIT adds better manageability for Java programs by avoiding recompilation in some scenarios and providing dynamic recompilation when necessary. By default, the JIT is enabled. You can disable it dynamically by using the **alter system** command to set the **java_jit_enabled** parameter to FALSE (default: TRUE).

## Oracle JVM Improved User Interface

Many improved interfaces make their debut in Oracle 11*g*. In this section, we'll review the following improvements:

- Command line–like interface from within the database

- Shell access directly to session namespace within Oracle JVM

- JAR files stored as objects

- Output redirection

- Setting session-persistent system properties

- Two-tier duration for Java session state

- Controlling session termination

**Command Line–Like Interface**   A command line–like interface is introduced in Oracle Database 11*g*. This new interface allows more flexibility for session state control, ability to set system properties, JAR support, output redirection, and immediate session termination. The interface is implemented by two functions in the **dbms_java** package.

```
FUNCTION runjava(cmdline VARCHAR2) RETURN VARCHAR2;
FUNCTION runjava_in_current_session(cmdline VARCHAR2) RETURN VARCHAR2;
```

The **runjava** function parameter runs the command provided in the **cmdline** parameter as though it were running the command in the shell. That is, a new invocation of the JVM is started that contains only the state and properties established by the command given. In the second function, **runjava_in_current_session**, the previous state established by previous **runjava** or **runjava_in_current_session** calls is retained and the new command (**cmdline**) is executed in the previously established Java state.

**Shell Access to Session Namespace**   When at the command line outside the SQL prompt, you can also connect to the database's JVM directly and interact with it directly. This facility is provided via the **ojvmjava** command-line interface.

To connect to the session namespace of the database instance, you would use **ojvmjava** like this:

```
ojvmjava -u scott/tiger -runjava -d dbserverhost:1521:ORCL -t
```

**JAR Files Stored as Objects**   Prior to Oracle Database 11*g*, when a .jar file was loaded into the OJVM using the **loadjava** utility, the classes in the .jar file were extracted and there was no stored association between the .jar file and the classes inside it. Starting in Oracle Database 11*g*, Oracle JVM now supports JAR files as database objects. The primary benefit of this feature is the ability to preserve the signature on signed JAR files and the ability to preserve namespaces when the same class may already be loaded in the database.

**Output Redirection**   When operating at the command line, the Java executable maps System.out and System.err to the stdout and stderr streams, respectively. However, in Oracle Database versions prior to Oracle Database 11*g*, such a mapping was missing and all OJVM output was sent to trace files in the **user_dump_dest** location on the filesystem. Starting with Oracle Database 11*g*, a new set of functions, **set_output_to_sql**, **set_output_to_file**, and **set_output_to_java**, allow you to configure where output from the OJVM is sent.

**Setting Session-Persistent System Properties**   Additional functions in the **dbms_java** package allow you to set system properties for your Java session before any executable code is run. The **dbms_java** functions responsible for setting, reading, removing, and inspecting system properties are

```
FUNCTION set_property(name VARCHAR2, value VARCHAR2) RETURN VARCHAR2;
FUNCTION get_property(name VARCHAR2) RETURN VARCHAR2;
FUNCTION remove_property(name VARCHAR2) RETURN VARCHAR2;
FUNCTION show_property(name VARCHAR2) RETURN VARCHAR2;
```

**Two-Tier Duration for Java Session State**   Prior to Oracle Database 11*g*, Java session state duration was from first invocation until the JVM process exited. A JVM process exit is an explicit exit by calling **java.lang.System.exit**, calling **dbms_java.endsession**, an uncaught exception, a fatal error, or the end of the database session. With the introduction of settable Java session state parameters, Oracle has introduced an additional level of duration for the Java session state.

First, when a session ends for any of the reasons described in the preceding paragraph, session state information related to specific classes or other java state is lost. However, assuming that the reason for the Java session termination was not the end of the database session, configuration settings like output redirection or system properties persist. When the **dbms_java.endsession_and_related_state** function is called, the session is completely ended, all configuration settings including output redirection and system properties are purged, and these settings are no longer available.

# Enhancements to Existing Utilities

The pre-existing Oracle JVM utilities have been enhanced in Oracle Database 11*g*. This section describes the following enhancements:

- URL support for **loadjava**

- List-based operation with **dropjava**

- Enhancements to **ojvmjava**

## URL Support for loadjava

The **loadjava** utility is used to create database objects for java objects. Before Oracle 11*g*, the file(s) you wished to load had to be on the local filesystem and locally accessible to the **loadjava** utility. Starting with Oracle Database 11*g*, this enhancement allows the **loadjava** utility to retrieve a class that is not on the local filesystem, but instead may be available via a remote HTTP server. To support this, **loadjava** also supports use of a proxy server with the new **-proxy** flag. See the following example of using **loadjava** with a URL:

```
loadjava -u scott/tiger -r -v -proxy myproxy.domain.com:8080 \
http://someserver.com/path/to/my.jar
```

## List-Based Operation with dropjava

The **dropjava** utility has improved usability by adding the ability to operate on multiple objects using a single command. This enhancement adds two more arguments to the ten other documented command-line switches: **-list** and **-listfile**. The **-list** argument allows you to specify multiple, space-separated arguments as the names of classes that are to be dropped. The **-listfile** switch allows you to specify the pathname to a file containing the list of classes to be dropped. Here are examples of each syntax:

```
dropjava -list -u scott/tiger -v class1.class2.class3 class4.class5.class6
dropjava -listfile /path/to/list.txt -u scott/tiger -s -v
```

## Enhancements to ojvmjava

The **ojvmjava** utility makes it much easier to manage Java in the database by connecting you to the session namespace in the OJVM in the database. The utility then provides an interactive shell where you can enter commands to be run by the OJVM. In previous releases, the result of entering an unrecognized command at the **ojvmjava** prompt was to get a prompt back again. In the Oracle Database 11*g* release, this behavior has been enhanced to provide an appropriate error message.

Another enhancement to the **ojvmjava** utility also has to do with error handling. When Java stack traces are received as the result of a command, the stack trace information can fill several screens with references. In Oracle Database 11*g*, the standard behavior has been updated to display a reduced amount of the stack trace. In order to obtain the complete stack trace, you can use the **-debug** command-line option (this option was also available in previous releases).

Finally, a new keyword has been added to the interactive shell provided by **ojvmjava** to allow users to change the database connection without having to exit the **ojvmjava** interactive shell. Users can now use the **connect** keyword from within the interactive shell to connect to a different database's OJVM session namespace. The options for the **connect** command are the same as those used for the **ojvmjava** command-line utility itself. Here are some examples of valid uses of the **connect** keyword from within **ojvmjava**:

```
connect -o -u scott/tiger  ### to connect locally using $ORACLE_SID
connect -t -u scott/tiger@dbserver:1521:orcl ### connect using thin driver
connect -o -u scott/tiger -d remote_db ### connect to remote descriptor
remote_db
```

## The ojvmtc Utility

The **ojvmtc** utility is new in Oracle Database 11*g* and offers the ability to resolve external references before running **loadjava**. Previously, unresolved references weren't discovered until attempting to use the loaded classes. This utility makes it possible to find potential problems earlier in the process and avoid runtime issues. The syntax includes options for the list of classes to be included in the closure set (the set to be loaded into Oracle JVM and a list of classes and archives to be used in resolution of the references (the set that will be available in Oracle JVM already). It is also possible to connect to the database in order to obtain the list of classes available to help resolve references. The syntax for the **–server** argument (which allows database connectivity) is unusual and follows the following pattern: **<driver_type>:<user>/<password>@<connection_information>**.

Here are some examples of valid syntax. Note that when using the **oci driver_type**, valid connection_information may be host:port:sid or TNS connect descriptor (resolved by SQL*Net client).

```
ojvmtc -server thin:scott/tiger@dbserver:1521:ORCL -classpath \
/path/to/my.jar:/path/to/your.jar app.jar
ojvmtc -server oci:scott/tiger@orcl_tns -classpath /path/to/my.jar
-list app.jar
ojvmtc -server oci:scott/tiger@orcl_tns -classpath /path/to/my.jar -jar \
loadthis.jar app.jar
```

# JDBC 4.0 Support

Oracle Database 11*g* fully supports JDBC 4.0. This section describes the most significant new features for JDBC 4.0 developers:

- Annotations
- Wrapper interface
- Support for java.sql.RowId
- Improved LOB support

In this section, we'll describe each of these features in more detail.

## Annotations

Annotations are metadata embedded in Java code and are associated with a class, method, or field. Annotations are processed at runtime and can be used to make runtime decisions by inspecting annotations via provided APIs. Coding and maintenance can both be reduced by effective use of annotations. Oracle Database 11*g* supports use of annotations as specified by J2SE 1.5.

## Wrapper Interface

Wrappers have been commonly implemented as custom implementations with slightly different APIs and varying levels of visibility to the classes that have been wrapped. Java has standardized the wrapper interface and provided methods to inspect and unwrap the wrapper to provide direct access to the wrapped class. These methods, **isWrapperFor()** and **unwrap()**, are documented in Oracle's *JDBC Developer's Guide and Reference* as well as in Java's standard class documentation. Oracle supports the **Wrapper** interface in its JDBC drivers.

## Support for java.sqlRowId

The **java.sql.RowId** interface is a new feature in JDBC 4.0. Oracle provides the **oracle.sql.ROWID** data type as a JDBC extension and it is related, but not the same as the **java.sql.RowID**. There are methods to get the rowid in the **ResultSet** and **CallableStatement** interfaces. Additionally, the **PreparedStatement** interface offers a **setRowId** method to set the value for a parameterized statement.

## Improved LOB Support

Previous JDBC versions had support for LOBs and with Oracle Database 11*g*, previous interfaces have been improved to make LOB manipulation easier. New methods **createBlob**, **createClob**, and **createNClob** have been added to the **Connection** interface to enable creation of objects for each of the respective LOB types. Here are some examples:

```
Connection con = DriverManager.getconnection(url, props);
Blob aBlob = con.createBlob();
in numWritten = aBlob.setBytes(1, val);
```

## JDK Support in Oracle Database 11g

Oracle Database 11g introduces changes to the support status of the JDK. Oracle client-side JDBC drivers support JDK 1.5 and 1.6. Server-side Java code running in Oracle JVM is run using JDK 1.5. Oracle JDBC drivers no longer support JDK versions below version 1.5.

# New Oracle Supplied Packages and Procedures

There are a number of new Oracle supplied packages introduced in Oracle Database 11g that we have not discussed yet in this book. Here are some quick highlights of some that would seem to be the most usable:

- **Dbms_addm**   Provides procedures that allow you to manage ADDM operations.

- **Dbms_comparison**   This package provides the ability to compare two Oracle databases and define the differences between the two. The package then provides the ability to converge the databases, making one look like the other.

- **Dbms_cube and dbms_cube_advise**   The packages provide additional abilities to manage online analytical processing (OLAP) cubes and dimensions.

- **Dbms_result_cache**   This package provides the ability to manage the database result caches (SQL and PL/SQL).

**Arup Says…**

The package **dbms_addm** is a great tool for analysis in an RAC environment. The ADDM reports were available earlier too, but they were instance-specific, not database-wide. In 11*g*, the new package **dbms_addm** allows you to get a report for the entire database. Here is a simple example to get the ADDM report for the period between snapshots 612 and 659:

```
SQL> var task_name varchar2(20)
SQL> exec :task_name := null;
SQL> begin dbms_addm.analyze_db (:task_name, 612,659); end;
  2> /
SQL> set long 99999
SQL> select dbms_addm.get_report (:task_name) from dual;
```

The second statement gets the report on the screen that shows the ADDM report for the entire database. Doing so allows you to get a true representation of metrics for the database, not just for a specific instance.

Perhaps the most interesting is the **dbms_comparison** package, which allows two databases to be compared. Remember the **compare** utility available in Enterprise Manager in 9*i*? In 10*g*, that functionality disappeared in the browser version of EM, but it was a much-sought-after feature. It appeared in many third-party database management tools. In 11*g*, this tool is part of the database code. The utility of the tool is extended even more by the fact that, although the local database where you are running the package must be 11*g* (of course, this package is available in 11*g* only), the remote database can be 10*g*R1 or later.

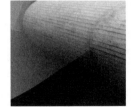

# APPENDIX

## Arup's Top Ten Features

I n the not-so-recent past, I bought a new car. No, it's not a sports car (I'm too young to retire and blow all my money on one); not a Beemer or a Merc or even a Saab (can't afford any one of them). Actually, the exact name is not really relevant for what I am trying to say, but the manufacturer is perceived to be very quality-conscious. The car has a number of features, displayed prominently on glossy brochures, that undoubtedly attracted my attention. The salesman went through the detailed features with a fine-toothed comb: How the speakers at the back of the trunk would enhance my sensory experience and how the sporty-looking exhaust pipe would make me feel years younger, and so on. Well, I was sold and got the car. Needless to say, almost all those features worked as expected, but some failed, notably the ones like enhancing my sensory experience. But, to my pleasant surprise, I discovered a number of features worth writing home about. Almost all the cars with power windows have a feature allowing the window to automatically roll down when the button is pressed for a tad bit longer, but how many cars have you seen, especially in the non-[*ahem*]luxury market, that offer the automatic window roll-*up* function? Well, this car does. You can flick the window button and the window rolls up automatically, just as it rolls down.

Well, what's the big deal about a little feature? Little, yes; but consider picking up carryout while trying to navigate through the precarious lanes of the drive-in window of a fast food chain in New York, especially in the rain or snow. Being able to keep both hands on the steering wheel certainly helps. Or consider rolling up the window after paying toll or picking up mail from the mailbox; many everyday activities offer a new perspective on usability and convenience, all because of that little feature. But that feature didn't make it to the brochure; it did make it to the manuals but into some quaint corner. The salesman didn't rave about it. Some marketing whiz kid from the manufacturer probably thought this little feature would not make that much of a difference and so relegated it to near-obscurity. But, from the perspective of the users, like me, that little feature is god-sent.

The story has a lot of parallels to the introduction of a new database version from Oracle. Like my car, the new database version has a lot of gee-whiz features; but how useful are they? The intelligent folks at Oracle's massive marketing machinery pick and rave about a few. We the users may have our eyes on another set of features. Mostly these two overlap, but sometimes they don't. We users dismiss a much-touted feature like the extra speakers in the rear of the car while salivating over the little-known details like the automatic window roll-up. In this book, Robert and I (actually, Robert mostly) have tried to present to you, the user, which of these features will make the biggest difference to our tasks, not the ones that the marketing folks at Oracle think are good for us. And all those have been presented with enough details for you to get going as soon as possible.

I have provided a commentary throughout the book where I added complementary content to what Robert has provided. In this appendix, I will elucidate the top ten features that I feel will change your experience as a user. Bear in mind that I have culled my 12 years of experience exclusively as an Oracle DBA in separating the chaff from the wheat for this list; this may not be the top ten list Oracle's top execs mentioned during the launch or even afterwards, nor are they promoted heavily by the Oracle product managers. So, they may have been prominently featured everywhere, or equally likely, hidden in some manual pages.

Happy reading!

# Arup's Top Feature # 1: Database Replay

What's one thing that does not change in your interaction with the Oracle database, regardless of the type of user you are—DBA, developer, or even sys admins and storage admins? It's the need to change—creating an index, applying a patch, changing a table from nonpartitioned to partitioned (or changing the partitioning scheme from hash to range, for instance), changing the storage layout from raw to ASM, and so on. Business keeps on changing and your database must keep in step with the changes, so tasks like gathering stats and the need for new indexes are not just avoidable hassles; they are bare necessities and very much a part of life. And on every change you probably invariably bite your nails, or do whatever your form of expressing anxiety is—pondering over the inevitable question of whether this change will break something somewhere else. Determination of the holistic effect of change is difficult, if not downright impossible. How can you assess the risk to the whole system as a result of the change?

If you had a way to perform the changes on a test system prior to making them in production, it would certainly be one way to have a good night's sleep. But although it is easy to replicate a database, it's not possible to faithfully duplicate the activities, especially the queries. Relying on a third-party load generator tool typically used by QA people does not solve the problem. While the tool can run a lot of load, bear in mind that it's performing synthetic transactions that may or may not resemble the actual SQL statements and thus will not be an accurate representation of the production workload.

This is the sweet spot for Database Replay. You turn it on, by a few mouse clicks or by calling a supplied package, and voilà! you start recording the workload from your production system like a camcorder. Later you can replay what was captured on a test system. The whole process is as easy as operating a camcorder even your grandmother can operate. Robert has explained it quite splendidly in Chapter 5, so I'm not going to repeat the usage here. But I will highlight some of the wonderful use cases. The best use of the tool is when you are concerned about any change in the environment of the database—the host was changed from Solaris to HP-UX, say; or the effect of a patch, such as the quarterly CPU patches; or the effect of converting the database from a single instance to an RAC one, and so on. In all these cases, you capture the workloads of the production system, which are recorded in some prespecified directory. You can then transfer these to a test system where they are replayed, or even replay on the same system when you get some outage. Either way, you are assured of one thing—whatever you are replaying is an accurate reflection of what goes on in your production database. Therefore the effect of the changes will be a truthful prediction of the effect of the same changes on the production system.

# Arup's Top Feature # 2: SQL Performance Analyzer

Database Replay is a part of a suite of tools Oracle provides as an option—called Real Application Testing (RAT). A very close second place in my favorite list is the second member of the RAT family—SQL Performance Analyzer (SPA). It's very similar to Database Replay; but with some important differences. SPA doesn't record anything; you can capture the SQL statements from the SQL Tuning Sets or the library cache, or you can write your own SQL statements. Once it gets a number of SQL statements, it replays them against the database after changing some parameter you specify. For instance, suppose you want to find out the effect of the parameter **optimizer_index_cost_adj** on the execution plans. You can capture all the SQL statements in the library cache and make them part of a SQL Tuning Set (STS). Later you can use SPA to replay the statements in STS while the parameter is changed. SPA will replay the statements one by one. Because the SQL statements are replayed, SPA can be used in the production databases to gauge the impact of parameter changes on SQL statements without actually making these changes. There is another difference: Database Replay must be run on the entire database and you can't decide the exact statements that will be executed.

At the end of the replay session, you get a report of the impact of those changes on performance—positive, negative, or no impact. The ability to preview the effect of the changes without making them beforehand is a powerful tool in your arsenal, and therefore it's my second choice, very close to the first, in the Top Ten list.

# Arup's Top Feature # 3: Partitioning

Actually there are several enhancements worth mentioning in partitioning. All those are important and I don't want you to lose focus on any one of them. So, I have grouped them all under one section. Let's see the first one—*interval partitioning*. One of the challenges in partitioning is to create new partitions to accommodate new records. Of course, it's a small challenge, but it is one that needs to be addressed throughout the life of the database instead of a one-time deal as in the case of design. If you don't add the new partition, a newly inserted row goes into the default partition; if you have defined one, or the insert fails—both situations are unpalatable. That's where interval partitioning shines. You define the interval, and Oracle automatically creates the partitions. Here is an example:

```
create table reservations (
     res_id        number(12),
     res_dt        date,
     hotel_id      number(4)
)
partition by range (res_dt)
interval (numtoyminterval(1,'MONTH'))
(
     partition nov07
     values less than (to_date('01-12-2007','dd-mm-yyyy'))
)
```

Once the table is created, it will have only one partition—NOV07—to hold the records for Nov 2007 and earlier. When a new record comes in to the table for Dec 2007, Oracle will automatically create a new partition for you. Read all about it in Chapter 7.

The names of these Oracle-created partitions are, however, something like SYS_P41—not very intuitive to target-specific partitions in a DML statement. So, Oracle Database 11*g* provides a new syntax for partitions:

```
select * from reservations partition for (to_date('3-dec-2007','dd-mon-yyyy'));
```

Here you didn't have to specify the partition name; all you did was to reference the value that will be in the partition and let Oracle get the name for you.

The second important partitioning enhancement is *reference partitioning*. Consider the classic example of EMP and DEPT tables. Suppose DEPT is partitioned on a column called ZONE.

```
create table dept (
        dept_no         number(2),
        dept_name       varchar2(20),
        zone            varchar2(5)
)
partition by list (zone)
(
        partition east values ('EAST'),
        partition north values ('NORTH')
)
alter table dept add constraint pk_dept primary key (dept_no);
```

The table EMP is a child table of DEPT, with DEPT_NO as the foreign key:

```
create table EMP (
        emp_id              number(10) not null,
```

```
        dept_no         number(2) not null,
        constraint fk_emp_dept foreign key (dept_no)
              references dept (dept_no)
)
partition by reference (fk_emp_dept)
```

Note the code carefully, especially the last line. The table is partitioned, but all you have given is the name of the foreign key constraint. This partitions the table exactly as the parent table—DEPT. But also note that the parent—DEPT—has been partitioned on the column ZONE, while there is no ZONE column in EMP. That is the beauty of reference partitioning. The child table does not need to have the partitioning key. This feature allows virtually any table to be partitioned on the scheme you want, without making too many structural changes.

The other notables in partitioning enhancements are: the ability to composite partition tables with RANGE as subpartition (so you can use RANGE-RANGE, LIST-RANGE, and so on) and the ability to partition on virtual columns. Virtual columns are not stored in the table; they are computed at run time. So, because you can define partitions, you can choose the best partitioning column without making changes to the application to populate these columns.

# Arup's Top Feature # 4: Transparent Tablespace Encryption

Encryption at rest, that is, on the database, has been around for a long time in Oracle databases, in the form of the supplied package **dbms_obfuscation_toolkit**. In Oracle 10*g* R1, we saw the successor to this package—**dbms_crypto**. But these packages provided only some APIs to build your own encryption infrastructure. In 10*g* R2, Oracle provided Transparent Database Encryption (TDE), which allowed a column to be encrypted in the database using only a single command. While that was a relief for most folks, it was not a solution for most cases. The biggest issue was performance. If you issue a query like this where the column SSN is encrypted and has an index:

```
select * from emp where SSN like '123%'
```

the optimizer will not choose the index. Why? In the database the column is stored in encrypted format, which has no predetermined pattern to it. For instance, we know that SSN 123456789 comes after 123456788; so the optimizer will be able to do an index range scan to find all records with pattern '123%'. But if the column is encrypted, the pattern will be really random; '12346789' and '123456788' may be stored as '0d345f754wf43e23e22b' and 'e3af456b39d348234ec' respectively. Examine the pattern of the encrypted values—they are worlds apart. So an index range scan is not possible. Instead a full table scan will be faster. Therefore, if you issue a query such as '123%' on a TDE-enabled column, the index is ignored and a full table scan is used, causing performance degradation.

The issue is solved in Oracle Database 11*g* by a new facility called Transparent Tablespace Encryption (TTE). You just create a tablespace as encrypted:

```
create tablespace secure_ts
datafile '...'
encryption using 'AES128'
default storage (encrypt);
```

After this tablespace is created, all you have to do is create a table in this tablespace, and that will be encrypted automatically. So far it sounds like TDE; what's the difference? The difference is the way the cache operates. The blocks of a table in an encrypted tablespace in the database cache in the SGA are not encrypted. So, when an index scan occurs, it can scan the index blocks in cleartext and a pattern-matching query such as "like '123%'" can access the index just like any clear-text table. So, you get the best of both worlds—you have the data encrypted while not making any sacrifices in performance. Read all about Transparent Tablespace Encryption in Chapter 6.

# Arup's Top Feature # 5: Flashback Data Archive

In Oracle 9*i*, we were introduced to a shiny new feature called flashback transactions. When data is updated, the past image of the block is stored in the undo segments, even if the data is committed. Why so? It's because a long-running query that started before the data was changed should see the pre-change data, even if the changes are committed now. The pre-change data is available anyway in the undo segments; so why not expose it to the users? That was the foundation of flashback queries, which allowed you to get the data as of a specified time (or SCN). In Oracle 10*g*, we saw flashback transactions that actually gave us a history of data changes, how they changed, who changed it, and so on; a great auditing tool, at least for debugging purposes.

However, there was a big caveat: The data came from undo segments. Undo data is not kept forever; it is flushed if it's not needed and there is a demand for space from new transactions. So, the flashback transaction fails when the undo data evaporates. That's why you resorted to writing your own triggers if you wanted to keep a record of changes permanently. In Oracle 11*g*, you don't have to; a new feature called flashback data archive does the trick. All you do is to define a flashback archive and add a table to that:

```
create flashback archive far1
tablespace ts_far1
quota 1g
```

```
retention 1 year
/
alter table emp flashback archive far1
/
```

That's it. You have added the table EMP to the flashback archive called FAR1. Now, whenever the table is changed, the past image will be stored in the flash recovery area. Internally Oracle implements several tables where this data is stored. If you explain a flashback query you can see that those unpublished internal tables are used. So, in effect, when you enable a table for flashback archive, Oracle performs the functional equivalent of writing triggers to capture the pre-change data and populate those internal tables.

Then, you may ask, we can accomplish the same using triggers; so what's the big deal, apart from the fact that we are relieved of the task of writing the triggers? Fair question, and there are two very good reasons.

First, those internal tables to record history are not done using triggers, but by the Oracle software code itself. So, there is no trigger-related performance impact—no context switching or checking for dependencies.

Second, you can continue using the queries as you did for flashback queries all along. There is no change to access the flashback archives. This gives you the flexibility of flashback queries while not limiting you to undo segments only.

You can use this feature in many scenarios. This will be a very quick auditing tool, without turning on auditing. Both auditing and flashback archives are written to disk, so IO is involved in both cases. However, in case of auditing, the writing is almost instantaneous (almost, since the operation is an autonomous transaction), while flashback archives are written by a special process called flashback data archiver (FBDA), which is completely asynchronous and does not affect the transaction. This should be a very good reason to use it over auditing. The other good reason is that you specify whatever tablespaces you like for flashback archives; auditing is still on the SYSTEM tablespace. So, you can define flashback archives on cheaper storage and Oracle will autopurge it after the specified duration. Read all about Flashback archives in Chapter 2.

# Arup's Top Feature # 6: SQL Plan Management

What is your biggest concern while collecting statistics on objects? Is it the fear of breaking something, and more specifically, breaking a perfect execution plan? If that is the case, you are not alone; this is a concern expressed by DBAs all over the world. What if there was a way to ensure that the newly calculated execution plan will be in effect only if it is better than the previous one?

In Oracle Database 11*g*, this is a reality, through a feature called SQL Plan Management (SPM). Whenever a new execution plan is calculated, it is baselined in a store called SQL Management Base. Once baselined, the SQL execution plan is attached to the query and is the plan used for the query from that point onwards

To start the baselining of all queries, you will simply issue this command:

```
alter system optimizer_capture_sql_plan_baselines = true;
```

This will cause the execution plan of all queries to be baselined. After that, if you change something that might potentially affect the execution plan, the plan will not change. If you issue an autotrace on the query, you will see a line such as the following:

```
- SQL plan baseline "SYS_SQL_PLAN_a3185cea611ea913" used for this
statement
```

This line indicates that the optimizer did not calculate the plan again; it merely used one of the cached plans. Well, this is good, but don't you want to make sure the plan reflects the current conditions, for example, newly updated stats and/or optimizer environments? Sure you do. That's where SPM excels too. You can choose to "evolve" a plan to see how the newly calculated plan compares to the existing one:

```
SQL> var rep clob
SQL> exec :rep := dbms_spm.evolve_sql_plan_baseline( -

sql_handle=>'SYS_SQL_353e8c17a551f70c')
SQL> print rep
```

The report will be printed in the SQL*Plus prompt. You can decide if the plan is better than the previous one. If so, you can accept it; otherwise, it remains in the SMB as a historical record of the plan that was once calculated. So, not only do you have an option to "lock" the best plan, but you have the option to constantly compare it against others and make sure you always get the best possible plan. You can see more on SPM in Chapter 9.

# Arup's Top Feature # 7: Private Statistics

One of the problems with optimizer statistics collection is the potential issue of resource consumption. The collection of statistics, whether by the **analyze** command or by using the **dbms_stats** package, consumes CPU and IO. You can somehow curtail this by using Resource Manager so that the task does not overwhelm the system and doesn't cause the other processes to starve. What if you want to collect the stats when the system is relatively free but do not want to make them effective immediately? Later you want to make them effective at some predetermined time. In Oracle Database 11*g*, you can do that rather easily. The task of stats gathering has been divided into two parts—collection and publishing (when they are made effective). By default, the stats are published as soon as they are collected, but you can change that. To change that property for the table PROP in the OREF schema, use the following:

```
begin
        dbms_stats.set_table_prefs ('OREF','PROP','PUBLISH','FALSE');
end;
```

Now, you can check it:

```
SQL> select dbms_stats.get_prefs('PUBLISH','OREF','PROP') prefs from dual;

PREFS
-----
FALSE
```

After that, delete all rows from the table and then gather the stats as usual. After the stats gathering, if you check the table for the stats, you will see

```
select last_analyzed, num_rows
from user_tables
where table_name = 'PROP'
/

LAST_ANAL    NUM_ROWS
---------  ----------
01-SEP-07      68131
```

Why do the stats show that there are 68131 rows when we just deleted all the rows? It's because the stats have not been "published" yet. They are in a "pending" state, which you can see as

```
SQL> select num_rows, last_analyzed
  2  from user_tab_pending_stats
  3  where table_name = 'PROP';

NUM_ROWS LAST_ANAL
---------- ---------
        0 01-SEP-07
```

Here you can see that the pending stats show the accurate picture—0 rows. You can decide now to "publish" these stats:

```
begin
    dbms_stats.publish_pending_stats('OREF', 'PROP');
end;
```

Now if you check the stats, they show

```
LAST_ANAL    NUM_ROWS
---------    ----------
01-SEP-07           0
```

The stats correctly show the accurate number of rows—0. This brief demonstration should be enough to show that the statistics can be private until you decide to make them public. The most useful scenario I can think of is stats collection on partitions. You can collect stats on partitions one by one using different slack times on the system and then publish all of them at one time. You can get a history of the stats collection on tables and if needed, you can "roll back" the stats to as they were some point in the past:

```
begin
        dbms_stats.restore_table_stats (
                ownname         => 'OREF',
                tabname         => 'PROP',
                as_of_timestamp => '01-SEP-07 06:15:00 PM'
        );
end;
```

This will restore the stats as of that time. So don't worry if you want to collect stats at the most opportune time and then publish them at another time. In case of issues, you can always revert to the previous version of the stats using just one call to the supplied package.

# Arup's Top Feature # 8: More Concurrency

You want to alter a table to either add a column or modify a new column, but alas, it has been frustrating. It has constantly been failing with this error:

```
ERROR at line 1:
ORA-00054: resource busy and acquire with NOWAIT specified
```

This is occurring because the table has been locked by some transactions, so the other session can't get an exclusive lock on the table to execute the DDL statement. In a highly active environment there will be an infinitesimally small amount of time when you can get an exclusive lock on the table; so unless you stop the apps, any type of DDL on active tables will be pretty much impossible. This artificially reduces availability of the system even when the database itself is already available.

In Oracle Database 11*g*, there are two major enhancements:

1. First, you can add a column to the table even when another transaction holds row locks on the table.

2. Second, you can instruct the session executing the DDL to wait for some specified time, say, 30 seconds, before giving up. You have to issue this statement:

```
alter session set ddl_lock_timeout = 30;
```

After this command has been issued, the ALTER TABLE statement will not error out if it is unable to get the lock. It will keep on trying for 30 seconds to get that lock. Even in an active system, there is a strong possibility that an exclusive lock will be available for the very small duration for the DDL statement. You can read all about it in Chapter 2.

The other enhancement is in dependencies. Suppose there is a view called VW1 on the table T1. When you add a column to the table T1, in 10g, the view would have been invalid. In 11g, that view will *still be valid*. The addition of a column to the base table does not change the view in any way, so there was no reason why the view would be invalidated. It took Oracle a while to get that logic, but thank heavens they finally got it in 11g. Modifying a column of the base table used in the view, however, still invalidates the view. On a similar note, if a function (or procedure) calls a package and some new procedures or functions are added to the package after all the other subprograms there, the calling function is not invalidated. In 10g it would have been. These features make the infrastructure truly available.

# Arup's Top Feature # 9: Result Cache

Remember Materialized Views (MV), aka snapshots? They are very useful when you want to store the result of a query in a permanent form. When the users issue that query, Oracle does not re-execute it; rather, it pulls the results out of the MV and passes it on. While the system works fine, it has some serious limitations. First, the results are computed only once, when the DBA refreshes the MV. When the users select from it, the data is as of the time of refresh, not current; so it may not be accurate. Second, there is no way of knowing if the data in the MV is stale and if so, how much behind. But the appeal of the MVs is much too attractive to ignore—by serving the data from a table rather than executing the query saves CPU and IO and thus is a boon in repetitive and resource-consuming queries.

So, how can you have your cake and eat it too? Oracle 11g provides the best of both worlds—in the form of result cache. You invoke it by a hint:

```
select /*+ result_cache */ p.prop_desc, v.province_name, c.country_name
from properties p, provinces v, countries c
where c.country_code = p.country_code
and v.province_code = p.province_code;
```

When the query is executed for the first time, it has to go to all the base tables, but the result is cached and subsequent executions go against the result cache, not the base tables, much like MVs. But that's where the resemblance with MVs ends. When the underlying table data changes, the result cache is automatically refreshed without the DBA's intervention, so results are always accurate.

This is best suited for tables that do not change frequently, such as the ones shown earlier. There is a very similar concept in PL/SQL function outputs as well, known as function cache. You can learn more about result cache in Chapter 8.

# Arup's Top Feature # 10: Better-Quality PL/SQL Code

In Chapter 8, Robert showed you how to identify a potentially buggy coding practice in PL/SQL, by making the compiler catch the use of the **when others then null** construct. The compiler can catch these types of coding practices when the session parameter **plsql_warnings** is set to ENABLE:ALL. When the session parameter is set and you recompile the procedure where you have used something like this in the exception section:

```
when OTHERS then NULL;
```

the compiler shows a warning:

```
PLW-06009: procedure "P" OTHERS handler does not end in RAISE or
           RAISE_APPLICATION_ERROR
```

But the usefulness of the compiler warning does not end there. Consider the following code:

```
SQL> create or replace procedure p
  2  as
  3  begin
  4     null;
  5  exception
  6     when others then null;
  7  end;
  8  /
Procedure created.
```

Now recompile the procedure with the new flags:

```
SQL> alter procedure p compile plsql_warnings = 'enable:all';
SP2-0805: Procedure altered with compilation warnings
```

When you describe the error

```
SQL> show error
Errors for PROCEDURE P:

LINE/COL ERROR
-------------------------------------------------------------------
6/7       PLW-06002: Unreachable code
SQL> alter procedure p compile;

Procedure altered.
```

This is a very useful message. Note the code segment carefully. Line 4 says NULL, which means nothing gets done in that line; no exception will be ever reached and hence there rest of the procedure is pretty much useless. The compiler warns you of that. All these help you write better, more efficient code.

As I mentioned earlier, it's a Herculean task to boil down all that glitters in Oracle Database 11*g* into just ten items. I have tried to present the ones I think will give the biggest bang for the buck for the users. These choices by no means belittle so many others that have not been mentioned. If I had more space, I would have talked about them. Some notables worth mentioning are—virtual columns, PL/SQL inlining, case-sensitive passwords to meet some regulations that require those, ASM instance affinity, and many others. A book is by no means a substitute for self-experimentation, which is exactly what I hope you will do, with this book providing some initial thrust. On Oracle Technology Network, I have authored a series on 11*g* new features. Some of the articles carry a video of the activities that might help you to get a jumpstart on the usage. Read the book and the articles, watch the movies; but above all, experiment on your own with twists and variations, without which you will never really grasp the essence of some of the functionalities provided in Oracle Database 11*g*.

# Index

## B

# C

# D

## E

# P

# Q

# R

# S

# X

# Z

# GET YOUR FREE SUBSCRIPTION
# TO ORACLE MAGAZINE

*Oracle Magazine* is essential gear for today's information technology professionals. Stay informed and increase your productivity with every issue of *Oracle Magazine*. Inside each free bimonthly issue you'll get:

IF THERE ARE OTHER ORACLE USERS AT YOUR LOCATION WHO WOULD LIKE TO RECEIVE THEIR OWN SUBSCRIPTION TO ORACLE MAGAZINE, PLEASE PHOTOCOPY THIS FORM AND PASS IT ALONG.

- Up-to-date information on Oracle Database, Oracle Application Server, Web development, enterprise grid computing, database technology, and business trends

- Third-party vendor news and announcements

- Technical articles on Oracle and partner products, technologies, and operating environments

- Development and administration tips

- Real-world customer stories

## Three easy ways to subscribe:

### ① Web
Visit our Web site at otn.oracle.com/oraclemagazine. You'll find a subscription form there, plus much more!

### ② Fax
Complete the questionnaire on the back of this card and fax the questionnaire side only to +1.847.763.9638.

### ③ Mail
Complete the questionnaire on the back of this card and mail it to P.O. Box 1263, Skokie, IL 60076-8263

Oracle Corporation © 2003. All rights reserved. Oracle is a registered trademark of Oracle Corporation and/or its affiliates. All other names may be trademarks of their respective owners.

# FREE SUBSCRIPTION

○ **Yes, please send me a FREE subscription to *Oracle Magazine*.**     ○ **NO**

To receive a free subscription to *Oracle Magazine*, you must fill out the entire card, sign it, and date it (incomplete cards cannot be processed or acknowledged). You can also fax your application to +1.847.763.9638. **Or subscribe at our Web site at otn.oracle.com/oraclemagazine**

○ From time to time, Oracle Publishing allows our partners exclusive access to our e-mail addresses for special promotions and announcements. To be included in this program, please check this circle.

○ Oracle Publishing allows sharing of our mailing list with selected third parties. If you prefer your mailing address not to be included in this program, please check here. If at any time you would like to be removed from this mailing list, please contact Customer Service at +1.847.647.9630 or send an e-mail to oracle@halldata.com.

signature (required)                                           date

**X**

name                                            title

company                                         e-mail address

street/p.o. box

city/state/zip or postal code                   telephone

country                                         fax

## YOU MUST ANSWER ALL TEN QUESTIONS BELOW.

**① WHAT IS THE PRIMARY BUSINESS ACTIVITY OF YOUR FIRM AT THIS LOCATION?** (check one only)
- □ 01 Aerospace and Defense Manufacturing
- □ 02 Application Service Provider
- □ 03 Automotive Manufacturing
- □ 04 Chemicals, Oil and Gas
- □ 05 Communications and Media
- □ 06 Construction/Engineering
- □ 07 Consumer Sector/Consumer Packaged Goods
- □ 08 Education
- □ 09 Financial Services/Insurance
- □ 10 Government (civil)
- □ 11 Government (military)
- □ 12 Healthcare
- □ 13 High Technology Manufacturing, OEM
- □ 14 Integrated Software Vendor
- □ 15 Life Sciences (Biotech, Pharmaceuticals)
- □ 16 Mining
- □ 17 Retail/Wholesale/Distribution
- □ 18 Systems Integrator, VAR/VAD
- □ 19 Telecommunications
- □ 20 Travel and Transportation
- □ 21 Utilities (electric, gas, sanitation, water)
- □ 98 Other Business and Services

**② WHICH OF THE FOLLOWING BEST DESCRIBES YOUR PRIMARY JOB FUNCTION?** (check one only)
Corporate Management/Staff
- □ 01 Executive Management (President, Chair, CEO, CFO, Owner, Partner, Principal)
- □ 02 Finance/Administrative Management (VP/Director/ Manager/Controller, Purchasing, Administration)
- □ 03 Sales/Marketing Management (VP/Director/ Manager)
- □ 04 Computer Systems/Operations Management (CIO/VP/Director/ Manager MIS, Operations)
IS/IT Staff
- □ 05 Systems Development/ Programming Management
- □ 06 Systems Development/ Programming Staff
- □ 07 Consulting
- □ 08 DBA/Systems Administrator
- □ 09 Education/Training
- □ 10 Technical Support Director/Manager
- □ 11 Other Technical Management/Staff
- □ 98 Other

**③ WHAT IS YOUR CURRENT PRIMARY OPERATING PLATFORM?** (select all that apply)
- □ 01 Digital Equipment UNIX
- □ 02 Digital Equipment VAX VMS
- □ 03 HP UNIX

- □ 04 IBM AIX
- □ 05 IBM UNIX
- □ 06 Java
- □ 07 Linux
- □ 08 Macintosh
- □ 09 MS-DOS
- □ 10 MVS
- □ 11 NetWare
- □ 12 Network Computing
- □ 13 OpenVMS
- □ 14 SCO UNIX
- □ 15 Sequent DYNIX/ptx
- □ 16 Sun Solaris/SunOS
- □ 17 SVR4
- □ 18 UnixWare
- □ 19 Windows
- □ 20 Windows NT
- □ 21 Other UNIX
- □ 98 Other
- 99 □ None of the above

**④ DO YOU EVALUATE, SPECIFY, RECOMMEND, OR AUTHORIZE THE PURCHASE OF ANY OF THE FOLLOWING?** (check all that apply)
- □ 01 Hardware
- □ 02 Software
- □ 03 Application Development Tools
- □ 04 Database Products
- □ 05 Internet or Intranet Products
- 99 □ None of the above

**⑤ IN YOUR JOB, DO YOU USE OR PLAN TO PURCHASE ANY OF THE FOLLOWING PRODUCTS?** (check all that apply)
Software
- □ 01 Business Graphics
- □ 02 CAD/CAE/CAM
- □ 03 CASE
- □ 04 Communications
- □ 05 Database Management
- □ 06 File Management
- □ 07 Finance
- □ 08 Java
- □ 09 Materials Resource Planning
- □ 10 Multimedia Authoring
- □ 11 Networking
- □ 12 Office Automation
- □ 13 Order Entry/Inventory Control
- □ 14 Programming
- □ 15 Project Management
- □ 16 Scientific and Engineering
- □ 17 Spreadsheets
- □ 18 Systems Management
- □ 19 Workflow

Hardware
- □ 20 Macintosh
- □ 21 Mainframe
- □ 22 Massively Parallel Processing
- □ 23 Minicomputer
- □ 24 PC
- □ 25 Network Computer
- □ 26 Symmetric Multiprocessing
- □ 27 Workstation
Peripherals
- □ 28 Bridges/Routers/Hubs/Gateways
- □ 29 CD-ROM Drives
- □ 30 Disk Drives/Subsystems
- □ 31 Modems
- □ 32 Tape Drives/Subsystems
- □ 33 Video Boards/Multimedia
Services
- □ 34 Application Service Provider
- □ 35 Consulting
- □ 36 Education/Training
- □ 37 Maintenance
- □ 38 Online Database Services
- □ 39 Support
- □ 40 Technology-Based Training
- □ 98 Other
- 99 □ None of the above

**⑥ WHAT ORACLE PRODUCTS ARE IN USE AT YOUR SITE?** (check all that apply)
Oracle E-Business Suite
- □ 01 Oracle Marketing
- □ 02 Oracle Sales
- □ 03 Oracle Order Fulfillment
- □ 04 Oracle Supply Chain Management
- □ 05 Oracle Procurement
- □ 06 Oracle Manufacturing
- □ 07 Oracle Maintenance Management
- □ 08 Oracle Service
- □ 09 Oracle Contracts
- □ 10 Oracle Projects
- □ 11 Oracle Financials
- □ 12 Oracle Human Resources
- □ 13 Oracle Interaction Center
- □ 14 Oracle Communications/Utilities (modules)
- □ 15 Oracle Public Sector/University (modules)
- □ 16 Oracle Financial Services (modules)
Server/Software
- □ 17 Oracle9*i*
- □ 18 Oracle9*i* Lite
- □ 19 Oracle8*i*
- □ 20 Other Oracle database
- □ 21 Oracle9*i* Application Server
- □ 22 Oracle9*i* Application Server Wireless
- □ 23 Oracle Small Business Suite

Tools
- □ 24 Oracle Developer Suite
- □ 25 Oracle Discoverer
- □ 26 Oracle JDeveloper
- □ 27 Oracle Migration Workbench
- □ 28 Oracle9*i* AS Portal
- □ 29 Oracle Warehouse Builder
Oracle Services
- □ 30 Oracle Outsourcing
- □ 31 Oracle Consulting
- □ 32 Oracle Education
- □ 33 Oracle Support
- □ 98 Other
- 99 □ None of the above

**⑦ WHAT OTHER DATABASE PRODUCTS ARE IN USE AT YOUR SITE?** (check all that apply)
- □ 01 Access
- □ 02 Baan
- □ 03 dbase
- □ 04 Gupta
- □ 05 IBM DB2
- □ 06 Informix
- □ 07 Ingres
- □ 08 Microsoft Access
- □ 09 Microsoft SQL Server
- □ 10 PeopleSoft
- □ 11 Progress
- □ 12 SAP
- □ 13 Sybase
- □ 14 VSAM
- □ 98 Other
- 99 □ None of the above

**⑧ WHAT OTHER APPLICATION SERVER PRODUCTS ARE IN USE AT YOUR SITE?** (check all that apply)
- □ 01 BEA
- □ 02 IBM
- □ 03 Sybase
- □ 04 Sun
- □ 05 Other

**⑨ DURING THE NEXT 12 MONTHS, HOW MUCH DO YOU ANTICIPATE YOUR ORGANIZATION WILL SPEND ON COMPUTER HARDWARE, SOFTWARE, PERIPHERALS, AND SERVICES FOR YOUR LOCATION?** (check only one)
- □ 01 Less than $10,000
- □ 02 $10,000 to $49,999
- □ 03 $50,000 to $99,999
- □ 04 $100,000 to $499,999
- □ 05 $500,000 to $999,999
- □ 06 $1,000,000 and over

**⑩ WHAT IS YOUR COMPANY'S YEARLY SALES REVENUE?** (please choose one)
- □ 01 $500,000,000 and above
- □ 02 $100,000,000 to $500,000,000
- □ 03 $50,000,000 to $100,000,000
- □ 04 $5,000,000 to $50,000,000
- □ 05 $1,000,000 to $5,000,000

100103

# Are You Oracle Certified?

Professional development and industry recognition are not the only benefits you gain from Oracle certifications. They also facilitate career growth, improve productivity, and enhance credibility. Hiring managers who want to distinguish among candidates for critical IT positions know that the Oracle Certification Program is one of the most highly valued benchmarks in the marketplace. Hundreds of thousands of Oracle certified technologists testify to the importance of this industry-recognized credential as the best way to get ahead—and stay there.

For details about the
Oracle Certification Program, go to
oracle.com/education/certification.

Oracle University —
Learn technology from the source

ORACLE

UNIVERSITY

# Learn Oracle Database 11g
# from Oracle University

Ready to learn from the experts?
Only Oracle University offers a complete
curriculum to take you from beginner
through Certified Master.

Our training offerings for Oracle Database
11$g$ include courses on identity and access
management, infrastructure grid, change
management, security, Real Application
Clusters, SQL and PL/SQL, building JavaEE
applications, BI and data warehousing,
high availability, and much more.

Oracle Database 11$g$: making information
more manageable, more available, and more
secure. Learn all about it from Oracle
University: oracle.com/education.

Oracle University —
Learn technology from the source

ORACLE

**UNIVERSITY**